The Next Step in Guided Reading

Focused Assessments
and Targeted Lessons
for Helping Every Student
Become a Better Reader

by Jan Richardson

■SCHOLASTIC

New York • Toronto • London • Auckland • Sydney
Mexico City • New Delhi • Hong Kong • Buenos Aires

Dedications

To God who strengthens me,

My husband who encourages me,

My three sons who inspire me,

And to my parents who have always loved me

and cheered for me.

~Jan Richardson

Acknowledgments

If I could live my life over, I would still be a teacher. Why? Because of all the delightful young learners who have so beautifully graced my life. I wish I could go to each one and tell them what an honor it was to be their teacher. I want to thank the many talented and hardworking teachers who have labored alongside me through the years, especially those from Greenwood, South Carolina, and Chattanooga, Tennessee. I also want to thank the following administrators: Lori Cothern, Jill Levine, Aimee Randolph, Madeline Bell, and my dear friend Ron Hughes, the first person to encourage me to write this book.

Four people had a direct influence on the final product of this book. I am so grateful for Eileen Judge's invaluable contributions as copy editor and her commitment to this work. Holly Grundon, interior designer, gave expert advice and shaved the manuscript to fit the required number of pages. Finally, I extend my deepest appreciation to my awesome editors, Gloria Pipkin and Lois Bridges.

Cover design: Jorge J. Namerow
Interior design: Holly Grundon
Acquiring Editor: Lois Bridges
Copy Editor: Eileen Judge
Development and Production Editor: Gloria Pipkin

ISBN-13: 978-0-545-13361-6
ISBN-10: 0-545-13361-0

Table of Contents

Introduction

Even after teaching elementary and middle school for years and earning a master's degree in reading, I found myself struggling to understand the reading process. I recall using basal readers, worksheets, and computer programs that were supposed to "fix" a student's reading problem, only to see the same children in my remedial reading classes year after year. I knew there had to be a better way, but I had no idea what it was.

The reading process finally began to make sense when I trained to be a Reading Recovery® teacher leader. But Reading Recovery® (Clay, 1993), as good as it is, focuses on individual tutoring of struggling readers in the first grade. I wanted to reach children of all ages and at all stages of reading development.

My doctoral work and my experience teaching thousands of children through the years have helped me discover the answer: *small-group guided reading.* Small-group instruction has been growing in popularity since the 1990s and is now included in virtually every reading program. In fact, it is mandated in Reading First classrooms. As a teacher and an educational consultant, I have taught or observed thousands of small-group lessons. This book is a step-by-step guide to teaching guided reading across all grade levels using the following four elements:

* Analyzing reading assessments to identify an instructional focus

* Prompting students to use reading strategies when they encounter difficulties

* Teaching skills that are necessary and appropriate for a specific reading stage

* Utilizing guided writing to support and accelerate the reading process

How to Use This Book

The simplest way to use this book is to begin with the first chapter and read it sequentially. As you read about a specific reading stage, you can apply the strategies in your guided reading lessons. You might also consider reading the book strategically. For example, if you have emergent readers in your classroom, you would read Chapter 3 and follow the lesson plan description. If you have fluent readers, you would look to Chapter 6 for specific strategies for teaching comprehension. As your students progress, you will find yourself shifting to different chapters to find strategies your students need to learn to become better readers.

Chapter 1 focuses on getting ready for guided reading. It provides a general overview of a balanced reading program and offers suggestions for schedules and management. I have included ideas for fostering student independence and literacy workstations.

Chapter 2 presents practical suggestions for using assessments to inform guided reading instruction. There are guidelines for analyzing a running record and streamlining the assessment process so that classroom time can be used efficiently.

Chapters 3, 4, 5, and 6 offer detailed descriptions and lesson plans for all stages of reading: emergent, early, transitional, and fluent. I have used the alphabetic reading levels created by Fountas and Pinnell (2008) to help teachers find the stage that best matches their students' reading levels.

Reading Stage	Alphabetic Levels	Text level range
Emergent	A–C	K
Early	D–I	1st
Transitional	J–P	2nd–3rd
Fluent	Q–Z	4th–6th

The lesson plans target reading strategies and skills appropriate for each reading stage so you will be able to differentiate your instruction based upon the needs of your students. I have also included word study and guided writing activities to give students an opportunity to apply skills and strategies that have been taught in the lesson.

Chapter 7 is designed to support you as you pinpoint specific reasons—and develop intervention plans—for students who are not accelerating. There are guidelines for involving a coach or colleague to help you and suggestions for analyzing the reading process of emergent, early, and transitional readers. I have included a "fix it guide" similar to what you find in an auto repair manual: "If you see this . . . try this." Every child can be a reader, no matter what challenges he or she has. We just have to figure out what the obstacle is and find a way to help the child overcome it.

Appendix A contains charts for each reading level, A–J+. The charts give you the big picture of behaviors and strategies you should expect to see at each level. It also offers suggestions for word study and writing activities. Many teachers copy the chart and insert it in their lesson-plan notebooks to help them plan their lessons. Appendix B has words to use at each level for word study, and Appendix C has reading-strategies cards useful for teaching decoding and vocabulary strategies.

I believe this book is the "next step" you have been searching for as a teacher. By following the lesson plans and selecting a purpose for your guided reading groups, you will see radical improvements in children's reading progress. Your focus will determine your effectiveness.

Preparing

FOR GUIDED READING

Guided reading is a key part of a balanced reading framework and an essential element of a successful reading workshop. But before you can begin small-group instruction, your students must be able to work independently for sustained periods of time. Like most things, this will take some preparation.

During the first few weeks of school, children need to learn to work together, read together, laugh and play together. Consequently, you should plan whole- and small-group activities that build classroom community and establish a climate where each student participates and every response is valued. Such an environment is essential not only to classroom management but to learning itself. This is especially true when it comes to the important work and learning being done in your reading workshop.

From the very beginning of the year, establish firm routines for your reading workshop: Students must know how to work in teams, how to solve problems without asking for your help, and how to use workstations or do other independent literacy activities. With routines and procedures clearly established, students will be able to begin working independently, allowing you to introduce the guided reading aspect of the reading workshop.

What follows are steps and guidelines for fostering independence and getting your students ready for guided reading, suggestions for scheduling and management, and an overview of approaches to a balanced reading program.

Balanced Reading Approaches

Introduce your students to read-alouds, shared reading, and independent reading. Each instructional approach has a specific purpose and varies in grouping, text level, and the manner in which the text is read.

Read-Aloud

Reading aloud to students is an important component of any reading program. It provides opportunities to foster interest and motivation, model fluent reading, engage students in discussing and analyzing a text, and demonstrate comprehension strategies. An interactive read-aloud (Fountas & Pinnell, 2001; Hoyt, 2007) is a slightly different approach. Its focus is to encourage reflective thinking and enhance comprehension by guiding students in discussing the text.

During an interactive read-aloud, you read a text to the students and stop two or three times during the reading to pose questions that encourage deep thinking. As students turn to a neighbor to talk about the book, they are learning to think deeply about the book, listen to each other, and value the opinions of their classmates. Be sure to employ a variety of genres, including nonfiction and poetry, so children can experience different linguistic patterns.

Shared Reading

Shared reading is usually done with the whole group using a grade-level text. In the primary grades, the teacher commonly uses big books or charts. With intermediate students, shared reading can be done with poetry charts, content area textbooks, short texts on an overhead projector, novels, or anthologies. As with read-alouds, you should use a variety of genres.

The purpose of shared reading is to teach skills and strategies, increase reading fluency, learn content information for social studies and science, and support developing readers. As you read the text aloud, students should follow along with their eyes and join in with their voices when they can. The challenge of shared reading is keeping the students engaged and focused. Limiting the shared reading experiences to 10–15 minutes helps students stay on task.

Independent, Self-Selected Reading

Each day students should have the opportunity to read books they select themselves. Teach them how to choose books they **can** read and **want** to read, books that will capture their interest and keep them reading. Extended time spent reading independently increases the amount or volume of reading, improves automaticity with sight words, increases fluency, and gives students the opportunity to practice the strategies they have internalized. Additionally, you want to create a love for reading. Remember to monitor the texts students select to ensure they are not too difficult. I have found that intermediate students will often select a text that is too challenging because they see someone else reading it. The problem is, students will lose interest if they encounter too many unknown words. Individual reading conferences provide an opportunity for you to discuss book selection, teach needed skills or strategies, and evaluate progress. To assess comprehension and monitor accountability, you might also require a weekly written response related to the student's independent reading book.

Summary of Balanced Reading Approaches

Approach	Grouping	Text Level	How Text Is Read	Purpose
Read-aloud	Whole	Above grade level	By the teacher	Model fluent reading & reading strategies Motivate students to read
Shared reading	Whole	On grade level	Students read <u>with</u> the teacher	Teach strategies Support language
Guided reading	Small	Instructional level (varies by student)	Students read text independently while teacher coaches	Practice reading strategies with teacher support Differentiate instruction based upon need
Self-selected reading	Individual	Independent level	Independently	Enjoyment & fluency Practice strategies that have been internalized

Framework of the Reading Workshop

The reading workshop often begins with a whole-group mini-lesson that focuses on teaching a procedure, reading strategy, or genre. The mini-lesson can incorporate either a read-aloud or shared reading experience. The students then move into the guided reading block for 45–60 minutes. As the teacher works with small groups, the other students do literacy-related activities. At the end of the reading block, students meet together to discuss their books or share what they learned in the literacy centers.

Independent Literacy Activities

Before guided reading can occur, students must be taught how to work independently for 30–60 minutes. Literacy centers or workstations provide an opportunity for students to engage in purposeful learning activities while you work with individuals or a small group. In primary grades, workstations give students the opportunity to practice skills and strategies that have been taught to the whole class. Intermediate teachers can create centers that relate to content instruction or simply have children read and write independently. No matter what format or activity the students are doing during reading workshop, it is important they understand the procedures and expectations for each activity.

The following six-week routine for primary grades gradually releases responsibility to the students and teaches classroom routines and workstation procedures. If students have used literacy workstations in previous grades, you may not need the full six weeks to establish procedures; however, I strongly recommend you follow this plan if you teach kindergarten. The time you invest in teaching independence will be well worth it when you begin your guided reading groups.

The First Six Weeks (K–1): Teaching Routines and Procedures

Week 1:
Build community and collaboration by having students work in small groups, or teams, doing activities they can manage with little direction from you.

* Plan a variety of engaging, small-group activities (puzzles, math manipulatives, clay, coloring books, Legos, blocks, simple art projects). Put each activity in a plastic container/tub and give each group a different tub.

* Set the timer for 10 minutes.

* Step away from the teams and observe how they interact with each other.

* Signal students to come to the gathering place and praise them for working together and solving their own problems.

* Each day, redistribute the tubs so that teams can work on a different activity.

Week 2:

Teach a literacy workstation, or center, each day to one team while other teams work with tub activities.

✳ Set the timer for 10 minutes.

✳ Assign a tub activity to all but one team.

✳ Pull one team into the workstation and demonstrate all aspects of the station. Then give students in the team the opportunity to practice the station while you observe and clarify any confusions.

✳ On each consecutive day, introduce the workstation activity to another team until all students have been instructed in how to use that workstation.

	Monday	Tuesday	Wednesday	Thursday	Friday
Team 1	**Center 1**	Tub #2	Tub #3	Tub #4	Tub #5
Team 2	Tub #1	**Center 1**	Tub #5	Tub #3	Tub #4
Team 3	Tub #2	Tub #3	**Center 1**	Tub #5	Tub #1
Team 4	Tub #3	Tub #4	Tub #1	**Center 1**	Tub #2
Team 5	Tub #4	Tub #5	Tub #2	Tub #1	**Center 1**

Week 3:

Introduce a second workstation and lengthen workstation time to 15 minutes.
For example, here's the plan for Monday:

✳ Team 1 does the workstation activity taught in the previous week (Center 1).

✳ Team 2 learns the new workstation activity (Center 2) with your support.

✳ Other teams work with a tub activity.

Encourage students to solve their own problems!

	Monday	Tuesday	Wednesday	Thursday	Friday
Team 1	**Center 1**	Tub #2	Tub #3	Tub #4	**Center 2**
Team 2	**Center 2**	**Center 1**	Tub #4	Tub #3	Tub #5
Team 3	Tub #2	**Center 2**	**Center 1**	Tub #5	Tub #1
Team 4	Tub #3	Tub #4	**Center 2**	**Center 1**	Tub #2
Team 5	Tub #4	Tub #5	Tub #2	**Center 2**	**Center 1**

Week 4:

Lengthen reading workshop to 20 minutes and introduce a new workstation to one team each day.

    ✳   Each day three teams work in workstations.

    ✳   Each day two teams do tub activities.

    ✳   Develop and explain the management system students will follow during reading workshop. The management system is a visual display of the center activities for each student. Options for management systems are explained later in this chapter.

	Monday	Tuesday	Wednesday	Thursday	Friday
Team 1	**Center 1**	Tub #2	Tub #3	**Center 3**	**Center 2**
Team 2	**Center 2**	**Center 1**	Tub #4	Tub #3	**Center 3**
Team 3	**Center 3**	**Center 2**	**Center 1**	Tub #5	Tub #1
Team 4	Tub #3	**Center 3**	**Center 2**	**Center 1**	Tub #2
Team 5	Tub #4	Tub #5	**Center 3**	**Center 2**	**Center 1**

Week 5:

By this time, students should be able to work for 25–30 minutes without your direct supervision. You will continue to assess, adjust, and clarify expectations at the centers.

    ✳   Add two new workstations (C4 & C5).

    ✳   Students will rotate to two workstations, each lasting 10–15 minutes. Some teams will still work with tubs (T) for one of the rotations.

    ✳   Teach the additional workstations to each team, always including demonstration and practice of routines and procedures.

	Monday		Tuesday		Wednesday		Thursday		Friday	
	10 m	10 m	10 m	10 m	10 m	10 m	10 m	10 m	10 m	10 m
Team 1	T1	C1	C2	C3	C4*	C1	C2	C3	C4	C5*
Team 2	C1	C2	C3	C4*	T1	C2	C3	C4	C5*	C1
Team 3	C2	C3	C4*	T1	C1	C3	C4	C5*	C1	C2
Team 4	C3	C4*	T1	C1	C2	C4	C5*	C1	C2	C3
Team 5	C4*	T2	C1	C2	C3	C5*	C1	C2	C3	C4

* The teacher works with this team to demonstrate the new center and provide guided practice.

Week 6:

All students are working in **literacy** stations. The tubs are no longer required.

* Continue to assess and adjust activities. You often have to tweak a center by adding more activities, changing its location, or limiting the number of students allowed at the station. Remember to transfer activities you have used with the whole class to the workstations.

* Lengthen time to 40 minutes, 20 minutes for each rotation.

* As you prepare to introduce guided reading, hold a class meeting and explain that students are not allowed to interrupt you when you work with a small group. Create a signal that lets students know when they are not supposed to interrupt. You might put up a stop sign at the guided reading table or wear a scarf, fancy boa, or outrageous tie that signals you should not be interrupted. A kindergarten teacher I know wore a sports visor during guided reading. On the bill of the visor she wrote, *Go away.* That is pretty direct, but it is one way for students to learn sight words. You might change the sign to read *stop*, *not now*, or *sit down*. One intermediate teacher surrounded his guided reading table with crime-scene tape. Students understood they were not to step across that line unless it was an emergency.

* After you get the students started in workstations, work with one guided reading group while other students work independently. If a student approaches you while you are working at the guided reading table, do not acknowledge his or her presence. Do not look at or speak to the student. If you do, it will only encourage him or her to come back next time. Simply hold up your hand and continue to teach your guided reading lesson. The student will eventually go away. Be sure you explain the conditions when students **may** interrupt. For example, if there is a fire, or someone is bleeding or sick, they can tell you. If students need permission to use the restroom, teach them to use a hand signal (such as crossing their fingers). When you see the signal, you can nod your head and continue with your lesson. The goal is to teach guided reading without interruption while other students are engaged in purposeful literacy activities.

	Monday		Tuesday		Wednesday		Thursday		Friday	
	20 m	20 m	20 m	20 m	20 m	20 m	20 m	20 m	20 m	20 m
Team 1	C5	C1	C2	C3	C4	C5	C1	C2	C3	C4
Team 2	C1	C2	C3	C4	C5	C1	C2	C3	C4	C5
Team 3	C2	C3	C4	C5	C1	C2	C3	C4	C5	C1
Team 4	C3	C4	C5	C1	C2	C3	C4	C5	C1	C2
Team 5	C4	C5	C1	C2	C3	C4	C5	C1	C2	C3
Teacher	GR1	GR2	GR3	GR4	GR1	GR2	GR3	GR4	GR1	GR2

Following Weeks:

Gradually lengthen the time for reading workshop and teach more guided reading groups until students are working independently for 60 minutes and you are working with at least two to three guided reading groups. If students have difficulty staying independently engaged at the workstations for 60 minutes, you can divide the reading workshop into two segments and do them at different times during the day.

Literacy Workstations for Primary Grades

Literacy workstation activities will vary according to grade level and time of year. It makes sense to reuse whole-group demonstrations in the literacy workstations. For example, if you read a big book and focused on compound words, put the big book in the workstation and have the students use Wikki Stix® or highlighting tape to frame compound words. The students can also write the compound words in their "workstation folders" if you want to hold them accountable for the skill.

Gaily Boushey and Joan Moser (2006) have developed a simple framework for their literacy block. Students not meeting with the teacher for reading instruction do one of the following activities: read to self, read to someone, listen to reading, work on writing, and do word work. The beauty of this approach is that it is easy to manage. Students choose three or four of these activities each day.

There are many books on literacy centers and workstations (Diller, 2003, 2005; Ingraham, 1997; Morrow, 1997). You can also search the Internet for ideas. Below are some easy workstation activities that can be adapted for any grade level.

Book Boxes

Students have a personal box or bag that contains a variety of books for independent reading. Include books students have read during guided reading and other easy books students can read without support. This activity gives students an opportunity to develop fluency and practice strategies on easy, familiar texts. For kindergarten students, include easy picture books in the book boxes and teach them to "read" the pictures. Although the children will probably not be able to read the book, they can practice book-handling skills and oral language.

Buddy Reading

Students choose a book from their book box to read with another student. The children often sit next to each other so they can see the text at the same time. Buddy reading can be done in several ways: Students can share one book and take turns reading a page; they can take turns reading an entire book from their box; or they can share a book and read chorally. After students read a book, they should briefly retell what they read or heard. You must, of course, teach children how to whisper read.

Writing

Students write individually or with a partner and usually continue the work they are doing during writing workshop. Motivation increases if children are allowed to choose their own topics. Some teachers add special writing tools, such as colored pens, markers, stamps, stickers, sticky notes, colored paper, and fancy stationery, to the writing center. You might also establish a message board or post office for students to leave messages for friends and teachers, and include the covers of used greeting cards and invite students to add a personal message.

Readers Theater

This is a highly motivating way to get students to reread a text. Students prepare for a performance by reading and rereading a script with their group at the workstation. They are not required to memorize or act out the play but are encouraged to use their voices, facial expressions, and hand gestures to interpret the dialogue. Scripts for Readers Theater are available in books and on the Internet. Teachers and students may also adapt favorite stories through collaborative script writing activities. If you schedule a performance time every Friday, all you have to do to maintain this center is make new scripts available on Monday. You could assign a script to each group or allow the groups to choose the script they want to perform that week. Obviously, each group should have a different script.

Poems and Songs

Children can reread poems and songs that have been introduced in whole-group demonstrations. To increase interest and engagement, allow them to use quiet musical instruments such as bells, triangles, sandpaper blocks, and finger cymbals during the reading. Students can copy the poem in a special poetry notebook and add their own illustrations.

ABC/Word Study

Alphabet books, magnetic letters, white boards, alphabet charts, and a class list of names or spelling words are a few of the items used in this center. Kindergarteners can use magnetic letters to match letters to an alphabet chart, match upper/lowercase letters, make classmates' names, or practice easy sight words you have introduced to the class. To practice letter formation, they can trace their names with colored markers. Older students could practice their weekly spelling words using magnetic letters, colored markers, letter stamps, white boards, small chalkboards, or Magna Doodles™.

Pocket charts can be used for a variety of word study activities such as matching words and pictures, or sorting words or pictures by the number of syllables (1, 2, or 3 syllables), vowel patterns (*ew* or *ai*), initial blends or digraphs (*cl*, *sh*), inflections (*–ed*, *–ing*, *–ly*, *–ily*), parts of speech (nouns, verbs, adjectives), etc. The students can also match a word and its definition, find antonyms and/or synonyms, or put words in alphabetical order. After each vocabulary activity is modeled for the class, put the word cards and category cards in a large manila envelope. When students go to the workstation, they select one of the envelopes there.

Word Wall

Kindergarten students can use special materials such as glitter markers, magnetic letters, Magna Doodles™, or rubber letter stamps to copy the wall words. In first or second grade, students can find words that have short or long vowel sounds, silent *e*, initial or final consonant blends, one-syllable/two-syllable words, words within a word, nouns/verbs, etc. Any phonic skill that has been taught to the whole group can be practiced using the words on the word wall.

Read the Room (or Word Hunt)

Students use a variety of child-friendly pointers (chopsticks, feathers, straws, plastic rods, magnifying glasses) to read material posted on the walls. This activity assumes you have a literacy-rich classroom environment with interesting and readable text on your walls. Interactive writing charts are a great source of readable texts for reading the room.

It usually works best if students read in pairs composed of different reading abilities. This provides support for less able readers and increases accountability.

Children in first or second grade can search the room and then write words that fit a particular feature such as these:

* Find a word for every letter in the alphabet.

* Find (and write) as many *b* and *d* words as you can.

* Find words that begin with a blend.

* Find compound words.

* Find words with an ending (e.g., *–ing, –ed, –s, –ful*).

* Find words that are nouns (or verbs or adjectives, etc.).

* Find words that have three syllables.

* Find words that begin with a prefix.

* Find words that fit a particular vowel pattern (*oo, ea*, etc.).

Oral Retelling

I think every classroom should have a retelling center. Once you read a book to the class, place it in the retelling center. To make this activity fun, copy and laminate the covers and put them in the workstation. Teach students how to play "Guess the Story." One child chooses a familiar book cover from the box (without the other children seeing) and describes the beginning, middle, and end of the story. The other children guess the title of the book. The child who guesses correctly takes the next turn at retelling a different story.

Include some retelling props such as three paper plates that have the words *beginning, middle,* and *end* written on them. Or you can take a new garden glove and write a story element on each finger: characters, setting, problem, events, and solution. This becomes the "five-finger retell."

Listening

Students listen to taped stories and follow along with copies of the text. After the reading, they can respond to the story by softly retelling it with a partner, drawing a picture of their favorite part, writing three sentences that retell the beginning, middle, and end (B-M-E), writing a five-finger retell (second or third grade), or doing a story map. You can also copy three pictures from the book and have the students sequence the pictures (without the text). Students in second and third grade could then write a short summary for each picture.

Computer

Use software that reinforces skills you have already taught the class. Never expect computers to teach new skills or strategies. Computers cannot take the place of teacher instruction, but they can be useful in reinforcing learning. Students can type spelling words, write stories, or use educational software that focuses on phonemic awareness.

Overhead Projector

Students can use magnetic letters to make words that fit a particular phonics skill you are teaching. They can also sort words that have been written on transparency film and cut apart. Children enjoy practicing letter formation on transparencies made from handwriting books. Add some transparencies of familiar poems, rhymes, and songs so children can choose their favorites to reread. To reinforce phonological awareness, students can circle rhyming words or words that reflect a specific focus you have recently taught the class.

Geography

This workstation has maps, a globe, atlas, postcards, magazines, coins, stamps from other countries, travel brochures and posters, fiction and non-fiction books, bilingual trade books and dictionaries, alphabet books in various languages, etc. Activities would complement the unit of study and could include making flags, writing travel brochures, doing a map puzzle, or preparing a report.

Science

Create a center that relates to your science unit. Children can use a magnifying glass to study an item (plant, ant farm, aquarium, insect, bird's nest) and then draw and/or write about it. To encourage research and exploration, include informational texts that match the unit.

Big Books

Children use pointers to reread familiar big books. They could use Wikki Stix® or highlighting tape to find sight words or words with a special phonic element.

Library

Students select a book and "read" it to another student or a stuffed animal. Usually books in the library workstation are sorted by theme (animals, space, sports, food, etc.) so children can find books that interest them. Although some children are not really reading these books, they are practicing oral language skills by using the pictures to tell a story.

Managing Workstations

Many teachers want to use the same groups for literacy centers as they do for guided reading. That makes the rotation smoother, but having all the lowest-level readers in one workstation can cause problems. I have found that centers work best if there is a range of reading levels in the group. That way there is at least one student able to read the workstation directions and help other students. This means students may have to leave a workstation to work with the teacher for guided reading. After the guided reading lesson, the students return to their workstation team and move on to the next rotation activity.

There are many ways to manage literacy workstations. Whatever system you choose, be sure you model and have students practice the procedures. The best systems do not require verbal directions by the teachers. One such management tool is a task board, a visual display of the workstation assignments. Students should be able to see the task board from their seats and understand how to follow the directions. The most commonly used is the team task board, but I have found the individual task board generates greater excitement and engagement.

Team Task Board

This board shows groups, or teams, of students which stations they need to do each day. The children spend about twenty minutes at each workstation and may be called out of the workstation to come to the guided reading table. At the beginning of each day, you move the team cards to the right so students have the opportunity to go to different stations each day. The following is an example of a task board for one day.

Team 1	Team 2	Team 3	Team 4	Team 5
Cheryl Nanci Sandi Will Sam	Veronica Ana Carlos Alfonso Tom	Brian Rocio Joanna Tara Sarah	Karlina Arthur Jarod Chris Patty	Timmy Mike Katlin Ben Kendra
Word Station	Readers Theater	Read the Room	Computer Station	Big Books
Science Station	Overhead Projector	Vocabulary Station	Book Boxes	Retelling Station
Buddy Reading	Listening Station	Computer Station	Readers Theater	Word Station

Individual Task Board

This is my favorite management system for all grade levels. Students are highly motivated to follow procedures because they have individual tasks for that day listed next to their name. Each day the teacher uses familiar icons to identify three activities each student will do. Guided reading is one of the activities, which eliminates the need to call a student out of a workstation to come to the guided reading table. The students know ahead of time which rotation will be used for guided reading.

Name	Activity #1 (20 min)	Activity #2 (20 min)	Activity #3 (20 min)
Jack	Guided Reading	Poetry Station	Computer Station
Sarah	Listening Station	Guided Reading	Vocabulary Station
Will	Readers Theater	Listening Station	Guided Reading
John	Guided Reading	Listening Station	Overhead Projector

Literacy Activities for Intermediate Grades

For the past few decades most intermediate teachers have relied on whole-class instruction to teach reading. Although whole-class instruction is one part of a balanced literacy program, it is not the best way to diversify instruction or scaffold students who need more support. Guided reading is the small-group component that allows teachers an opportunity to assess students' strategic abilities and scaffold them so they can internalize reading strategies. In order for guided reading to be effective, however, the teacher must work without interruptions. So, what are the other students doing while the teacher does guided reading? Students must be independently engaged in literacy activities. Independent reading should always be one of the activities for reading workshop.

Encourage Independent Reading

A well-stocked classroom library is essential for independent reading. There should be a wide range of levels and genres. Realistic fiction is great, but you also need informational books, biographies, magazines, comic books, and picture books. I once interviewed a reluctant reader in middle school and discovered he loved to read cookbooks. I brought a few cookbooks from home (they were never used much anyway!), and I put them in my library. It worked! Many reluctant readers can be reached with comic books or even video game magazines. Eventually, you can nudge them towards other genres.

Reserve a corner of the classroom for the library, preferably far from your guided reading table. To help your students find books quickly, sort the books by genre, authors, topics, etc., and place them in labeled containers. Establish routines for browsing the classroom library and have students select several books at a time. Give each student a plastic bag or magazine holder to use as a personal book basket. If students finish reading a book during reading workshop, they can go to their plastic book bag or basket and select their next book. This eliminates the need for students to browse the classroom library during reading workshop.

If you are a new teacher and do not have a lot of books, there are several inexpensive ways to build a classroom library. Check out as many books from your public library as they will allow. Stop by garage sales and used book stores, or ask your avid readers to donate books they have already read. Classroom book clubs (such as Scholastic's Firefly, SeeSaw, Lucky, Arrow, TAB, and Club Leo) that offer bonus books with each order are a great source of attractive paperbacks. Another idea is to ask your librarian to set aside 30–40 "good" books for your classroom. Students who have trouble finding a book they like will have better luck browsing through a box of "really good books."

"I hate to read." Most children who say they do not like to read are struggling readers who have not been successful with reading. Our job is to help them find a book they like, one that is easy for them to read. Get to know the interests of your reluctant readers so you can offer them some choices. Say, "I found this book I think you will like. Will you please read the first chapter and let me know what you think about it?" Most children will not refuse a personal invitation.

Book Teasers

A book teaser is when you read only one or two chapters of a book to get students interested. Then you put the book, along with others by the same author, in a special place so students can find them during independent reading. When I taught elementary school, I used to read from a chapter book each day. I thought it was a good way to calm children down after lunch or recess. When I moved to middle school, I still wanted to read to the students, but I didn't have time to read an entire book. I discovered that if I read the first chapter of a good book, I could get the students hooked into reading the rest of it on their own.

Book Talks

The purpose of a book talk is to entice students to read a specific book. It is similar to a movie trailer. The teacher spends three to five minutes giving enough information so that students are excited and eager to read the book. Teachers need to be familiar with *current* children's literature so they can recommend these books to their students.

Ideas for Intermediate Literacy Stations

Although I prefer that the other students read while the teacher does guided reading, it is not unusual to find students who cannot stay focused on independent reading for 45 minutes. To solve this problem, develop a literacy workstation format that engages students in several activities. Be sure one of the 20-minute rotations is self-selected reading. Literacy activities should be modeled by the teacher and practiced by the students to ensure procedures are understood. Here are some literacy activities that are easy to implement and work at any grade level:

Buddy Reading

Students pair up and read the same book or short text. It could be a novel they both want to read or a passage that correlates to a unit of study in science or social studies. Students love to work together and will be more motivated to read the passage if they can do it with a partner. You might also include a few questions they can ask each other after they have read for 15 minutes. If you teach children how to create their own questions, you are helping them build comprehension skills.

Word Study

Students do activities related to their spelling words for the week. They could sort words according to spelling features, search for other words that have the same spelling feature, make their spelling words out of magnetic letters, put their words in alphabetical order, or think of antonyms or synonyms.

Vocabulary

Students do activities related to the week's vocabulary words (antonyms, synonyms, prefixes, suffixes, parts of speech, homophones, etc.). Pat Cunningham's (2009) book on vocabulary has dozens of activities for teaching vocabulary in math, science, and social studies that could be easily adapted for an independent vocabulary workstation.

Writing

Students can continue the work they are doing during writing workshop or write a thoughtful response to their self-selected book. You may decide to require a weekly or biweekly letter children write to you that explains the thinking they are doing during independent reading.

Readers Theater

Students rehearse a script with a group and perform it for the class later in the week. Students can be taught how to write their own Readers Theater script based upon a traditional tale, familiar novel, or historical event you have taught in social studies.

Research Related to Content Areas

Students work on projects related to science or social studies units. They can work individually or in small groups to research a topic and prepare a presentation that summarizes their learning.

Weekly Reading Workshop Contract

Many teachers prefer a record or contract that holds students accountable for the literacy activities they do during reading workshop. The example below was created by a classroom teacher in South Carolina and is based on a 60-minute guided reading block with three 20-minute rotations. While the teacher works with three guided reading groups, the students not in the guided reading group do independent reading or a literacy activity. Students are always required to read for one 20-minute rotation. If the student has guided reading during one rotation, he or she would have only one other literacy activity that day. If the student does not have guided reading that day, he or she would read for 20 minutes and do two other literacy activities. Here is an example of the contract for one week.

Reading Workshop Contract

Name _____   Date _____

	Literacy Activity #1	Literacy Activity #2
Monday Independent Reading Title: _____ Pg. ____ to ____	☐ guided reading ☐ vocabulary station ☐ project or research ☐ response journal ☐ Other: _____	☐ guided reading ☐ vocabulary station ☐ project or research ☐ response journal ☐ Other: _____
Tuesday Independent Reading Title: _____ Pg. ____ to ____	☐ guided reading ☐ vocabulary station ☐ project or research ☐ response journal ☐ Other: _____	☐ guided reading ☐ vocabulary station ☐ project or research ☐ response journal ☐ Other: _____
Wednesday Independent Reading Title: _____ Pg. ____ to ____	☐ guided reading ☐ vocabulary station ☐ project or research ☐ response journal ☐ Other: _____	☐ guided reading ☐ vocabulary station ☐ project or research ☐ response journal ☐ Other: _____
Thursday Independent Reading Title: _____ Pg. ____ to ____	☐ guided reading ☐ vocabulary station ☐ project or research ☐ response journal ☐ Other: _____	☐ guided reading ☐ vocabulary station ☐ project or research ☐ response journal ☐ Other: _____
Friday Independent Reading Title: _____ Pg. ____ to ____	☐ guided reading ☐ vocabulary station ☐ project or research ☐ response journal ☐ Other: _____	☐ guided reading ☐ vocabulary station ☐ project or research ☐ response journal ☐ Other: _____

Reading Notebooks

A Reading Notebook contains all the forms and responses students use for reading workshop. Not only is it a tool for monitoring and assessing independent reading, but it also contains responses from guided reading. I suggest using a one-inch plastic three-ring binder, one flexible enough to fold back the cover but durable enough to last the entire year. Some schools compile and bind a notebook for each student with the required number of pages for the year. The Reading Notebook has the following five parts: reading record, independent reading responses, guided reading notes, notes from whole-group lessons, and new word list.

Part 1: Independent Reading Record

Insert five copies of the reading record (page 24). Students record the title, author, and genre of books they read. When they finish the book, they record the date. You may decide to use this log as part of a student's reading grade.

The following chart may be inserted into the reading notebooks so students understand the different genres.

Description of Genre	
Fiction	
Genre (code)	**Definition**
Fantasy (F)	A story that is completely make-believe; may include talking animals, unusual creatures, and magic
Science Fiction (SF)	A fantasy story that includes scientific features (robots, time machines, superhuman characters, etc.)
Realistic Fiction (RF)	A story that uses made-up characters but could happen in real life
Historical Fiction (HF)	A fictional story based upon some event that happened in the past
Traditional Literature (TL)	Favorite stories that have been passed down throughout history; includes fairy tales, tall tales, legends, fables, and myths
Mystery (M)	A suspenseful story about a problem not solved until the end

Nonfiction	
Informational (I)	Texts that give factual information about a topic (sports, animals, history, science, weather, etc.)
Biography (B)	A story of a real person's life written by another person
Autobiography (AB)	A story of a real person's life written by that person

Reading Record

Title	Author	Genre	Date Completed

Genre codes:

Fiction: Fantasy (F), Science Fiction (SF), Realistic Fiction (RF), Historical Fiction (HF), Traditional Literature (includes folktales, fairy tales, myths & legends) (TL), Mystery (M)

Nonfiction: Informational (I), Biography (B), Autobiography (AB)

Part 2: Independent Reading Responses

Insert 35 pages of lined paper. Each week students write a one-page response to the book they are reading in the form of a letter to the teacher. This is a way to make students accountable for their independent reading. Some teachers prefer to leave the response open-ended; others like to give specific requirements, such as having students make connections or analyze a character. These weekly responses are usually in a letter format, but you might vary the response assignment to make it more interesting. Whatever approach you choose, model your expectations clearly. Write a sample response letter for a book you have shared with the class. Do the writing in front of the students and think aloud as you write. It is critical that you read the student letters and write back to them each week. Your response does not need to be lengthy, but it should be positive and personal. The independent reading response can be scored and used as part of the student's reading grade.

By the middle of second grade, students should be able to complete a simple reading response that includes a picture and short description of their favorite part of the book. Since children at this level may be reading a short book every day, they would only respond to one of the books they read that week. The following reading response would be completed each week. The menus that follow for fiction and nonfiction texts give students nine options for their reading responses. Each week students can choose one response. When the next grading period begins, they start over with a clean sheet.

Guidelines for Response Letters (Grades 3–5)

Students will need ideas for writing their response letters. You can duplicate the following suggestions for responding to fiction and nonfiction and have students insert the ideas in a sheet protector at the beginning of Part 2 in their notebooks. It is always best to model each of these responses to get the maximum performance from your students. Do not try to introduce them all at once or students will become overwhelmed and confused.

Ideas for Responding to Fiction

1. Write about some connections you made while you read. How did your connections help you understand the story?

2. Tell me something that surprised or interested you.

3. Tell me about your favorite character. What do you like about this character?

4. How is the main character changing throughout the story?

5. Write about a character, compare characters, or compare a character with yourself or someone you know.

6. Compare your book to another story.

7. Illustrate a favorite scene and describe the events leading up to it.

8. Write about what you liked or disliked. Always explain why.

9. Write about what you wish would happen in the story.

10. Tell about something you think the author should have included in the story.

11. What parts of the book puzzled you? Write any questions you have about what you read.

12. Write about the inferences you have made this week. Did you make the inferences from dialogue or characters' actions?

13. Tell me about the author's message (theme).

14. Tell me how you feel about the ending. What changes, if any, would you have made?

15. Summarize the part you read this week.

16. What would you like to remember about this book?

17. What did the author do that you might like to try in your writing?

Ideas for Responding to Informational Text

1. What were some important things you learned from your reading?

2. What connections did you make as you read?

3. Illustrate and write about the main idea and details.

4. What facts did you enjoy learning about most?

5. What pictures or illustrations did you find interesting?

6. Is this book like another you have read? If so, how are they alike? How are they different? Which did you like better? Why?

7. What kind of research do you think the author had to do to write the book?

8. What questions would you ask the author if you met him or her?

9. What more do you want to know about the topic? How will you learn more about it?

10. Would the book be different if it had been written ten years ago? One hundred years ago?

11. By reading and investigating, what did you discover that can help you outside of school?

The Next Step in Guided Reading © 2009 by Jan Richardson, Scholastic Professional

Grading:

You do not have to grade every reading response, but you need to write a short, encouraging note to the student. If you are genuine with your praise and sincere in your questions, students will be eager to write another response the next week. Reading and grading the responses can be easily managed if the class is divided into four groups (Monday, Tuesday, Wednesday, and Thursday). Each group is responsible for turning in a response on their assigned day so the teacher only has to read a few responses each day. If you use this plan, you will not have 25 response letters to read over the weekend. I have included some sample rubrics, but the best rubrics are those that have been constructed with your class.

Part 3: Guided Reading Notes

Insert 40 sheets of blank, lined paper. During guided reading, students are asked to write a short response that relates to the comprehension strategy focus. These responses are usually not graded; however, you should use them to assess individual student's comprehension and guide instruction. More explanation is provided in the descriptions of the guided reading lessons.

Part 4: Notes (from read-alouds, shared reading, or mini-lessons)

Insert 40 sheets of blank, lined paper. During whole-group instruction, students record their thoughts and questions or practice a strategy you have modeled.

Part 5: New Word List

Insert fifteen copies of the New Word List (page 37) for direct vocabulary study during guided reading. Words will vary according to the guided reading group. Students are tested every two weeks on ten of the words.

Select one or two new words per guided reading lesson. The words should be highly useful ones that come from the guided reading text being read that day. At the end of the lesson, the students write the new words in the first column of the New Word List. After the word is discussed, the students write a synonym or short definition for the word. Before the students leave the group, they receive a small colored slip (or slips) of paper for their "vocabulary bag." When they go to their seats, they write each new word on one side of a slip and the definition on the other side, like a flashcard. The new word slips go into a self-sealing plastic bag that contains previously learned words. The students use their vocabulary bags to do practice activities in school and at home.

Independent Practice Activities for the New Word List

Students need multiple experiences reading, writing, and speaking new vocabulary before they "own" it. Each day students can spend 20 minutes of the reading workshop doing one of the following activities using words from their New Word List:

✳ Turn and Talk: Students work with others from their guided reading group and take turns talking about the words on their list. They should use a word in a sentence and relate it either to the story they read in guided reading or to personal experiences.

✳ Guess This Word: Students work with a partner from their guided reading group and give clues about one of the words on their New Word List. "I'm thinking of a word that . . . ."

✳ High Five: One student writes down a word from the list, and the other(s) try to guess it by asking questions. The goal is to guess the word in less than five questions.

✳ How Do These Go Together? (Cunningham, 2009): Students pick two words from their vocabulary bags and write a sentence using both of the words.

✳ Picture This: A student draws an illustration for one of the new words, and the other students try to guess it.

Review Activities to Use During Guided Reading

Spend a minute during each guided reading lesson to review a few of the words on the New Word List.

✳ Option #1: Students cover the right (definition) column. The teacher *gives the definition* for a word and asks the students to point to the correct word on their list.

✳ Option #2: Again, students cover the right (definition) column. The teacher *asks for the definition* of one of the words. The students who know the definition put their thumbs up, and the teacher calls on one of the students.

✳ Option #3: Students take 6–10 vocabulary cards and place them on the table, word-side up. The teacher gives a definition, and the students point to one of the vocabulary cards.

✳ <u>Option #4</u>: The teacher distributes a different vocabulary word to each student. The students must either give a definition for their word or use it in a sentence that demonstrates the meaning of the word.

Assessing Students on Their New Words

Every week or so, test the students on the most recently learned words, plus additional words learned in previous weeks. An easy way to test is to have the students fold back or cover the definition column on their New Word List so they see only the word column. If you say a word, the students must write a definition for the word. If you say the definition of the word, the students have to find the matching word on their list and write it on their paper. Quickly score the test and let students highlight the words they got right on their New Word List. Highlighting is a great motivator!

Questions Teachers Ask About Classroom Management

How do I get everything done in the allotted time?

✳ Use a timer! It is easy to unintentionally extend any guided reading lesson or other whole-group activity beyond the scheduled time. If you truly want to get everything in, you need to keep to your schedule.

✳ Analyze your schedule and set priorities. Eliminate activities that have little educational value (such as worksheets). Make every minute count. Use the beginning or end of the day for writing workshop or shared reading. I have found that precious minutes are lost with meaningless board work or the lunch count. Practice morning routines and teach children how to take their own attendance and select their lunch choice.

✳ Be sure workstation materials are accessible to children, and make the children accountable for putting materials in their proper place. You don't want to waste time trying to find materials or cleaning up a station because the last team did not follow procedures.

✳ Work with your colleagues and principal to reduce intercom interruptions.

✳ Practice transitions until students can rotate between activities in less than one minute. Believe me, it is possible! You will get what you expect. If you expect children to take five minutes to move between workstations, then it will take students five minutes.

✳ Organize guided reading materials so they are easily accessible. Many teachers use a plastic dish tub for each reading group and put the books and other materials they will use for that group in the tub.

How can I keep the noise level in my classroom within reasonable limits during independent work/guided reading time?

✳ Teach students how to use a whisper voice. If students touch their throat, they will not feel a vibration if they are whispering. They will feel a vibration, however, when they are talking softly. You could even have a whisper monitor who reminds loud students to use their whisper voice. If you teach children to whisper, I guarantee you will have fewer headaches at the end of the day. Expect whisper voices in the centers and at the guided reading table. Again, you will get what you expect.

✳ Remember to use a soft voice when you speak to the students at the guided reading table. I have watched the noise level in a classroom rise because the teacher was using a "teacher voice" during guided reading.

✳ Use a soft bell, a song, a rhyme, etc. to get the attention of the whole class when it is time to rotate. One great idea is to place a music box next to the guided reading table. When it is time to rotate, open the box to let the music play. As soon as children have moved to their next rotation, close the music box. If there is still music in the box at the end of reading workshop, you can award a point. Create some type of class reward for collecting a certain number of points.

How can I keep children from interrupting me when I am working with small groups in guided reading?

✳ Demonstrate and practice routines so students know exactly what to do at the workstations. Teach children how to ask other members in the group for help when they have a problem.

✳ If students keep coming to you for help while you are teaching a group, analyze the work you assign. Is it too hard, too complex? Can every student be successful?

✳ Make workstation activities multi-leveled so every student can find an activity appropriate for his or her reading abilities.

✳ Record the interruptions you receive and analyze them. Is there a pattern to the interruptions? What can you do to encourage more student independence?

✳ Develop a signal so children know when they must not interrupt you.

✳ Do not respond to children who interrupt you during guided reading. Do not look at them and do not speak to them.

✳ Put two chairs on either side of the guided reading table and label them, "Observation Chairs." If a student is disruptive during your guided reading lesson, motion the student to sit in the Observation Chair until your guided reading lesson is over and you can deal with the problem.

How do I know students are reading their self-selected books?

It is impossible to know for certain that students are reading and understanding their self-selected books, but one way to monitor self-selected reading is through individual conferences. Ideally, you would like to meet with each student at least once a week to discuss his or her self-selected book. Another way is for the students to keep a reading log that lists books they have read independently. You can further monitor independent reading by requiring students to write letters to you about the books they read.

Reading Response, Grade 2

Directions: Select one of the books you read this week and draw a picture of your favorite part.
Below the picture, tell why this was your favorite part.
Tell me what books you read each day.

_____

_____

_____

Monday I read _____ by _____.

Tuesday I read _____ by _____.

Wednesday I read _____ by _____.

Thursday I read _____ by _____.

Friday I read _____ by _____.

Reading Response Choices for Fiction, Grades 2–3

Each week, choose one of the activities for your response letter.
Put a check in the box when you have used the response.

Name _____		Grading Period 1 2 3 4
Which character deserves an award? Why?	Draw a picture that describes the setting. How is the setting important to the plot?	How was the problem solved?
Use 5-finger retelling to retell the story.	Describe and illustrate your favorite part.	Compare two characters in the story. How were they alike?
Contrast two characters in the story. How were they different?	Make a connection. What did the story remind you of?	Draw three pictures to describe events that happened in the beginning, middle, and end of the story. Write about each picture.

Reading Response Choices for Nonfiction, Grades 2–3

Each week, choose one of the activities for your response letter.
Put a check in the box when you have used the response.

Name _____		Grading Period 1 2 3 4
What questions do you have about the topic?	What connections did you make as you read?	Write about some facts you learned from your reading. Share your opinion about something you read.
Pick three events from your book and write about the things that caused those events to happen.	Describe the main ideas and details you read this week.	Compare or contrast ideas from the book. Write about two things that are similar or different.
Draw a picture that summarizes what you learned this week. Label your drawing to identify important ideas.	What information was most interesting to you?	Write a letter to the author. What did you like? What questions do you have?

Figure 1-2

Reading Response Rubric—Option #1

	4	3	2	1	Score
Ideas	More than three interesting ideas	Two or three interesting ideas	One or two ideas	Does not make sense	
Organization	Well organized, logical sequence	Organized but a weak beginning or ending	Lacks transitions or logical flow	Not organized; no beginning or end	
Letter Form date, greeting, closing, signature	All letter components included	Lacks one letter component	Lacks two letter components	Lacks three or more letter components	
Neatness	Presentation is clean and neat; easy to read	Easy to read but not as neat	Somewhat challenging to read	Very difficult to read	
Spelling	No errors	One or two errors	Three to five errors	More than five errors	
TOTAL					

Reading Response Rubric—Option #2

Developed by Debbi Rosenow's fifth grade students

TOTAL Score: _____

Appearance and Format

_____ date   _____ greeting

_____ closing   _____ capitalization (beginning of sentences & proper nouns)

_____ spelling   _____ punctuation (including underlining the title of the book)

_____ paragraphs are indented

4 = complete and neat; response is easily understood	3 = almost complete and neat; response is mostly understood	2 = incomplete; weak; somewhat accurate so that parts of response are understood	1 = not attempted; inaccurate; response is difficult to read and understand

What should be in the first paragraph?

_____ Give name of book & author.   _____ Give a brief summary of what you read this week.

_____ Write three–four sentences.

4 = complete; briefly tells what is happening in the story; includes four ideas	3 = almost complete; briefly tells what is happening in the story; includes two or three ideas	2 = incomplete; weak attempt; briefly tells what is happening in the story; includes one or two ideas	1 = not attempted; inaccurate; does not tell any events from the story

What should be in the second paragraph?

_____ Think deeply about your reading.   _____ Write three or four sentences.

_____ Include your connections, inferences, or questions.

4 = complete; shows deep understanding by providing evidence and making connections	3 = almost complete; shows adequate understanding of the text and includes at least one connection	2 = incomplete; weak attempt; shows some understanding of the text but no connections	1 = not attempted; inaccurate; shows little or no understanding of the text with no connections

What should be in the third paragraph?

_____ Tell something you would like your teacher to know about your reading this week.

_____ Share your opinion of the book.

_____ Would you recommend this book to a friend? Why or why not?

4 = complete	3 = almost complete	2 = incomplete	1= not attempted

New Word List

Name _____   Date Begun _____

New Word	Definition

chapter

2

Assessment

AND GROUPING

Most teachers hate assessment. I think it's because many mandated assessments do not have instructional value. Assessment is paramount, however, to delivering effective guided reading instruction. If you want to help children learn to read, you simply must do assessment. Assessments should help you answer the following questions: How should I group my students? What text should I use with each group? What strategy should I teach next?

I suggest you use a variety of reading and writing assessments to identify reading levels and expose skills and strategies the students need to learn. The assessments you use will differ according to each student's reading level. Emergent and early readers will require a greater variety of assessments than transitional and fluent readers.

Assessments for Emergent and Early Readers

For a child just entering kindergarten, it is helpful to know if the student can identify the letters of the alphabet and write his or her first name. It the student does well on those two skills, I follow up with a word list, running record, dictated sentence, and writing sample. The word list and running record are individual tests, but the dictated sentence and writing sample can easily be completed in small groups.

Just make sure the students don't copy from each other. The following chart lists some assessments that are useful for forming emergent and early guided reading groups:

Primary Assessments	Information Provided
Letter identification (K–1)	Known letters and visual discrimination
Sight word list (K–2)	Known words and visual memory
Dictated sentence (K–1)	Sound/letter knowledge, phonemic awareness, and letter formation
Writing sample (K–2)	Oral language, vocabulary, visual memory, phonemic awareness, concepts of print
Running record (K–2) Oral retell	Reading level and strategies Recall

Letter Identification

Show the student an alphabet chart in which the letters are out of sequence. Ask the student to name the letters on the chart. It is important to record both incorrect and correct responses so you can help the child sort out any confusion. Letter knowledge is directly related to experiences the child had prior to entering kindergarten, so a meager knowledge of letters doesn't mean the child has a learning disability. However, strong letter knowledge indicates the student has visual memory and discrimination abilities. If a student scores well on the letter test, there is no need to repeat it.

Sight Word List

Ask the child to read and write a short list of easy words common in emergent-level texts. Record both correct and incorrect responses. Most beginning kindergarten students know few, if any, sight words, but this test is helpful in grouping mid-year kindergarten and first-grade students for guided reading. A child who recognizes sight words is strong in visual memory and should be able to read these words when they appear in text.

Dictated Sentence

This assessment could be administered in a group of four or five students and is especially useful for emergent and early readers. Ask the children to write a sentence you dictate and encourage them to stretch out each word as they write the sounds they hear. Be careful not to stretch any words for the students. It is critical that you find out what the child can do without any help. The following sentences are appropriate for kindergarten and first-grade students.

Kindergarten Sentences (easiest to hardest)	First Grade Sentences (easiest to hardest)
A. My name is _____. B. I am happy at school. C. I like to eat oatmeal for breakfast. D. I have to sit on a rug. E. I wish I had peanut butter on my sandwich. F. This is a fine day for swimming at the beach.	A. I want to go to the playground today. B. My teacher is going to read me a story. I will sit on the rug and be quiet. C. I have great friends in my class. I think I will share my snack. D. Next year I want to do even better at school. I will try my hardest in second grade.

Although most teachers like to score these sentences by awarding one point for every sound the child records correctly, the real benefit in this assessment is determining how the student processes and records sounds. Is the student hearing consonants? Does the student hear sounds at the beginning or end of a word? Does the student hear any vowel sounds, digraphs, blends, or endings? I actually learn a lot more about children if they misspell a word than if they already know how to write it. That is why I include words kindergarteners and first graders would not normally know how to spell. You want to learn how they hear sounds, not if they can spell. Additionally, you will learn how the child forms letters and which letter formations you need to teach. All this information is useful when you plan the word study component of your guided reading lessons.

Writing Sample

In addition to the dictated sentence, I like to see an unedited writing sample from writing workshop. With a writing sample, I can assess the child's phonemic awareness and analyze language structure, vocabulary, and concepts of print. In my analysis I ask these questions to uncover more of the child's processing system:

✳ **Oral language and vocabulary:** Did the child create his or her own story? Did the story make sense and fit Standard English structure? Did the student use interesting vocabulary?

✳ **Visual memory:** Did the student spell any sight words correctly?

✳ **Phonemic awareness:** Did the student hear and record sounds in sequence? Is the child hearing vowels, digraphs, endings, and/or blends?

✳ **Concepts of print:** Did the student write left to right? Did he or she put spaces between words and appropriately use capital letters and punctuation?

Analyzing a Running Record

Running records (Clay, 2000) are valuable assessments for guided reading. In addition to telling you what text level is appropriate for instruction, they indicate strategies and skills you need to teach. There are several commercial assessment kits for administering a running record. *Leveled Books for Readers* (Fountas & Pinnell, 2002), *Developmental Reading Assessment* (Beaver, 2006), *Rigby PM Benchmark Kit* (Nelley & Smith, 2000), and the *Qualitative Reading Inventory* (Leslie & Caldwell, 2005) all have leveled passages for assessing a child's reading level. However, you don't need a kit to take a running record. Any text and a blank sheet of paper will do.

During my doctoral studies, I worked with a woman named Winnie, who had contacted the university to get help with reading. Winnie was 74 years old and could not read. I met her in a local restaurant and asked her why she wanted to learn to read now, at her age. She told me she wanted to read the Bible to the old folks in the nursing home. Right then I made a commitment to her and myself that I would teach her how to read. I hadn't brought an assessment kit with me so I asked Winnie to do the best she could to read the menu. She smiled shyly and said she might not do too well because she needed new glasses. I grabbed a napkin off the table and took a running record as she read the menu. As I analyzed her attempts and errors I realized she knew quite a few sight words but had no strategies for figuring out unknown words except looking at the pictures. For six weeks, I went to Winnie's house to teach her how to read. We specifically worked on strategies such as using meaning, finding known parts, and using analogies to figure out tricky words. At our last visit, I gave her a new Bible, a contemporary version written at the fourth-grade level. Tears filled her eyes as she read a few verses and said, "I would never go to a Bible study before because I was afraid they would call on me to read. I guess I can start going now." A running record taken on a napkin was the first step to helping Winnie become a reader.

The fact that a student can read a passage does not mean he or she comprehends it. It is always a good idea to ask the student to retell after a running record to find out how much the student remembers. I remember taking a running record on a sixth grade girl who had been identified as needing help with reading. She read the passage perfectly with appropriate intonation and expression. Then I said, "Tell me what you just read." She gave me a puzzled look and responded, "Am I supposed to remember what I read?" She was serious, and I knew we had work to do.

Step 1: Determine the Accuracy Level

The first step in analyzing a running record is determining the accuracy level. Divide the number of words read accurately (including errors that were corrected) by the total number of words in the passage. This will give you a percentage. Use the accuracy score below to identify the text as being at an independent, instructional or frustration level. Remember, this is only the first step of analysis and does not consider comprehension.

Level	Accuracy	Appropriate approach
Independent	95–100%	Independent reading or literature circles
Instructional	90–94%	Guided reading
Frustration	Below 90%	Read-aloud or shared reading

Step 2: Analyze Errors

Take a close look at the errors the student made. You want to determine which information systems the student is using and which he or she is ignoring. There are three information systems to consider (Clay, 2006):

- Meaning (M): Does the student's error make sense? If so, the student is using meaning (also called semantics).

  Example Child says: *The boy <u>ran</u> down the <u>street</u>.*
  Text says: *The boy <u>runs</u> down the <u>road.</u>*

- Structure (S): Does the student's error follow the rules of grammar in Standard English? If so, the student is using structure (also called syntax). Most of the time, if the error makes sense it also matches structure.

Example Child says: *The boy hides in the cabinet.*
Text says: *The boy hid in the cabinet.*

♦ Visual cues (V): Is the error visually similar to the word in the text? If so, the student is using visual information (also called graphophonics).

Example Child says: *Kristen talks smoothly to the world dog.*
Text says: *Kristen talked soothingly to the wounded dog.*

Many struggling readers in the intermediate grades use visual information and ignore meaning. In the third example, the student said "world" for "wounded." Her error did not make sense, but "world" and "wounded" look similar.

Sometimes students will use all three information systems but still be wrong. In the same example, the child said "smoothly" for "soothingly." The error makes sense, fits standard structure, and looks similar. This error would be coded MSV. If the student ignores a particular information system, the teacher should prompt the student to use that system during guided reading. Teachers should not prompt students during a running record.

During guided reading . . .
If the student ignores meaning, say, "What would make sense?"
If the student ignores structure, say, "What would sound right?"
If the student ignores visual cues, say, "What would look right?"
More prompts are provided on the lesson plans in later chapters.

Step 3: Analyze Strategies

A strategy is an action a reader takes to solve a problem in the text. Emergent and early readers tend to be overt in their use of strategies. You will often see them look at the picture, reread, or try to sound out a word. Transitional readers may be hesitant to try an unknown word. If a student appeals for help, always say, "I want you to try." You will learn more about a student's reading process if the student makes an attempt and is incorrect. Analyzing a student's strategies will help you to decide how to prompt the student during guided reading lessons. The following strategies are critical for every reading level:

✳ Self-monitoring: Does the student stop when the reading is not making sense? Is the student aware of his or her errors? To prompt the student to self-monitor, say, "Are you sure? Does that look right and make sense?" Self-monitoring should occur at every reading level. If the student does not notice an error has been made, there will be no attempt to fix it.

* Cross-checking: Does the student use more than one information system to problem-solve unknown words? Cross-checking at an emergent reading level would involve using initial letters and pictures to problem-solve an unknown word. However, whenever a reader uses both visual information and meaning, he or she is cross-checking.

* Self-correcting: Does the student fix an error if it does not make sense? A student may monitor but not be successful in correcting the error.

Step 4: Assess Fluency

Although running records aren't usually timed, Richard Allington (2009) suggests teachers calculate the reading rate to determine the number of words correct per minute (WCPM). To get this rate, simply divide the number of words read accurately by the total time it took to read the passage. The WCPM can be compared to the average grade-level reading rates; however, I do not recommend a strict pass-fail determination. Strategic readers often read slower if they reread to monitor or stop to figure out an unknown word.

Average Number of Words Correct Per Minute by Grade Level and Time of Year			
	Fall	**Winter**	**Spring**
Grade 2	51	72	89
Grade 3	71	92	107
Grade 4	94	112	123
Grade 5	110	127	139
Grade 6	127	140	150

Source: Hasbrouck & Tindal, 2006

Speed and accuracy should not be the sole measures of fluency. You need to consider the student's expression, intonation, and attention to punctuation. I have simplified the four-point fluency scale posted on the NAEP Web site (http://nces.ed.gov) to help teachers assign a fluency rating to the running record.

1: Reading is very slow, mostly word-by-word.

2: Reading is choppy, mostly two-word phrases.

3: Reading is mostly phrased, but lacks some aspect of fluency such as speed, intonation, expression, or attention to punctuation.

4: Reading is fluent and phrased with appropriate expression and intonation.

Step 5: Assess Comprehension

Most reading assessment kits include a comprehension check. If the student reads the text at 90% accuracy and exhibits some fluency, determine whether the student understood the basic information in the text. You should not expect 100% understanding at an instructional level, but the student should understand the gist of the story. Although it is difficult to quantify comprehension, most researchers consider 75–80% to be an instructional level. The following behaviors may also indicate the student probably understands what he or she is reading:

* The student substitutes words that make sense.

* The student rereads to confirm or repair meaning.

* The student reads with expression.

* The student retells the main ideas and some details in the text.

A word of caution: No single instrument can capture the total reading process. When making instructional decisions, always consider the student's day-to-day responses and reading behaviors during guided reading lessons.

Step 6: Select a Focus for Instruction

Use the information from the running record to decide the focus strategy for your guided reading instruction. The following issues are priority ranked and should be addressed during guided reading.

Risk-Taking: This is the most important teaching point. A student who constantly appeals for help and makes no attempt on unknown words is not developing independence. Telling the student the word will only encourage continued appeals for help. Teachers often equate a lack of risk-taking to a lack of self-confidence. This may be true, but the lack of self-confidence may also be a result of not being successful or having a teacher (or parent) correct every error. If a student does not try unknown words, the first step is to stop correcting the child. Instead say, "That was a good try." Or "I like the way you checked your picture. You must be thinking about what would make sense." If the student refuses to make any attempt say, "Try something." At this point, it is important to ask yourself, "Does the student know what to try? Does he or she know how to use the information in the picture and in the text?" Make sure you are explicit in modeling decoding strategies that are appropriate for the student's reading level.

Self-Monitoring: When a student makes an error that does not make sense, does he or she stop? This is the first strategy I look for on a running record, and I frequently notice it is missing with struggling readers in the intermediate grades. If the student does not realize that what is being said does not make sense, he or she will likely have very poor comprehension. To prompt for this strategy, allow the student to finish reading the sentence and then say, "Did that make sense?" If the student says, "Yes," then reread what the student said and ask him or her to find the tricky part. Once the student is monitoring for meaning, he or she can use the decoding strategies below. It is important to also occasionally ask "Did that make sense?" when students read accurately. Otherwise they will begin to depend on your prompting to monitor their reading.

Decoding: Good readers use many different strategies to figure out unknown words, even at the earliest levels. If you notice that a student is stopping at an error but does not figure out the new word, he or she needs to learn more decoding strategies. Here are some strategies that work with just about every stage of reader:

* Reread and sound out the first part of the word. What would make sense?

* Check the picture and think what would make sense and look right.

* Cover the ending. Is there a part you know?

* Chunk that word and sound each part. Think about what would make sense.

* Is there another word you know that looks similar? (This strategy takes a while for students to internalize because the student must know a large bank of words in order to make an analogy).

Fluency: Does the student read with phrasing and expression? Does the student stop at periods and use appropriate intonation? If the answer is no, then you probably need to work on fluency. I don't expect perfect fluency on a running record because the text is supposed to be at an instructional level, but you should see some evidence of short phrasing and expression. There are several things you can do to improve fluency, but first make sure the text is not too difficult. The student cannot be expected to be fluent if he or she is doing a lot of problem-solving. The following prompts target fluency:

    ❋   *Try reading it without your finger.*

    ❋   *How would the character say that? Can you read it like the character would say it?*

    ❋   *Read it smoothly.*

Oral Retell: Is the student able to recall the main events and some details of the story? It is not unusual to find students who read accurately and fluently but are not able to recall what they read. During guided reading, try the following prompts:

    ❋   *Look at the picture and tell me what you read.* (Retell with picture support.)

    ❋   *What did you read on this page?* (Cover picture & retell without support.)

    ❋   *What happened at the beginning of the story? Then what happened? Think about the pictures in the story.*

Comprehension: Although retelling is one level of comprehension, it does not explore deeper understanding. Once children are fluently reading with a literal level of comprehension, it is appropriate to prompt for higher-level thinking and inferencing. The chapter on fluent guided reading provides numerous strategies for improving comprehension.

Assessments for Transitional and Fluent Readers

For transitional and fluent readers, a leveled passage with comprehension questions is the most valuable assessment. I usually ask transitional readers to read the passage aloud so I can determine whether the student monitors for meaning and uses effective decoding strategies. Fluent readers can read the passage silently. After the reading (whether oral or silent), the student should give an oral retell and respond to some questions about the passage so you can assess comprehension. Since most transitional readers are still learning phonic skills, I recommend the following spelling inventory that pinpoints needed areas of word study.

Word Study Inventory for Transitional Readers

Directions: Dictate the following words as the student writes them on a blank sheet of paper. Then circle the skills that need further instruction. Teach short vowels and digraphs before you teach blends and endings.

Student Name _____ Date _____

	Short Vowel	Digraph	Initial Blend	Final Blend	Long vowel VCe	Vowel Team Diphthong	R-Controlled Vowel	Inflections
1. span	a		sp					
2. sled	e		sl					
3. chip	i	ch						
4. shot	o	sh						
5. thud	u	th						
6. brick			br	–ck				
7. plump			pl	–mp				
8. skunk			sk	–nk				
9. clasp			cl	–sp				
10. grope			gr		o-e			
11. twine			tw		i-e			
12. blade			bl		a-e			
13. stark			st				ar	
14. thorn		th					or	
15. chirp		ch					ir	
16. snare			sn		–are			
17. sprain			spr			ai		
18. dream			dr			ea		
19. croak			cr			oa		
20. fright			fr			igh		
21. glowing			gl			ow		–ing
22. talked						alk		–ed (/t/)
23. pouted						ou		–ed (/ed/)
24. broil			br			oi		
25. prowled			pr			ow		–ed (/d/)
26. flapped			fl					–pped doubling feature
27. tries			tr					y to i, add –es
28. hiking								e drop
Word-study activities	picture sorts, making words, sound boxes, and analogy charts				analogy charts			

The Next Step in Guided Reading © 2009 by Jan Richardson, Scholastic Professional

Streamlining Assessment for Intermediate Students

Because instructional time is precious and should be guarded, I have developed procedures that streamline the assessment process for intermediate readers.

Step 1: Initial Screening

If you do not have a previous assessment, give students a word list that matches their grade level. Divide students into two groups—those who can decode words at grade level and those who cannot.

Step 2: Assessment of Below-Grade-Level Decoders

* **Oral reading:** Begin with the leveled passage that is at the student's instructional level as determined by the word list. Ask the student to read the text aloud as you take a running record. If the text is too difficult (<90% accuracy), stop the reading and give the student an easier text to read. After you take the running record on the first reading, invite the student to read it again silently before you ask the student to retell the passage.

* **Retelling:** Remove the text and ask the student to tell you everything he or she can remember about the story. Do not prompt for specific information. You can say, "Is there anything else you remember?"

* **Comprehension questions:** Regardless of the retelling, ask the comprehension questions. Record the student's responses on the recording sheet. Do not allow the student to look back. After you ask all the questions, you may repeat the questions the student missed and invite the student to look back in the text for the answer. If the student tries to reread the entire text, discontinue the look-backs. Correct answers with look-backs *do not* change the student's comprehension score, but they *do* tell you whether or not the student can find answers to questions.

* **Determination of the instructional reading level:** Consider both the oral-reading accuracy and the comprehension questions (without look-backs) to determine an appropriate text level for guided reading. Your goal is to find the level at which the student reads with at least 90% accuracy and has 75–85% comprehension. If the student passes the oral reading, but is at the frustration level on the comprehension

questions, then that level is too difficult for guided reading. Ask the student to silently read a text at a lower level and then do the retell and comprehension questions.

If the student scores at the independent level on both the oral reading and comprehension, this level is too easy for guided reading but appropriate for independent reading. Give the student a text to read at a higher level. After the student reads this text out loud, check comprehension. You should take another running record because this text is more difficult than the previous passage.

Step 3: Assessment of On- and Above-Grade-Level Decoders

Now you should assess the students who passed the word list for your grade level. Since you already know these students can decode grade-level text, you do not need to take a running record. Ask the students to silently read the passage that matches their instructional level as determined by the graded word lists. After the silent reading, remove the text and ask the student to retell the text and answer the comprehension questions. If the student does well on the comprehension, give the student a passage at a higher level. If the student reaches the frustration level on the comprehension, give him or her a text at a lower level. Your goal is to find the instructional level for comprehension. You might want to do a comprehension interview to assess specific comprehension strategies.

Using a Comprehension Interview

The following assessment is adapted from Ellin Keene's (1997) "Major Point Interview for Reading" found in *Mosaic of Thought*. It can be completed during independent reading, although you do not need to do the entire assessment at one sitting. You may choose to give the entire class certain portions of the assessment to determine which students need more instruction in specific comprehension strategies. Some teachers have incorporated this interview into their reading conferences. The purpose of the interview is to identify which comprehension strategies the student has internalized and which ones still need to be taught. Information from the interview is useful in grouping students for guided reading. If you have several students who have trouble summarizing, they would be grouped together and taught this comprehension strategy.

Sit next to the student and ask him or her to tell you about the book. Check (✓) the story elements the student mentions. It is not necessary for you to have read the book to assess retelling. Simply scan the chapter titles and ask for more clarification on a specific chapter the student has read. Be aware that students will choose books they have already heard or seen in the theater. The retell in this case would be invalid.

Now have the student read a few paragraphs to you. There is space on the second page of the interview to record miscues and strategies. Your intent is to determine if the book the student has selected is easy enough for independent reading. I commonly come across intermediate students who select books that are too difficult. If this is the case, there is no need to continue the interview. Your job is to help the student find another book. I always tell students there are just two rules for selecting a book for independent reading: The book must be easy, and they must enjoy it. If the student does not like the book or cannot decode it easily, he or she will quickly lose interest and spend the entire reading workshop browsing the classroom library or daydreaming.

If the text is at an independent level, have the student continue reading a few more paragraphs. Stop the reading and assess one or more of the comprehension strategies listed in the interview. You can use the rubric to determine if the student has internalized a specific comprehension strategy (score of 3) or if the student needs more instruction on that strategy (score of 1 or 2).

I do not grade the interview. I use it as another tool for grouping students and identifying an instructional focus for guided reading. After you have assessed all your students and are ready to group students for fluent guided reading, you can input the data on the "Assessment Summary for Fluent Readers" described in Chapter 6.

Comprehension Interview

Adapted from Keene, E. (1997) *Mosaic of Thought*, "Major Point Interview for Reading"

Student Name _____

Date _____ Text (pg.) _____

Retell fiction: What has happened in the story so far?

_____ Setting   _____ Character   _____ Problem(s)

_____ Events   _____ Solutions

Retell nonfiction: What are you learning about? _____

_____

_____

Teacher says: Start reading where you left off. I'll listen. (Student whisper reads while teacher records miscues and self-corrections on back of interview sheet.)

Text level:

_____ Easy (95–100%)

_____ Instructional (90–94%)

_____ Frustration (< 90%)

Teacher says: Keep reading, and I'll stop you once in a while and ask you some questions.

Strategy	Questions	Student Response	Rubric
Self-Monitors Uses fix-up strategies when meaning breaks down	• What can you do to make the sentence make sense? • What else can you do to help yourself?		1. "I don't know." 2. Fix-up strategies do not clear up confusion. 3. Fix-up strategies help clarify meaning.
Connects Makes connections to personal experiences, previous knowledge, or other texts s/he has read	• What did you think about when you read that part of the story? • Did it remind you of something you already know, an experience you've had, or another book? Tell me.		1. "I don't know." 2. Response is not related to text. 3. Response relates background knowledge & personal experiences to text and enhances comprehension.

Comprehension Interview *(continued)*

Strategy	Questions	Student Response	Rubric
Summarizes Provides a concise summary that captures the main idea and important details	• What is this part mainly about? • Can you tell me in one or two sentences what you just learned?		1. No response or incorrect 2. Recalls some events in random order 3. Synthesizes succinctly, recalling main idea and details in sequence.
Predicts Makes logical prediction(s) based on events	• What do you think will happen next? • What might you learn next? • What in the text helped you make that prediction?		1. No response or "I don't know." 2. Prediction is not substantiated with text. 3. Prediction is consistent and logical with text. It is plausible.
Questions Asks questions while reading to clarify meaning or extend the meaning	• What did you wonder about as you were reading? • What questions did you ask yourself? • What confusions did you have?		1. No response or an unrelated question 2. Literal question with short answer 3. Higher-order question that represents complex thinking about the text
Infers Reads "between the lines" to capture unstated but implied information	• What did the author mean by _____? • What are you thinking about the character? • What were you thinking when the text said _____?		1. No response or "I don't know." 2. Response is stated in the text or not logical. 3. Response is logical and shows inferential thinking.
Visualizes Creates mental images of characters, events, and/or ideas	• What did you picture in your mind? • What did the characters look like? • What could you draw to illustrate that idea?		1. No response 2. Image is unrelated to the text. 3. Image is closely matched with the text and further clarifies complex ideas.

Miscues and Self-Corrections

Questions Teachers Ask About Assessment

What assessments should I use?

As long as you have a leveled text, you can find the instructional level with a running record and an oral retell. If you prefer a commercial assessment package, select one with short, leveled passages and a comprehension component. When assessing emergent and early readers, use passages or books with pictures.

Why should I take a running record?

Running records capture the reading process of emergent, early, and transitional readers. An analysis of the errors reveals the strategies a child uses at difficulty and the strategies the child needs to learn next. Running records are not useful with fluent readers because fluent students make few, if any, errors. When assessing fluent readers, I have them read the passage silently and then do the retell and comprehension questions.

Should I introduce the text used for an assessment?

Always state the title and a main idea sentence. These introductions are usually printed on the testing forms. The student quickly looks through the pictures (if available) and begins reading. *Do not* introduce any vocabulary.

Should the student read the text silently first?

Again, assessments will differ on this point, but there is more to be gained by taking the running record on a cold read because you can capture all the strategic processes. If you let the student read the story first, he or she will likely score better, but you will lose the opportunity to observe the strategies the child uses at difficulty. It is always appropriate to give the student the opportunity to reread the text silently before you ask comprehension questions or ask for a retelling.

What if the student asks for help?

It is always best to maintain an objective position in assessment. Do not give prompts or helpful hints. If the child gets stuck, say "Try it." If the student refuses to go on reading, say, "Go on." Some assessments allow you to give unknown words to students, but that can distort the reliability of the test. Stay as neutral as possible.

How do I assess comprehension?

First ask the student to retell the story. You can prompt for general information such as, "Can you tell me about the characters (or the setting)?" Or you can say, "Do you remember anything else?" After the oral retelling, ask the comprehension questions included with the assessment.

How are texts leveled?

Most publishing companies give a recommended guided reading level for their texts— but leveling texts is not an exact science. Some companies use a readability formula that considers sentence length and number of syllables in words. These formulas, however, do not make allowances for challenging vocabulary and background knowledge. This is especially important at the intermediate levels. A text should be matched to the needs of the group, not just the reading level. In other words, when selecting an informational text at levels above M, you need to consider both prior knowledge and decoding skills.

How do I know when to move a student to a higher-level guided reading group?

You do not need to formally assess students before moving them to a different guided reading group. When you notice a student reading with fluency, accuracy, and understanding, put him or her in a higher group. In guided reading, the text needs to be slightly challenging so the student can practice using strategies. If you find there is little for you to teach, then the text is probably too easy. It is obvious when the text is too difficult.

chapter 3

Pre-A and Emergent

GUIDED READING

Emergent readers are typically kindergarten and first-grade students; however, children at higher grade levels who are learning to speak English or have special learning needs may also need emergent skills and strategies. The lesson plans described in this chapter are appropriate for children at any age or grade who are reading between level Pre-A (nonreader) and level C (DRA 4). This chapter includes two kinds of lessons: the Pre-A lesson and the Emergent Guided Reading lesson.

Understanding Emergent Readers

The Pre-A lesson is for children not ready for traditional guided reading lessons because they know fewer than 40 upper- and lowercase letters and hear few, if any, sounds. If these students have had limited experiences with books prior to entering school, they probably lack early concepts of print such as left-to-right tracking and the concept of a letter or word. The Pre-A lesson framework is especially useful for students learning to speak English. Students who need these nascent literacy skills learn a great deal from whole-group activities such as read-alouds, shared reading, and interactive writing. Their specific needs, however, are best addressed in small groups with the Pre-A lesson plan. The framework includes four components:

* ❋ Working with letters and names
* ❋ Working with sounds
* ❋ Working with books
* ❋ Interactive writing

Once students know most of their letters and have enough English to understand simple directions, they are ready for emergent guided reading lessons. The emergent reading stage includes students who are reading at levels A–C. Each emergent guided reading lesson focuses on teaching appropriate skills and strategies.

Reading skills and reading strategies are not the same. A strategy is a behavior or thought process a reader uses to construct meaning especially when the reader is confused. A skill is an item of information, such as a letter sound, ending, or vowel combination. Skills are important and need to be taught, but they are useless if the student does not have the necessary strategies to use the skills.

Emergent Reading Skills	Emergent Reading Strategies
• Letter formation • Know all letters and sounds • Read and write sight words • Segment sounds in sequence (consonant-vowel-consonant) • Space between words during writing	• Employ one-to-one matching • Use meaning (picture clues) and initial letters to figure out unknown words • Segment sounds to write unknown words • Use meaning, known words, and initial letters to self-monitor during reading and writing • Discuss a story with teacher prompting

Trace an Alphabet Book

Students who cannot identify at least 40 upper- and lowercase letters in the alphabet (counting both uppercase and lowercase letters), should trace an alphabet book with a tutor every day. The sooner these children learn the names of the letters, the sooner they will benefit from whole-group and small-group instruction. You can use a simple published alphabet book or alphabet cards, but the process works best if the pictures in the student's ABC book are the same pictures you have on your classroom alphabet chart or frieze. The goal of the tracing is to teach the name of each letter and create a picture link for the letter sound. The tracing occurs outside the Pre-A small-group lesson and is usually done by a teaching assistant, a volunteer, or an upper-grade student. Each page of the alphabet book should have the capital and lowercase letter along with a picture. Select pictures familiar to the students. Do not include the word for the picture, as this can be confusing.

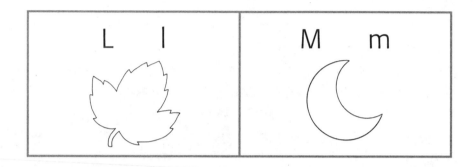

Tracing Procedures

The student uses his or her pointing finger to trace each upper- and lowercase letter in the ABC book, saying the name of the letter each time. Then the student points to the picture and names it (e.g., "A, a, apple"). Do not allow students to trace with a pencil or marker. The tactile experience is essential for building a memory trace. The student traces every letter in the book as long as he or she knows at least ten different letter forms. If a student knows fewer than ten letter forms, have the student trace only the letters he or she knows and the letters in his or her first name. The tutor helps the student when necessary.

Tutor Support

The tutor sits next to the student (not across the table) and observes the student trace each upper- and lowercase letter. The tutor should only help if the student struggles with the name of the letter, letter formation, or the picture.

　＊　If the student does not know the name of the letter, the tutor says the letter name. Then the student should repeat the name of the letter while tracing it in the book with his or her finger.

　＊　If a student does not know how to form a letter correctly, the tutor lightly holds the student's hand and helps the student trace the letter. Always have the student trace the letter from top to bottom. Release the student's hand when the student no longer needs the tutor's support with letter formation.

✳ If the student does not know the concept in the picture, the tutor should explain the concept and have the student repeat the picture.

Does Tracing the Alphabet Book Work?

I have been collecting data on tracing the alphabet book for ten years. It is by far the fastest and easiest way for children to learn their letters even if they are learning English as a second language. Kindergarten teachers from Greenwood, South Carolina, tried this procedure on 45 students who, even after two months of school, did not know at least 40 letters (upper- and lowercase letters were counted separately). After 18 tracing sessions, the group gained an average of 18 letters.

For the most part, the students who began with fewer known letters took the longest to learn the letters. Individual learning rates varied, but on average, students who began kindergarten knowing fewer than five letters took three months of tracing to learn the letters. Students who knew between 6–15 letters in August took two months, and those who knew at least 16 letters when they entered kindergarten, took only one month of tracing to learn their letters.

One more piece of data: This year, I worked closely with 52 kindergarten teachers from school districts in South Carolina and Tennessee. All the teachers used the tracing procedures on their students who didn't know the alphabet. In this group of over 1,000 students, there were many children learning English as a second language and others who were already coded for special education. At the end of the school year, only one student did not know at least 40 letters, and that child had severe learning challenges.

Preparing for Pre-A Lessons

In addition to tracing an alphabet book every day, students who know fewer than 40 letters should receive small-group instruction with the classroom teacher. It works best if you group students according to their letter knowledge, but do not put more than four students in one group. For example, the four children with the fewest known letters will be in the same group so you can better target their needs. The Pre-A lesson has four distinct components that are designed to improve visual memory, phonemic awareness, oral language, and concepts of print. These four areas are the building blocks of emergent literacy (Clay, 1991) and strong predictors of reading success, according to the National Early Literacy Panel. The following chart lists the parts of a Pre-A lesson and the target skills for each component.

Pre-A Lesson Framework	
Lesson Component	**Target Skills**
Working With Letters and Names	Visual memory (with children's own names) Letter names Visual discrimination Visual scanning (left to right across a word)
Working With Sounds	Phonological awareness (hearing syllables and rhymes) Phonemic awareness (hearing initial consonants) Auditory discrimination (hearing the difference between sounds)
Working With Books	Concepts of print (left-to-right tracking, one-to-one matching, concept of letter/word, first/last, capital/lowercase) Oral language and English syntax Vocabulary (high-frequency words and picture concepts)
Interactive Writing	Phonemic awareness (hearing consonant sounds) Linking consonant sounds to letters Letter formation Concepts of print (left-to-right tracking, spacing between words, capital/lowercase letters, concept of letter/word, and first/last)

The entire lesson lasts 15–20 minutes and should include one activity from all four components. The four components support emergent literacy development and need to be integrated throughout the lesson. The greatest challenge you will likely face is getting all four components done in one 20-minute lesson. Teachers frequently ask me if they can spread the lesson over two days and do one or two components each day, but it is best if you address all four activities in one session. That way you are able to make connections between skills and strategies and bring meaning to the emergent reading process. This format is not just about learning letters and sounds; it is about learning all of the important early literacy skills and strategies. In order for you to complete the lesson plan in the time allotted, you should spend only three to five minutes with each component. Changing the activity every few minutes keeps students engaged and focused. I have two suggestions for keeping the quick pace: Use a timer and limit teacher talk. Remember the student is also tracing an alphabet book every day outside the Pre-A lesson time.

Letter/Sound Checklist

Before you begin your Pre-A group instruction, you should prepare one letter/sound checklist for each group. The checklist should have space for four students because this is the maximum recommended group size for Pre-A lessons. Use the initial letter identification assessment to highlight known letters and sounds onto the Letter/Sound Checklist. As you work with the students, you will update the chart when you see evidence a student has learned a new letter or sound. Because you are working with a small group, it is easy to observe these new discoveries.

Letter/Sound Checklist

Directions: Highlight the letters and sounds the student knows.

Student Name _____

Letters:

A	B	C	D	E	F	G	H	I	J	K	L	M	N	O	P	Q	R	S	T	U	V	W	X	Y	Z
a	b	c	d	e	f	g	h	i	j	k	l	m	n	o	p	q	r	s	t	u	v	w	x	y	z

Sounds:

a	b	c	d	e	f	g	h	i	j	k	l	m	n	o	p	q	r	s	t	u	v	w	x	y	z

As you plan your lesson, use the chart to determine which letters and sounds should be taught that day. During the first lesson component, you will teach the letter formation for one new letter. For sound-sorts you will select two letters most children know by name but not by sound. I never do a sound-sort if the students do not know the name of the letter. Often the name of the letter helps students learn the letter sound.

Additionally, the letter/sound chart will help you know how to prompt individual children throughout the lesson. For example, during a "Working With Books" segment, you might ask a specific child to locate a known letter (from his or her chart) or give you the sound of a letter. Getting children to transfer item knowledge to text reading is important. They need to learn to use what they know about letters as they read text.

Materials for Pre-A Lessons

Put the following materials in a plastic tub for each group:

* Alphabet charts (one per student)—Each child should have his or her own alphabet chart that has a picture for each letter. Place the alphabet chart inside a clear, heavy sheet protector. Students will use the alphabet chart throughout the lesson.

* Name template for rainbow-writing—Print each child's first name on a sheet of paper. Place the name template inside the same sheet protector that holds the alphabet chart. The alphabet chart is on one side and the child's first name on the other. The name template will be used during the first component called, "Working With Names."

* Personal letter bags—Label a quart-size bag with the student's name and insert the magnetic letters the student *knows*. If the student knows fewer than ten letters, include both the capital and lowercase forms of

the letters. Once the student knows ten lowercase letters, only use the lower-case magnetic letters in the bag. As students learn new letters, add these to the bag. The students will use their personal letter bags during "Working With Letters."

* Letter/sound checklist—Highlight each student's known letters and sounds, and update daily.

* Dry-erase markers and erasers (one per student)

* Wooden craft sticks or straws for pointers (one per student)

* Pictures for initial consonant sorts—Collect 6–8 pictures that begin with each consonant in the alphabet (excluding the letter *x*). Avoid pictures with beginning blends. Label 20 envelopes with the consonant letters and put the pictures in the corresponding envelope.

* Sentence strips and scissors for interactive writing

* Easy, Level A books with one line of print to use during "Working With Books"

* A timer

Description of the Pre-A Lesson Plan

Important Note: Keep the letter/sound checklist handy throughout the entire Pre-A lesson. You will use it to record new letters and sounds the students learn in the lesson. You will also use the checklist to determine which letter formation you should teach that day and which sounds you should work on with picture sorts. Additionally, when you do the interactive writing, you should use the checklist to decide which students should help you write a specific letter. Call on the student who knows the letter. If the student can't recall how to make the letter, direct the student to use the alphabet chart.

Part 1: Working With Letters and Names (3–4 minutes)

Research has shown that phonetic writing in young children starts with letters from their name (Both-de Vries & Bus, 2008). Therefore, the child's name should be the proper starting point for the development of basic knowledge of letter names and sounds. The purpose of this component is to teach visual discrimination, build rapid recall for letter names, improve visual memory, create some letter/sound links, teach letter formation, and teach students how to write their first name without a model. Do not spend more than four minutes working with letters and names. It is imperative that you have time to do all four activities during every lesson.

Pre-A Lesson Plan (Teacher uses one plan per group.)

Students _____ Date _____ Lesson # _____

Activity Options (select activities that target the needs of the group)	Observations/Notes
Eight Ways of Working With Letters Letter activity: #_____ Letter formation: _____	
Working With Names (Choose 1) (This component may be omitted once each student can write his/her name without a model and knows all the letters in his/her name.) • Use name puzzles. • Make names out of magnetic letters. • Do rainbow-writing with names.	
Working With Sounds (Choose 1) Clapping syllables 1 2 3 Rhyming words _____ Picture sorts _____	
Working With Books Do shared reading with a Level A book. Encourage oral language and teach print concepts (choose one or two): • Concept of a word (students frame each word in a sentence) • First/last word (students locate in text) • Concept of a letter (students frame a letter or count the letters in a word) • First/last letter (students locate in text) • Period (students locate in text) • Capital/lowercase letters (students locate in text)	Title:_____ Observations:_____ _____ _____ _____ _____
Interactive Writing & Cut-Up Sentence Sentence:	

Name Activities

Do **one** of the following activities for about one minute. This component can be omitted once children know the letters in their first name and can write their first name without a model.

✳ **Name Puzzles:** Write each student's first name on tag board. Cut the name into two parts and put it in a legal-sized envelope. Print the student's name on the front of the envelope. Give the envelopes to the students and tell them to put their name puzzle together. They can use the front of the envelope as a model. When a student can put the puzzle together with the model, turn the envelope over and have him or her remake the puzzle without looking at the model. Then gradually cut the name into more parts. The goal is for the student to be able to put the puzzle together (without a model) when each letter is cut apart. As students put their puzzles together, work with individual students on the letters in their names. Possible prompts include the following:

   ◆ Show me the letter *a*.

   ◆ How many *a*'s are in your name?

   ◆ What is this letter? (Teacher points to a letter the student knows.)

   ◆ Let's say the letters in your name. (Teacher helps student spell name.)

✳ **Making names with magnetic letters:** Make a "Name Bag" containing one or two sets of magnetic letters for the student's first name. Students use the letters to make their first name. If necessary, students can use the model on the envelope of the name puzzle. Insist on left-to-right sequential construction of the name.

✳ **Rainbow-writing:** Write each student's name on a sheet of construction paper. Use large letters so students can easily trace over their name. Insert this paper into a clear, heavy sheet protector and distribute dry erase markers. Teach the students how to trace over their names letter by letter with the dry-erase marker. Once they trace their names with one color, they can choose another color to do it again. Writing on the sheet protector allows students to erase their writing easily and reuse the activity. Work with individual students on letter formation, reminding them to start at the top, guiding their formation by placing your hand on top of theirs if necessary.

Eight Ways of Working With Letters

Students spend about two minutes doing one of the following activities using the known letters in their individual letter bags and a personal alphabet chart. Circulate among the students and prompt children to name the letters as they sort them. The purpose of this activity is to build automaticity with *known* letters. Children will learn new letters as they trace the alphabet book with a tutor outside of the small-group lesson. It is important that you regularly communicate with the tutor so you know which new letters students have learned. You should add these letters to the student's letter bag.

1. **Match the letters in the bag.** This activity is only for children who have fewer than ten letters. You will put multiple sets of the letters they know in their bags. Ask the children to find the letters that are the same. For example, find all of the *c*'s and put them in a line. Find all the *o*'s and put them in a line. Students should say the name of each letter as they line them up left to right.

2. **Match letters to an alphabet chart.** Give each student an alphabet chart that has been placed inside a plastic sheet protector. Instruct them to match the letters in their bag to the letters on the chart and to name the letter and the picture as they place it on the chart. Ask students to give the letter sound if they know it.

3. **Match upper- and lowercase letters.** Put matching upper- and lowercase letters in their bags. Ask students to find the capital letter that matches the lowercase letter. They should name the letters as they line them up. Teach students how to use the alphabet chart for help.

4. **Sort by color.** You will need multicolored magnetic letters for this activity. Tell children to find the red letters and name them as they put them in a line. Then have them find all of the blue letters and name them as they line them up. Continue with other colors of the magnetic letters.

5. **Name letters left to right.** Tell children to put all their letters in a line and name them as they line them up. Encourage speedy recall. "Let's see how fast you can do it." There is no specified sequence for this activity. They just grab a letter from the bag, name it, and put it at the end of the line.

6. **Name a word that begins with that letter.** Ask the students to pick a letter from their bag, say the name of the letter, and say a word that begins with that letter. For

example, the child might pick a *b* and say, "*b*—book." If children have difficulty thinking of a word, prompt them to use their alphabet chart.

7. **Name the letter that begins that word.** The teacher says a word and asks the children to find the letter on the alphabet chart that makes the sound at the beginning of the word. For example, the teacher says, "Find the letter that you hear at the beginning of *book*." The children find a *b*.

8. **Find the letter that makes that sound.** Ask students to find a letter on the alphabet chart that makes a particular sound. For example, "Find the letter that says /t/."

Letter Formation

Each day spend about one minute teaching letter formation. Select a letter most of the students in the group know by name. It often takes several days for the students to learn one new letter formation. I have arranged the letters according to how they are formed. Teach the letters from one group before you work on the letters in another group. Students form the letter three ways: in the air with big movements, on the table using their finger, and on a whiteboard with a marker. Each time they form the letter they should say the letter name and the verbal directions listed next to each letter.

Group 1: Letters that start like a *c*

c – around like a *c*

o – around like a *c* and close

a – around like a *c* and down

d – around like a *c*, up and down

g – around like a *c*, down and hook left

q – around like a *c*, down

Group 2: Letters that start like an *l* (lowercase)

l – start at the top, down

t – start at the top, down, cross

h – start at the top, down and hump

k – start at the top, down, in, out

b – start at the top, down and around

r – start at the top, down, up, and over

n – start at the top, down, up, hump

m – start at the top down, hump, hump

i – start at the top, down, dot

j – start at the top, down, hook left, dot

p – start at the top, down, up and around

Group 3: Unique letters

e – over and around like a c

f – down, cross

s – around like a snake

u – down and up

v – down and up

w – down, up, down, up

x – like a cross

y – down, down

z – across, down, across

Part 2: Working With Sounds (2–3 minutes)

The purpose of this component is to teach three aspects of phonological awareness: hearing syllables, hearing rhyming words, and hearing initial consonant sounds. Students will also learn to associate sounds with a letter name. Each day select one of the following activities appropriate for the students in the group: clapping syllables, working with rhymes, or picture sorts. Do not use an activity if the students can already do the task. Your job is to support students as they do the activity. If they can already do the task without your help, you've just wasted precious time. You will spend only about 2–3 minutes with this component.

Clapping Syllables

You can use picture cards, the alphabet chart, or just say a word and have students clap the parts. Begin with words that have one or two syllables. Have students say the word and clap the parts in the word. When students can clap one and two syllables, include pictures or words with three syllables. You can also use pictures of students in the class and have students clap the names of their classmates. At first you will have to clap with the students, but the goal is for the students to clap the syllables without your support. Discontinue this activity when students are able to clap three syllables in a word.

Working With Rhymes

Tell students you are going to say two words. If the words rhyme, they should put their thumbs up. If the words do not rhyme, they should put their thumbs down. For example, if you say, "pig, wig," the students put their thumbs up. If you say, "pig, table," students put their thumbs down.

Another fun activity is to tell students you are going to say a word that rhymes with a body part. Tell them first which two body parts you are going to use. For example, *I am going to say a word. If it rhymes with "nose," touch your nose and say, "nose." If it rhymes with "chin," touch your chin and say, "chin."* Again, at first you will help children with hearing rhymes, but eventually, they should do the activity without your support. Discontinue the activity when children hear rhymes. You are not asking them to give you a word that rhymes with another word. This is a much more challenging task and requires children to have a large vocabulary.

Picture Sorts

Students sort pictures by their initial consonant sound. The following letters have the sound in the letter name so they are usually the easiest to learn: *b, d, f, j, k, l, m, n, p, r, s, t, v, z*. Also consider the names of the students in your classroom. If you have a Kaitlyn and a Zack in your class, it is probably a good idea to sort pictures that begin with a *k* and a *z*. Children who know few letters and sounds often make connections to the names of their classmates. Begin with distinctly different letter sounds (such as /t/ and /m/) and eventually sort sounds that are similar (such as /b/ and /d/ or /y/ and /w/).

Procedures for Picture Sorts

* Choose two consonants. Begin with letters the students already know by name but not by sound. The first picture sorts you do should have distinctively different sounds and should have the sound in the letter name.

* Give each student two pictures for each consonant you selected. Tell students the name of the picture as you pass it out. Do not waste time having the children figure out the pictures.

* Write the two consonants on a white board and say: *Listen to the sound at the beginning of each picture. If your picture begins with the /m/ sound, it will go under the M. If your picture begins with the /t/ sound, it will go under the T.*

* Do not let students put their pictures under one of the letters too quickly. They have a 50% chance of being correct just by guessing. Teach students to follow this procedure:

  Say the picture: *moon*
  Say the beginning sound: /m/.
  Say the name of the letter: M.
  Put the picture under the M.

✳ Students take turns saying their pictures, saying the beginning sound, saying the letter name, and putting the picture under the correct letter. Make sure the students follow each step. You are teaching them a process for hearing and recording sounds that will eventually transfer to independent writing. Scaffold when necessary.

Part 3: Working With Books (5 minutes)

The purpose of this component is to build oral language, teach early concepts of print, and improve book handling skills. Select a very simple, Level A guided reading book. It should have one line of print per page and known concepts. Do not use big books. I have tried using a big book with Pre-A students and found that children are not as engaged as when they hold a little book in their hands. It is important that students handle the book and turn the pages.

First, guide the students through the book and have them take turns discussing the pictures. Encourage using complete sentences as they describe what is happening in the picture. Avoid asking the student a question like "What is the boy eating in this picture?" that requires a one-word answer. Instead, model how you want children to talk about the picture by saying, "The boy is eating an apple. Now tell me about the picture on the next page." If students have trouble giving a complete sentence or respond with improper English structure, model a sentence about the picture and ask the student to repeat it.

Next, read the book with the students. This is choral reading, not guided reading. Give the students a small pointer so they can practice pointing to the words. As students read the book with you, circulate and help them with one-to-one matching. After students have read the book with you, they may read it on their own. During the second independent read, work with individual students and differentiate your prompting based upon need. Some students may need your help with one-to-one matching, while others may be ready to show you a specific letter or word.

Teaching Points

After students have had the opportunity to read the book on their own, teach the group **one or two** of the following print concepts.

✳ Concept of a word: *Put your fingers around each word on the page. How many words are on that page? Let's do it again on a different page.*

✳ First/last word: *Point to the first word on the page. Point to the last word.*

✳ Concept of a letter: *Show me one letter. Show me two letters.*

✳ First/last letter: *Point to the first letter of a word. Point to the last letter.*

* Punctuation: *Show me a period.*

* Capital/lowercase letters: *Find a capital* T. *Find a lowercase* a.

Part 4: Interactive Writing (5 minutes)

Interactive writing allows children to work alongside the teacher as they construct a text by "sharing the pen" (McCarrier, Pinnell, & Fountas, 2000). Interactive writing with Pre-A readers builds oral language and provides the opportunity to teach sound/letter links, print concepts, and letter formation.

* Dictate a simple sentence (four to six words). Do not waste time asking children what sentence they would like to write. With four children in the group you will likely receive four different responses. Say, *Today we are going to write . . . .* Most often the sentence will relate to the book they just read, but it doesn't have to be an exact sentence from the book. You will construct the sentence to include letters and sounds you have been teaching the group. You might say, *Let's write, "I can play the bells." Say that sentence with me.*

* As children repeat the sentence, distribute dry-erase markers and alphabet charts.

* Draw a line for each word in the sentence on a sentence strip while students repeat the sentence.

* Have students help you write each word. Teach them to say the word slowly and listen for the first sound. Once the students isolate the initial consonant sound, use a name chart or alphabet chart to link the sound to a letter. Students take turns writing the **dominant** consonant sounds in each word. While one student is writing on the sentence strip, the others should practice the letter on their alphabet chart, which has been inserted into a heavy, plastic sheet protector. You write the sounds the students are not ready to learn. Teach correct letter formation. The following example shows the students' writing (bold letters) and the teacher's contribution (standard letters). Student contributions will vary depending on their phonemic awareness skills. Some are able to hear long vowels easily; others are not. Tailor your instruction so that you are constantly teaching what they are ready to learn. Do not allow invented spelling; write the letters for the sounds the children cannot hear.

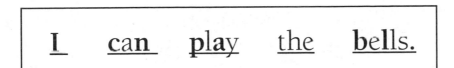

Cut-Up Sentence

When you finish writing the sentence with the students, cut the words apart. Give each student one or more words and have them work together to remake the sentence. At the end of the lesson, put a paper clip around the cut-up sentence and give it to one of the children to take home.

When to Discontinue the Pre-A Small Group Lesson

Students are ready to move from the Pre-A plan to emergent guided reading when they can do the following:

* Write their first name without a model

* Identify at least 40 upper- and lowercase letters by name

* Demonstrate left-to-right directionality across one line of print

* Understand enough English to follow simple directions

* Hear a few consonant sounds (at least five)

Rubric for Pre-A Small Group Lesson

This rubric can be used for self-evaluation, observation, or coaching.

Components	Evident (✓)
Classroom Environment	
Other students were working independently in literacy workstations.	
Small-group lesson materials were organized; table was free of clutter.	
Teacher was not interrupted by other students in the room.	
Each student had an alphabet chart.	
Teacher had an updated letter/sound chart for the students in the group.	
Working With Letters and Names	
Teacher gave each student a personal letter bag of known letters.	
Students did one of the letters/names activities using their known letters.	
Teacher worked with individual students asking for letters and/or sounds.	
Name activity (optional): Students did name puzzle, used magnetic letters to construct name or did rainbow-writing with name. (This activity is discontinued when students can write their first name without a model.)	
Time: 3–4 min.	
Working With Sounds	
Students did one of the following activities (circle): Clapped syllables, worked with rhyming words, did picture sorts	
Time: 3–4 min.	

Rubric for Pre-A Small Group Lesson *(continued)*

Components	Evident (✓)
Working With Books	
Students previewed the book by discussing the pictures.	
Students read the book with the teacher (first reading).	
Teacher worked with individual students prompting for concepts such as one-to-one matching, finding the first word on a page, finding a capital letter, etc.	
Students may have read the book independently as a second reading.	
After reading, the teacher addressed one or two teaching points from the lesson plan.	
Time: Not more than 5 min.	
Interactive Writing	
Each student had an alphabet chart and a dry-erase marker.	
The teacher dictated a simple sentence (four to six words).	
Children rehearsed the sentence as the teacher drew a line for each word on a sentence strip.	
Students took turns writing a letter in the sentence. The teacher supported correct letter formation.	
While one student wrote on a sentence strip, the others practiced writing the letter on their alphabet chart.	
Teacher cut the sentence apart and gave each student one or two words.	
Students used their word cards to remake the sentence.	
Time: Not more than 5 min.	
TOTAL LESSON: 15–20 minutes	

Using Assessments to Group Students and Select a Focus Strategy for Emergent Readers

It is appropriate to use several types of assessments to form emergent guided reading groups. The following chart lists information that can be gained from some of the most common assessments used in kindergarten and first grade. Since children should already know most of their letters by name before they begin the emergent guided reading lesson, the letter assessment is omitted.

Assessment	Information
Dictated sentence	• Phonemic awareness: ability to hear sounds in words, link sounds to letters, and write the sounds in sequence • Letter formation • Concepts of print: left-to-right directionality, spacing, return sweep, punctuation
Writing sample	• Language skills: English syntax, vocabulary, ability to construct an idea • Phonemic awareness/phonics skills: hearing sounds in sequence, sound/letter links, spelling of high-frequency words, letter formation • Concepts of print: directionality, spacing, return sweep, punctuation
Word list	• Sight-word knowledge, decoding skills
Running record	• Strategies, reading levels

Some teachers are overwhelmed by the volume of assessment data commonly required in kindergarten and first grade. Not all assessments are useful for grouping students for guided reading, but many can provide important information including reading level, strategies, and skills. The following assessment summary chart organizes the assessment information for Pre-A and emergent readers and makes it easier to group according to student needs, rather than just instructional level.

Assessment Summary Chart for Pre-A and Emergent Readers A–C

Name	Instr. Level	Known Letters	Known Words	Hears Sounds	Cues Used		Early Strategies				Oral Lang.
	90% or ↑	Record #	Record # Read Write	+ ✓ –	MSV	1:1	✓pic	GMR	X ✓		+ ✓ –

Directions for Using the Assessment Summary for Emergent Readers

Column 1 and 2: Name and Instructional Level

Write the student's name in the first column and record the instructional text level determined by the running record. Remember, this is the level at which the student reads with 90–94% accuracy. If the accuracy is higher than 94%, then the text is considered to be at an independent level. If the student knows at least 40 letters by name but is not able to read Level A text with at least 90% accuracy, the student should still be coded as Level A. Code the student as Pre-A only if he or she knows fewer than 40 letters.

Column 3: Known Letters

Write the number of letters (upper- and lowercase) the student is able to identify by name. The maximum score in this column would be 52, unless you expect the students to identify the printer's *g* and *a*; then the maximum score would be 54.

Column 4: Known Words

Record the number of sight words the student can read (R) and write (W). This is determined by giving the student a short list of frequently used sight words for kindergarten and first grade. You can make up a list from the following words or use a list that comes with your reading program.

> Words that appear frequently in emergent-level texts:

am	at	is	can	go	me	my	see	the
to	up	and	do	got	had	has	he	his
in	it	like	look					

Column 5: Hears Sounds

Put a plus (+) in this column if the student hears initial, medial, and final sounds. Put a check (✓) in this column if the student hears initial and final sounds. Put a check minus (✓-) if the student hears only a few initial or final sounds and a minus (–) if the student does not hear sounds in words. Most teachers use a writing sample or a simple dictated sentence to make this determination, but you could also use a phonemic segmentation test. Here are three examples of dictated sentences that have been useful for assessing kindergarten and first grade students:

* September/October: *I like to eat oatmeal.* (Assesses ability to hear consonants and long vowels)

❊ January/February: *I want peanut butter on my sandwich.* (Assesses ability to hear consonants, long and short vowels, and /ch/)

❊ May/June: *This is a fine day for swimming at the beach. I have my plastic shovel and my bucket.* (Assesses ability to hear digraphs, long vowels, blends, and /–ing/)

❊ More examples of dictated sentences are provided in Chapter 2. It is not necessary to attach a number score to these sentences, but you should analyze them to determine whether the student is hearing sounds in sequence and which phonic elements the student needs to learn next.

Column 6: Cues Used

Put an *M* if the student's errors are mostly meaning-related. Put an *S* if the student's errors match the structure of the text. Put a *V* if the student tries to sound out an unknown word or makes substitutions that are visually similar. Refer to the analysis of a running record on pages 42–43 in Chapter 2 if you need to review the meaning, structure, and visual information systems.

Column 7: Early Strategies

The running record can help you assess four emergent strategies: using one-to-one matching (1:1), checking the picture at the point of difficulty, getting the mouth ready for the initial letters (GMR), and cross-checking (× ✔).

> **1:1 Matching:** Put a plus (+) in this column if the student points to the words while he or she reads or if the student reads without making any insertions or omissions. Put a check (✔) in the column if the student appears to be looking at print but occasionally says extra words or leaves out words. Put a minus (–) in the column if the student invents a story or does not appear to be looking at the print.

> **Checks picture (✔ pic):** Put a plus (+) if the student consistently searches the picture when encountering an unknown word. Put a check (✔) if the student occasionally checks the picture, and put a minus (–) if the student does not use picture clues.

> **Gets mouth ready (GMR):** Put a plus (+) if the student consistently uses initial letter sounds at difficulty, put a check (✔) if the student occasionally uses initial letters, and put a minus (–) if the student ignores first letter cues.

Cross-checking (✗ ✓): This is a highly important strategy for emergent readers. It is the action of using the picture clues and the first letter of the word to figure out an unknown word. For example, if a child first says "bunny" for "rabbit" then stops and corrects the error because she notices "rabbit" starts with an *r* and not a *b*, the student is cross-checking. When a child uses only picture clues and does not use the letters in the word, the child is not cross-checking. Also, if a child tries to sound out an unknown word and never thinks about the meaning of the story, the child is not cross-checking. Put a plus (+) in this column if the student is consistent with this strategy. Put a check (✓) if the student occasionally cross-checks but is not consistent. Put a minus (–) in this column if the student shows no evidence of cross-checking. Very few Level A and B readers cross-check without teacher prompting. However, cross-checking should be an established behavior without teacher prompting before a student is moved to text level D.

Column 8: Oral Language

Record the child's command of English by using this simple rubric:

(+) Child has excellent oral language and uses Standard English structure.

(✓) Child speaks English but makes frequent grammatical errors due to immature language structure or nonstandard English dialect.

(–) Child is not fluent in English or has a severe language delay.

Grouping Students for Emergent Guided Reading

After you complete the assessment summary chart, use the information to group your students for guided reading. Place students together who are close to the same reading level (not more than one level apart) and have similar needs. For example, you may be able to put some A and B students together because they know many letters but no sight words. You might place B and C students together because they hear sounds in words but are not using them during reading to cross-check.

Although I recommended you put no more than four students in your Pre-A groups, your emergent guided reading groups can have up to six. Continue to update your assessment summary chart monthly and use the information to regroup students for guided reading.

If a student is unable to read Level A and has fewer than 40 letters, do not use guided reading. Use the Pre-A small-group lesson format to build expertise in oral language, phonemic awareness, letter knowledge, and concepts of print.

Materials for Emergent Guided Reading

* Alphabet charts (primarily to use during guided writing)

* Letter/sound checklist (if students do not know all of their letters and sounds)

* 6 dry-erase boards, markers, and erasers

* 6–8 sets of lower-case magnetic letters

* Pictures for sound sorts (initial consonants and short medial vowels)

* Assessment kit

* Leveled books

* Copies of lesson plans (see page 84)

* High-frequency word chart for each group: You will use this chart to record the high-frequency words students can write. I do not keep track of the words students are able to read in isolation. If children know how to write a word, they can usually read that word.

* Sound box template (place in a heavy plastic sheet protector): Students will use this template for segmenting words during word study.

* A timer

High-Frequency Word Chart

I have provided two options for the high-frequency word chart. One allows you to write the words as you introduce them to your group, the other lists recommended words for each guided reading level. During the sight-word review component, ask students to write three familiar words. Put a check under the student's name each time the student writes the word without teacher support. Once the student has correctly written the word six times you can assume it is a known word.

No matter which form you choose, keep a record of the words students know how to write. You will use this information to select guided reading books, to plan your word study, and to create your dictated sentence for guided writing.

High-Frequency Word Chart, Option 1

Sight Words	Name	Name	Name	Name	Name	Name

High-Frequency Word Chart, Option 2

This chart lists words that would be appropriate to teach at levels A, B, and C. There is no sequence for introducing sight words. Select a word that appears in the book, and put a check (✓) each time the student writes the word without support.

Level A (1)	Student 1	Student 2	Student 3	Student 4	Student 5	Student 6
am						
at						
can						
go						
is						
me						
my						
see						
the						
to						
up						
we						
Level B (2)						
and						
do						
got						
had						
has						
he						
his						
in						
it						
like						
look						
on						

High-Frequency Word Chart, Option 2 (continued)

Level C (3–4)	Student 1	Student 2	Student 3	Student 4	Student 5	Student 6
are						
come						
did						
for						
get						
have						
here						
him						
of						
play						
said						
she						
will						
you						
Adds –s						

Sound Box Template

Make six copies of this page and place the template inside a clear plastic sheet protector.
Use during sound-box activities to help students hear and record sounds in words.
Give students a phonetically regular word that includes your phonic skill for that lesson.
After students segment the sounds in the word, they use a dry-erase marker to write
the word in the boxes.

Emergent Guided Reading Lesson Plan

Title: _____   Level: _____   Lesson #: _____

Day 1 Date: _____	**Day 2 Date:** _____
Sight-Word Review–Writing: _____ _____ _____	**Sight-Word Review–Writing (include new word from Day 1):** _____ _____ _____
Introduction of New Book: This book is called _____ and it's about _____ New vocabulary: _____ **Text Reading With Prompting:** • Check the picture. What would make sense? • Get your mouth ready. • Does that make sense and look right? • Could it be _____ or _____? • Show me the word _____. (if a student is stuck on a sight word) • Check the word with your finger. Does it look right? • Try reading without pointing with your finger. • How would the character say that? (expression)	**Rereading of Yesterday's Book** Observations:
Teaching Points After Reading: • One-to-one matching (At Level C, discourage pointing.) • Use picture clues (meaning) • Monitor with known words • Get mouth ready for initial sound • Cross-check picture & first letter • Visual scanning (check the word left to right) • Expression	**Teaching Points After Reading:** • One-to-one matching • Use picture clues (meaning) • Monitor with known words • Get mouth ready for initial sound • Cross-check picture & first letter • Visual scanning (check the word left to right) • Expression
Discussion Prompt (if appropriate):	Discussion Prompt (if appropriate):
Teach 1 Sight Word: _____ • What's Missing? • Mix & Fix • Table Writing • Whiteboards	**Teach Same Sight Word:** _____ • What's Missing? • Mix & Fix • Table Writing • Whiteboards
Word Study (Choose just 1): • Picture sorts: _____ • Making words: _____ • Sound boxes: _____	**Guided Writing:** Dictated or open-ended sentence

The Next Step in Guided Reading © 2009 by Jan Richardson, Scholastic Professional

Selecting a Text for Emergent Readers

You will find a lot of variability in texts at levels A–C. Most books will use a repetitive pattern, which is helpful at Levels A and B but should be phased out by Level C. Books with repetitive patterns help students learn high-frequency words since the same words are usually repeated on every page. However, these patterned texts can also lead children towards thinking reading is about memorizing the pattern. You want emergent readers to look at print and not say, "I can read this with my eyes closed." Closely monitor children as they read these easy books to make sure they are still looking at the words. Having children use a pointer is one way to make sure they are matching the words on the page to what they are saying.

Consider the students' strengths and needs when you select a guided reading book. The new book should have some known sight words students can use to monitor their reading, but the text should also have at least one new sight word you can teach. If the book contains too many unknown words, the students will become frustrated or attempt to memorize the pattern. Another consideration for selecting the text is the language abilities of the group. If the students are just learning English, select books that have mostly familiar concepts. You will only impede the reading process if the students do not know the concepts in the pictures. Finally, look for texts that use complete sentences with natural language. This way students are able to lean on their oral language skills to predict text structure.

Text Considerations for Emergent Readers

- Story makes sense
- Strong picture support
- Mostly familiar concepts
- Some repetitive phrases
- Some familiar sight words
- One new sight word

Description of the Emergent Guided Reading Lesson (Two-Day Plan)

Use the same guided reading book for two consecutive lessons.

DAY 1	Explanations of Procedures: This lesson plan takes 20 minutes. If you have more time, you can expand the reading or word study/writing components.
Sight-Word Review (1–2 minutes) Students write three words you have previously taught them. Use the high-frequency word chart to select the words and to record student responses. I often select words in the new book that have been taught in previous lessons. That way I am reinforcing the known words they can use to monitor their reading.	Distribute whiteboards and markers to each student. Set up folders or teach children how to cover their writing with their hand so they do not copy. Tell the students to write the word you taught them yesterday. Say, "Write *said*. Think about what it looks like." Record student responses on the high-frequency word chart. Put a check mark if the student is able to write the word without help. This is not a test. If the student cannot write the word *said*, give a clue such as, "It has four letters. Do you remember that second letter? It is an *a*." If you help the student, do not put a check mark on the high-frequency word chart. Try to intervene *before* the student writes the word incorrectly. Usually children will hesitate when they aren't sure of the next letter. Ask, "What letter comes next?" If the child says the wrong letter, tell him or her the correct letter. It is better to help the student write the word correctly than allow him or her to write it incorrectly. The more the child writes the word correctly, the better chance of building visual memory for that word. However, I do not let children copy the word. Copying does not develop independence. Since you are working with a small group, you can scaffold students at the point of difficulty. You should also use this time to review two other words you have previously taught. Do not spend more than one minute on this task. The goal is fast writing of the words to build visual memory. I do not recommend using flash cards for this component because flash cards do not support learning the word in detail. Writing provides evidence of what each child knows and helps children control left to right visual scanning.

DAY 1	Explanations of Procedures
Introduction (3–4 minutes) Introduce the text and discuss new vocabulary.	**Main Idea Statement:** State the title and give a simple "gist" statement. For example, "This book is called *The Rock Pools*. It's about some animals and things you might see in a pool near the ocean. Let's look through the book and get ready to read the story." **Story Walk**: Have students talk about the pictures in the book. You do not need to discuss every page, but you do want children to have an idea of how the book is structured. For children who have limited English, encourage a complete sentence. Say, "Tell me who is in the picture and what they are doing." Model if necessary. ## Introduce New Vocabulary **Sight Words:** Introduce new sight words by having students predict the first letter and locate the word in the text. You do not need to write the word on the whiteboard or make the word out of magnetic letters. This happens *after* the reading. **Concepts**: Discuss unfamiliar concepts that are in the text, such as *path, hedgehog*, or *cabbage*. **Cross-Checking**: To encourage cross-checking behavior, give students choices when you come across pictures of familiar concepts. For example, you could say, "It might be a horse or a pony. You'll have to check the first letter when you read to figure it out." You do not need to write these words on the whiteboard or have the students locate them in the text. You are building background with the words so they can search meaning and visual cues when they see them in the book.

DAY 1	Explanations of Procedures
Read the Story Day 1—Students read the book independently with teacher prompting. (5–8 minutes) Day 2—Students reread the book and other familiar books. (8 minutes) Prompt for strategies when the student stops or makes an error. Prompt on accurate reading to assess student's skills and strategies.	The students read the book several times on Day 1 and Day 2. Students should read independently, **not chorally or round-robin**. If you notice two students reading the same words, ask one of the students to go back a page and read it to you. You want to discourage paired reading because it does not foster independent problem-solving. The goal of this component is not accurate reading but active processing. You want children to encounter challenges, and then observe the children as they try to solve problems. Listen to individual students and prompt for strategic behaviors when a child stops or makes an error. Use one or more of these prompts: • *Read it with your pointer and make it match.* • *What would make sense?* • *Get your mouth ready for the first sound.* • *Check your picture.* • *Could it be* puppy *or* dog? *How do you know?* • *Reread and think what would make sense and begin with that letter.* • *Show me* **said**. (Use this prompt on new sight words that cannot be easily decoded.) • *Try reading without pointing.* (fluency) • *Read it like the character would say it.* (expression) **If a student makes no errors**, it is still important to prompt for emergent strategies. You want to be certain the student is not just repeating something he heard from the child sitting next to him. For example, you might ask the student to show you a specific sight word you have taught or show you how to get his mouth ready for the first sound in a word. Prompting on accurate reading helps you assess whether the student is memorizing the book or actually applying strategies. Instruct students to reread the book until you tell them to stop. I usually let students read for 5–8 minutes, depending on the text level. On the back of the lesson plan, take notes on individual students.

DAY 1	Explanations of Procedures
Teaching Points (1–2 minutes) ❏ One-to-one matching ❏ Use picture clues (meaning) ❏ Monitor with known words ❏ Get mouth ready ❏ Cross-check ❏ Visual scanning ❏ Expression	After all students have read the story at least once, tell them you want to show them something that will help them be better readers. Use your notes to select your whole-group teaching points. You might teach them how to get their mouth ready or how to check the picture and think what would make sense. You could also have them locate some of the sight words in the story. At Levels A–B, **ALWAYS** do the **cross-checking strategy**. This is where you select a few random pages from the story, cover the picture, and have the students chorally read the text while you point to the words. Encourage students to sound the first letter when they come to the unknown word. Then show them the picture. Children should be able to cross-check the picture and first letter without your prompting before you move them to Level D.
Discussion Prompt	If appropriate, ask a question that explores deeper comprehension. Not all emergent books have enough of a story to warrant a discussion.
Teach One Sight Word: Days 1 & 2 (1–2 minutes)	**ALWAYS teach one sight word** during every lesson. The purpose of this component is to help students develop visual memory and increase their bank of high-frequency words. You will teach the same sight word for at least two days. If the students do not know the sight word after two days, teach it again with the next book. Don't introduce a new word until the first one is firm. It is critical that students develop a visual memory in these early levels. Follow these procedures *every* day with *every* word in this sequence: What's Missing?, Mix & Fix, Table Writing, and Whiteboards.

DAY 1	Explanations of Procedures
Teach One Sight Word: Days 1 & 2 (1–2 minutes) - What's Missing? - Mix & Fix - Table Writing - Whiteboards	**What's Missing?** Write the word on a whiteboard or make it with magnetic letters. Do this in front of the students so they can see the left-to-right construction of the word. Tell students the word and ask them to look at each letter. Have students spell the word as you point to each letter in sequence. This prompts students to study the word by scanning left to right. Some students develop a haphazard approach to looking at print, which can lead to serial order problems. Say, "Boys and girls, this was a word in the story. [Write the word]. The word is *the*." Turn the board towards you and erase (or remove) a letter. Show the board to the students and ask them to tell you what letter is missing. Ask, "What's missing?" The students tell you the missing letter, and you put it back in the word. Repeat the procedure two or three more times by erasing one or more letters at a time until the entire word is erased. Students then spell the word for you as you write (or make) the word on the whiteboard. **Mix & Fix**. Give each student the letters to make the new word. They should check your model to make sure they made the word correctly. Students check the word by sliding their finger under the word while they say it. Students should now pull each letter down to remake the word from left to right. Again, prompt for a slow check of the word. Now have students mix (or scramble) the letters and fix the letters to remake the word. **Table Writing.** Students use their finger to "write" the word on the table. The finger tracing helps them remember the word. Encourage them to say the word as they write it and then check it with their finger. **Whiteboards**. Students write the word on a whiteboard, saying the word as they write. You will normally teach the same sight word on Days 1 and 2. If students have extreme difficulty learning words, you may need to spend more than two days on the same word. Do not introduce a new sight word until students have learned the current word. To do so would only confuse them.

DAY 1	Explanations of Procedures
Word Study Day 1 only Select **one** activity (3–5 minutes)	There are three **options** for word study at this level: picture sorts, making words, and sound boxes. Choose only one activity and do it for the last 3–5 minutes of the lesson. There are specific skills you want to teach at each level: • Level A—hearing initial consonants • Level B—hearing medial short vowels (*a* and *o*) • Level C—hearing medial short vowels (*i, e,* and *u*) • Appendix A has specific examples of words to use for each word study activity.
Picture Sorts **Level A** Dd Hh Children should segment the initial sound in the picture and then say the name of the letter that makes the sound.	**Picture Sorts**. This activity should be used *before* making words and sound boxes because it actually teaches the target skill. Prepare for this activity by gathering pictures for initial consonants and *medial* short vowels. The consonant sorts should not have pictures with initial blends or digraphs such as *frog* or *ship*. This will only confuse the student. You will also collect pictures for short vowel sorts. These pictures should be one-syllable words with the short vowel in the middle such as *mop* and *cap*. For consonant sorts, select two letter sounds and distribute to each student three or four pictures that have those initial letters. Each student says the picture, sounds the first letter, names the letter that begins the word, and places his/her picture under the correct consonant. It is important that the student actually *names* the letter because this will help the student recall the letter during writing.
Level B o (log) a (cap) Children stretch the word and emphasize the vowel. This helps them hear the medial vowel sound.	**Level A:** Sort initial consonant sounds. **Level B:** Sort initial consonant sounds or short medial vowels *a* and *o*. When doing the vowel sorts, use pictures with one syllable that have a short vowel in the middle. Teach children how to stretch the word and "punch" the middle to hear the short vowel sound (e.g., *frog – fr-o-o-o-o-g*). Again, the children should follow the same procedures as they did with consonant sorts: • Say the picture (cap). • Stretch the word and punch the vowel (c-a-a-a-p). • Say the vowel (a). • Put the picture under the vowel that has been written on a whiteboard.

DAY 1	Explanations of Procedures

Picture Sorts Level C
i (ship)
u (bug)
 	
Work with other short vowels.
 	
Making Words
Target Skill for Levels A–C
 	
Examples for A:
hop-mop-top-bop
cat-rat-bat-hat-fat
big-wig-dig-fig-pig
 	
Examples for B:
rat-rag-ram-rap-map
cat-can-man-map
hot-hop-cop-cot-dot
 	
Examples for C:
can-cap-map
mop-big-wig-wag
hag-hog
	Level C: Work with all short vowels. Sort two vowels at a time: one familiar vowel sound and one new vowel sound.
	
	Making Words: Select several consonants and one vowel for this activity. Give each student his/her own set of letters. Tell the students to make a word. Always begin with a known word. After they make the word, have them check it by saying the word slowly as they run their finger under it. This activity strengthens visual scanning abilities. Then tell them to change a letter to make another word. At first, you may need to tell them which letter to change, but eventually they should be able to hear the dissonance and make the change without your support. There are different target skills for each level:
	
	        Level A: Exchange initial consonants.
	        Level B: Exchange initial and final consonants.
	        Level C: Exchange initial, medial, and final letters
	                in a CVC word.
	Here are some examples for each level:
	
	Level A: "Take two letters and make *am*. Say it slowly and check it with your finger. What did you make? Now add a letter to the beginning to make *Pam*. Check it. Change the first letter to make *Sam*. Check it. Change a letter to make *ham*."
	
	Level B: "Take three letters and make *can*. Check it. I am going to say a new word. You must say this word slowly so you know which letter you need to change. You may need to change the first letter or the last letter. Change a letter to make *cap*. Check it first. Which letter do you need to change? Take away that letter and get the letter to make *cap*.
	
	Level C: "Take three letters and make *cat*. [Allow time.] Now I'm going to ask you to make a new word. You might have to change the first letter, middle letter, or the last letter. You'll have to check it first to find out which letter you need to take away. I want you to change *cat* to make *mat*. First slide your finger slowly under the word *cat* and say *mat*. What letter do you need to change? Make it say *mat*. Now check it again. Are you right? Change a letter from *mat* to make *map*. Check it first to see what letter you need to change."

DAY 1	Explanations of Procedures

Sound Boxes
 	
Encourage noisy writing. Students should say each sound as they write the corresponding letter in the box.
 	
Level A:
 	
| s
	o |
	
	Level B:
	
	| a
		t |
		
		Level C:
		
		| w
			i	g		**Sound Boxes:**
						
						This is the most difficult activity. Students must hear some consonants and at least one vowel sound to be successful. Not all Level A students will be able to do sound boxes, especially if they have difficulty with letter formation.
						
						Distribute dry-erase markers and sound box templates that have been inserted into a plastic sheet protector. Tell the students you are going to say a word, and they must write one sound in each box as they say the word slowly. Model the following procedure: Say the word slowly and hold up one finger as you say each sound /b/ - /a/ - /t/. Students should eventually be able to segment the sounds without your support. After they segment the sounds on their fingers, have the students write the word in the sound boxes, saying each sound as they write the corresponding letter. It is important that they say the sound as they write the letter because this will build the letter-sound links and help them be more independent during writing.
						
						Use only phonetically regular words. Begin with two boxes and move to three boxes. As students write each letter in a box, they should say the sound (not the letter name) softly. Discourage spelling the word. The purpose of this component is phonemic awareness, not visual memory.
						   • Examples of two-box words for Level A: me, go, no, he, we
						   • Examples of two-box words for Level B: am, at, an, on, as
						   • Examples of three-box words for Level C: map, hit, hop, lap, cup, hat
						
						If students are having problems with the short vowels, do picture sorts first with vowels before you do sound boxes.

DAY 2	**Explanations of Procedures**
Sight-Word Review (1–2 minutes)	On the second day, begin with the sight-word review. Follow the same procedures as Day 1, but use different words. The sight word you taught them on Day 1 should be one of the review words for Day 2.

DAY 2	Explanations of Procedures
Familiar Reading (5–8 minutes)	Distribute yesterday's book and have students read it as you prompt individual students. If the students are able to read yesterday's book quickly several times, give them other familiar books they have read in previous guided reading lessons. This familiar reading should last about eight minutes.
Teaching Point (1 minute)	Do one or two teaching points following the same procedures as described for Day 1.
Sight Word (1 minute)	Teach the *same* sight word you taught the group yesterday. Be sure to follow all four procedures for teaching a sight word: • What's Missing? • Mix & Fix • Table Writing • Whiteboards You should have about 8–10 minutes left to do guided writing.

Guided Writing
 	
Day 2 only
 	
(8–10 minutes)
 	
Use a dictated or open-ended sentence.
 	
is   is   is
 	
the pez is ht
 	
(Ex.: The pizza is hot). *Pizza* and *hot* are unknown words. These are the words you want them to stretch.
	Make a writing journal for each student. Fold about 15 sheets of paper in half and staple. Students should write in these journals rather than on whiteboards so you have a record of their attempts and successes. Guided writing provides the opportunity for students to write a simple sentence that has been carefully crafted to include some known sight words and other words that provide an opportunity for stretching sounds. The sentence is dictated by the teacher to save time and to provide appropriate learning challenges. The new sight word you taught in this lesson must be in the dictated sentence. Gradually increase the number of words in the sentence so students can extend their auditory memory.
	
	      Level A: A simple sentence with 3–5 words.
	          Ex: I can run.
	
	      Level B: Sentence should be 5–7 words.
	          Ex: I go to the park to play.
	
	      Level C: Sentence should be 7–10 words.
	          Ex: My mom is going to take me to the park.

DAY 2	Explanations of Procedures
	After you dictate the sentence, have the students repeat it several times as you draw a line for each word in their journals. The lines will help children put spaces between their words. Once children are able to space without prompting, you do not need to draw the lines. (At this point, you may shift to using simple lined paper with about 3–4 lines on each page. I do not recommend handwriting paper because it is too confusing for children at this level.)
The and *is* should be spelled correctly because they are sight words you have taught the group in guided reading.	Sight words you have taught need to be spelled correctly. If students misspell a sight word, write the correct spelling on the top page of the journal and have them practice it. Sometimes it triggers the child's memory if you write the letters the child wrote correctly and put a line for the letters the child wrote incorrectly. For example, if the student wrote *sad* for *said*, you can write *sa_d* on the practice page and ask, "What letter is missing?" If the student does not remember, tell him or her.
Guided Writing • Encourage risks	When students ask you how to spell a word that is not one you have taught them, encourage them to take risks, say the word slowly, and write the sounds they hear. Here, you will accept invented spelling and prompt students to use what they know about sounds. If you spell words for the students, you are hindering independence and encouraging them to depend upon you for the next word.
• Accept invented spelling on unknown words	Use the top part of the journal for practicing a sight word, demonstrating correct letter formation, or writing a word in boxes. If the word the child is trying to write is phonetically regular but the child needs some support for hearing the sounds in the word, you can draw sound boxes and help the student segment the sounds. The child should then be able to write a word in the boxes. For Level A, I don't expect accuracy on vowel sounds. In fact, I am happy if the children hear and record the consonant sounds correctly. Vowels are target skills for Levels B and C. Expect what you have taught.
• Expect correct spelling for sight words you have taught the group	If any students forget the sentence, tell them to reread what they have written to see if they can remember the next word. If a student still cannot remember, dictate the entire sentence and have that student repeat it again. Avoid dictating the sentence word by word for the students.

Rubric for Coaching an Emergent Guided Reading Lesson (Levels A–C; 1–4)

This rubric can be used for self-evaluation, observation, or coaching.

Components	Evident (✓)
Classroom Environment	
Guided reading materials were organized; table was free of clutter.	
Other students were working independently in literacy workstations.	
Teacher was not interrupted by other students in the room.	
Sight-Word Review (1 min.)	
Students *wrote* three high-frequency words.	
Teacher prompted students who had difficulty.	
Teacher used chart to record progress.	
Book Introduction (not more than 5 min.)	
(Day 1 only) Teacher gave short introduction.	
Students looked through book to construct meaning of story.	
Teacher introduced new vocabulary.	
Reading With Teacher Prompting (8–10 min.)	
(Days 1 & 2) Students read the book *independently* (not chorally). On Day 2 students may read other familiar books.	
Book was at the appropriate level (slightly challenging).	

Components	Evident (✓)
Teacher listened to individual students read and *took anecdotal notes*.	
Teacher prompted students to use strategies.	
Teacher did one or two teaching points from lesson plan.	
Discussion prompt: Teacher asked one higher-level thinking question, if appropriate for the text.	

Sight Word (1–2 min.)

Lesson followed *all four* procedures: What's Missing? Mix & Fix, Table Writing, Whiteboards.	
New word was in the book.	
New word was appropriate for text level.	

Word Study (5 min.) – Day 1 only

Circle activity used: Picture sorts, making words, sound boxes

Students said the words slowly as they sorted, worked with magnetic letters, or wrote the words in boxes. (Teacher did not say the word for the children!)	

Guided Writing (5–8 min.) – Day 2 only

Students repeated sentence before writing it in their journals.	
Teacher prompted students to stretch sounds in words.	
Students reread their sentence to help them remember the next word.	
TOTAL LESSON – 20 minutes	

Ten-Minute Lesson for Emergent Readers (Individual Instruction)

There are occasions when you may want to do an individual guided reading lesson because a particular student does not fit into any group. This is often a short-term problem since groupings change frequently. The following lesson plan is designed for emergent readers and uses the same book for three days. Since you are working with only one student, you will be able to accomplish a lot in 10 minutes.

Day 1

Sight-Word Review (30 seconds): Keep a record of the high-frequency words you have taught the student and review three words each day by having the student write them on a whiteboard. Follow the procedures described in the emergent lesson.

Read a New Book (8 minutes): Do a quick picture walk before the student reads the book. Only dwell on new concepts that are not in the student's listening vocabulary. You do not need to discuss every page unless the student needs to increase oral language. During reading, use the prompts and teaching points listed on the bottom of the lesson plan.

Learn a New Word (1 minute): Teach one new sight word using all four procedures. Do not teach a new word until the first is known.

* *What's Missing?* Teacher writes word on board, student spells word, teacher erases one letter, student tells what letter is missing, continue erasing one, two, or three letters at a time.

* *Mix & Fix.* Student makes the word out of magnetic letters several times.

* *Table Writing.* Student writes the word on table with his or her finger.

* *Whiteboards.* Student writes the word on a whiteboard without copying.

Day 2

Sight-Word Review (30 seconds): Follow the same procedures as described in Day 1, but practice different words. Be sure to include the new sight word you taught in yesterday's lesson.

Finish or Reread Yesterday's New Book (4 minutes): The student reads the same book that was used in Day 1. If the student didn't finish the book in the previous lesson, begin where the child stopped. If the student did finish the book, he should reread the book. Prompt the student to use strategies appropriate for the reading level. Watch the timer! If you extend the lesson beyond 10 minutes, you will not have time to meet with other guided reading groups.

Reteach the Same Sight Word From Day 1 (1 minute): Follow the same procedures as listed for Day 1.

Word Study (4 minutes): Select **one** activity appropriate for the student's needs. You will do either a picture sort to firm up consonant or short vowel sounds; make words that focus on exchanging initial, medial and/or final letters; or use sound boxes to help students hear and record sounds in sequence. These procedures are described in the emergent lesson plan. Focus on the skills the student needs to learn. Teach consonants before vowels. The chart in Appendix A will help.

Day 3

Sight-Word Review (30 seconds): Review three more words from the high-frequency chart. Be sure to include the sight word you just taught.

Familiar Reading (10 minutes): At some time during the day, the student should read the new book to a buddy. It is best to focus this entire lesson on guided writing.

Guided Writing (9 minutes): Dictate a sentence that is carefully crafted to include the new sight word, other familiar sight words, and at least one unfamiliar word. You can get tremendous benefit from the guided writing component by designing sentences that allow students to apply the skills and strategies they have learned in other parts of the lesson. Follow the procedures described in the emergent lesson plan. The sentences should get longer as the student progresses. For Level A dictate a sentence with 3–5 words. Level B should be 5–7 words, and Level C should be 7–10 words. By gradually lengthening the sentence, you are helping the student build auditory memory.

Ten-Minute Lesson Plan for an
Individual Emergent Guided Reading Lesson

Student: _____ Date: _____

Day 1

Sight-Word Review: _____ _____ _____

Introduction:
This book is about _____

New vocabulary: _____

Reading and Teaching: Record observations and teaching points:

Discussion Prompt:

New Sight Word: _____

Day 2

Sight-Word Review: _____ _____ _____

Reading and Teaching: (Reread yesterday's book)

Re-teach same sight word: _____

Word Study (do one activity): Picture Sorts, Making Words, or Sound Boxes

Day 3

Sight-Word Review: _____ _____ _____

Guided Writing: Record sentence and teaching points
Level A: 3-5 words
Level B: 5-7 words
Level C: 7-10 words

Prompts and Teaching Points
During and After Reading

Emergent Level (A–C)

❑ 1:1 matching—*Lift up your pointer each time you say a word. Point to the word you are saying.*

❑ Use meaning—*Check the picture. What would make sense?*

❑ Use known words—*Show me "the." Now read that again.*

❑ Use first letter—*How would you get your mouth ready for the first sound?*

❑ Cross-check picture and first letter—*Get your mouth ready for the first sound and check your picture. What would make sense and start with that sound?* Always do the cross-checking teaching point after reading. Turn to a page in the book and cover the picture. Ask the student to read the page and get his/her mouth ready to say the first sound of the new word. Then reveal the picture.

❑ Blend little words (3 sounds) and think about what would make sense—*Check the word with your finger and say it slowly. What would make sense?* (Use this prompt only with phonetically regular words.)

❑ Phrasing & expression—Once children are matching voice to print accurately, ask students to read without pointing. You can also model appropriate expression and intonation and ask the child to read it like the character would say it.

Questions Teachers Ask About Emergent Guided Reading

When children are learning a new sight word, should they spell the word or say it slowly?

Both. Students should spell the word as they do "What's Missing?" and "Mix & Fix" and say the word slowly as they table write and write the word on the whiteboard. Some children are auditory learners; others are visual learners. You are covering both styles if you follow the procedures.

Why do you teach the new sight word after the reading of the book and not before?

Teaching the new word comes after the reading of the book because the students have had the opportunity to see the word in context. Now that they have some familiarity with the word, it is appropriate to teach it in depth using the four steps: What's Missing?, Mix & Fix, Table Writing, and Whiteboards. During the introduction, you should write the new sight word on the whiteboard or simply say the word and have students locate it in the book. If a student forgets a sight word during reading, say the word for the student and ask her to point to it. Then have the student reread the sentence.

Should I attend to every error the student makes during the reading of the book?

Usually with emergent readers at levels A–C, you *will* attend to every error because it gives you the opportunity to teach strategies. However, always remember that the more you correct a student, the less likely he is to take risks. If the student is still learning English, you should let some minor errors go and focus on the ones that distort the meaning. Your goal is not accurate reading, but strategic reading. Sometimes a student will use strategies and get the word wrong. Praise the student for using a strategy. Errors give you the opportunity to teach a strategy. Getting the word correct is not as important as using a strategy.

What should I do if I am listening to a student and she doesn't make any errors?

If the student is reading Level A or B and makes no errors on a page, it is usually very powerful to prompt the student to show you a specific sight word or demonstrate how to use initial letter sounds. The earliest books are often easy to memorize, so prompting for skills and strategies on accurate reading gives you valuable insight into what the student is attending to. You might say something like, "Show me *look*," or "How would you get your mouth ready to say this word?" Both of these prompts target the emergent skills you want students to learn at these levels. If the student is reading at Level C and makes no errors reading the page, you can take him or her to a different page that might offer a challenge, or prompt the student for comprehension or fluency.

When should I start teaching for fluency?

Children should use a pointer at Levels A and B until one-to-one matching is firm. Prompting for fluency at these very early levels may give students the impression that you expect them to read quickly without even looking at the words. Once students get to Level C, they should be consistent with one-to-one matching. Now it is appropriate to remove the pointers and tell children to read with their eyes. You want them to train their eyes to track print so they don't have to depend upon their finger to do that job. This will promote fluency. The most effective way to work on fluency at Level C is for the teacher to frame two words, such as *mom said*, and tell the student to read these words together. Continue to frame two or three words while the student reads. I usually do the framing for a page or two. Then I say, "Now I want you to read the next page and put two or three words together as you read." If the book has dialogue, prompt for appropriate expression. "How would the character say that?" Model if necessary.

Is it okay to teach the same sight word for more than two days?

Absolutely. Children who are slow to accelerate often have poor visual memory. They will take four or more days to learn one sight word. It is very important that you do not introduce a new sight word until the students firmly know the first one. Introducing too many words at one time will only add to their confusion.

Are there specific words I should introduce first?

Yes. Begin with words that are phonetically regular and appear often in the books at the emergent levels. This will allow them to quickly learn about twenty high-frequency words they can use both in reading and in writing. In the first few lessons, introduce words that look different and are not confusing. For example, I would not introduce *and* and *can* consecutively or even *am* and *me* because they have letters in common and could cause confusion. The second high-frequency word chart in this chapter has sight words that are appropriate for each text level, but there is no precise sequence to follow. Consider the words you have already introduced in your shared reading lessons and begin with those that are the easiest to learn. I strongly recommend that you teach the words on the Level A and Level B lists before you try to teach those on the Level C list. The Level C words require keener visual memory and are best taught when students know about twenty words.

Is it a big deal if students are writing words backwards?

YES! The student may have a problem with serial order. This means the student is not carefully scanning a word from left to right. Some children develop a haphazard approach to looking at words, which will cause serious problems in reading and/or writing progress. Visual scanning is a learned behavior that is important to teach early in the reading process. There are several techniques throughout the emergent lesson that help students control left-to-right scanning:

* Sight-Word Review: Have students say the word as they write it. When they say *am* slowly, they should use the /a/ sound to help them remember to write the *a* before the *m*.

* Learning a New Sight Word: All four procedures for teaching a new sight word help students control serial order. Be sure you do all four steps: What's Missing?; Mix & Fix; Table Writing; Whiteboards.

* Word Work: When students make a word with magnetic letters, they should check each word by saying the word slowly and sliding their finger under the letters to make sure they are right. You are teaching them to coordinate the visual and auditory processes. Don't let them whip their finger across the word without even looking at the letters. When students do sound boxes, they should say the sounds on their fingers and write each letter in a box **as** they say the sound of that letter. Do not let them say the letter name. After they write the word in the boxes, they should say it slowly and check it with their finger.

* Guided Writing: Tell children to say each word **as** they write it. This will eliminate writing words backwards. They won't write *og* for *go* if they are saying the word slowly.

If you follow all of these procedures, you will have very few children with serial order confusions.

Is it okay to do rhyming families during word work?

You will always do rhyming families at Level A. After Level A, students will work with words that do not rhyme. I have identified a phonic skill focus for word work at each level. At Level A, the focus is hearing and using initial sounds. When children change *cat* to *bat* to *fat*, they are focusing on the initial sound. After Level A, you will be focusing on other phonics skills, such as hearing and using consonants at the end of the word (Level B) and hearing and using medial vowels (Level C). Your sequence for word work will look something like this at Level B: *cat-fat-fan-man-map*. At Level C you will begin exchanging short vowels. A typical activity would look like this: *cat-mat-map-mop-top-tap.* The focus for every word work activity is not learning the words but rather learning how words work by hearing sounds in sequence and exchanging letters to match the sounds.

What can I do if a student is making slow progress?

There are several things you should consider: attendance, oral language, sight words, strategies, even teacher behaviors that could be interfering with the student's progress. I have devoted Chapter 7 to problem-solving for the students who are not accelerating. Collect assessments on the student, grab a colleague, and work through the questions in this chapter. I guarantee you will find something that will help.

How much progress can I expect?

No two classrooms are alike, and many factors affect student progress, but teachers who use my format consistently have 75–90% of their students reading at or above grade level by the end of the year. Currently I am analyzing data for a school in Tennessee that used my lesson format this year. The school is located in an urban area with 85% of their students qualifying for free or reduced lunch. There were four kindergarten classrooms with 17–18 students in each classroom and an instructional aide for one hour of the day. Two of the four teachers were new to teaching kindergarten and had never done guided reading. The other two teachers were veteran kindergarten teachers who were experienced with my lesson plan. The team worked closely together and provided many mentoring opportunities for the new teachers. Only 13 students (8%) came to school knowing the alphabet. At the end of the year, 86% of the grade were reading at text Level C or higher, and many students were reading and writing at first-grade levels. The graph shows the end-of-year reading levels for the 69 kindergarten children.

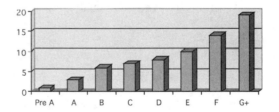

Figure 3-1, graph of end-of-year reading levels of kindergarteners

Of the ten students who did not reach the Level C benchmark, six were able to read a Level B text and knew how to read and write at least twenty sight words. Although I cannot guarantee these results with every school, I can say without reservation that consistent guided reading instruction that incorporates appropriate word study and guided writing is the best way I know to close the achievement gap in kindergarten.

4

Early

GUIDED READING

Most first grade students are at the early reading stage, which includes Levels D–I (DRA levels 5–16). It is relatively common, however, for advanced kindergarten readers and challenged second and third graders to be reading at an early level. Early readers know the letters and sounds but may still be learning how to apply these skills to attack challenges in texts. They should be able to read and write about 20–30 sight words; otherwise, they will struggle with fluency. As children progress through the early reading levels, they learn how to do the following:

* Monitor by checking the meaning of the story and scanning the word for a visual match

* Problem-solve new words using a variety of strategies

* Reread at difficulty to access meaning and structure

* Read for fluency, phrasing, and expression

* Make predictions

* Remember and retell what they have read

* Read and write a large bank of sight words

* Apply phonetic principles, such as blends, vowel combinations, silent e rule, and endings, in both reading and writing

As early readers build automaticity with sight words and decoding strategies, their fluency should improve (Allington, 2009). Teachers need to watch for self-monitoring behavior. It is extremely important that children listen to themselves as they read and stop if what they say does not make sense. Self-monitoring is the foundation for comprehension. When you say, "Does that make sense?" to a child, you are teaching comprehension.

When children reach Levels E and higher (8+), the stories grow more complex. There are usually several characters in the story, and the setting and plot become more important. If children have been taught to think about the story, check the picture, and make sense, comprehension usually comes naturally. Some children, however, have difficulty remembering and sequencing events and will need support to retell the story.

Preparing for Early Guided Reading Lessons

Each early guided reading lesson lasts 20 minutes and includes reading, discussing an instructional-level text, and either learning phonics skills through word study (Day 1) or writing a few sentences about the story with your support (Day 2). One book is used for two days.

Two things need to occur before you can begin working in small groups: (1) Students must understand the classroom routines for literacy workstations and be able to work independently for sixty minutes; and (2) you need to understand how to use assessments to group your students. Refer to Chapter 2 if you need ideas for literacy workstations. The following are suggestions for using assessments.

Assessing Early Readers

The most helpful assessment for analyzing early readers is a running record on an instructional-level text. This means the student should make some errors so the teacher can analyze the student's miscues, strategies, and reading behaviors. Include an oral retell or ask a few comprehension questions to make sure the student has some understanding of the story. Occasionally you will find an early reader

Early Guided Reading Lesson Plan—Levels D–I

Title: _____ Level: _____ Group: _____

Day 1 Date: _____	Day 2 Date: _____
Sight Word Review–Writing: (optional after Level E)	**Sight-Word Review–Writing:** (optional after Level E)
Introduce new book: This book is about _____ New vocabulary: _____	**Continue reading or reread book:** Notes:

Prompts for Early Readers: (Use for Day 1 and Day 2)
- Check the picture. Does it look right and make sense? Reread and think about the story.
- Check the end (or middle) of the word. What would look right and make sense?
- Cover the ending. Is there a part you know? Try that again and think what would make sense.
- Chunk the word and think what would make sense.
- Do you know another word that looks like this one?
- What can you try? What can you do to help yourself?
- Put some words together so it sounds smooth. (fluency)
- Try reading that like the character would say it. (expression)
- What is happening in the story? What is the problem? How might they solve the problem? How does the character feel now? (comprehension)

Teaching Points: Use anecdotal notes to select one or two teaching points each day.

Word-solving strategies:	**Fluency & Comprehension:**
• Monitor • Reread at difficulty • Attend to endings • Use known parts • Use analogies	• Attend to **bold** words • Reread p. _____ for expression • Recall information • Retell story (beginning–middle–end) • Discuss character's feelings
Discussion Prompt:	**Discussion Prompt:**
Teach Sight Word: (optional after Level E) _____	**Teach Sight Word:** _____
Word Study (Choose one activity): • Picture sorts: _____ • Making words: _____ • Sound boxes: _____ • Analogy Chart: _____	**Guided Writing:**

114   *The Next Step in Guided Reading* © 2009 by Jan Richardson, Scholastic Professional

Assessment Summary Chart for Early Readers (Levels D–I)

Name	Inst. Level	Cues Used MSV	Monitors for Meaning + ✓ -	Decodes + ✓ -	Fluency (1–4)	Retell + ✓ -

Cues Used: M=meaning, S=structure, V=visual

Monitors for Meaning: (+) always, (✓) sometimes, (-) rarely

Decodes: (+) Uses beginning, medial, and final letters; attends to parts and endings; (✓) Uses beginning and final letters; ignores medial sounds and some endings; (-) Uses some letter sounds; not consistent in attending to visual cues

Fluency: 4 = phrased & fluent with expression; 3 = phrased but without intonation, ignores some punctuation; 2 = mostly two-word phrases; 1 = word by word

Retelling: (+) complete, (✓) partial, (–) very limited/weak

who whips through a passage with few errors but does not remember what was read. If you need help analyzing a running record, refer to pages 41–47 in Chapter 2.

The running record will indicate the student's instructional level, reveal the cues and strategies the student uses, and provide valuable information on decoding skills, fluency, and ability to retell. Record this information on the Assessment Summary Chart for Early Readers to help you form your reading groups and select a focus strategy for your lessons.

Directions for Completing the Assessment Summary Chart

Columns 1 and 2: Name and Instructional Level. Write the student's name in the first column and record the instructional text level as determined by the running record. This is the level at which the student reads with 90–94% accuracy and with some comprehension. If the student fluently reads the text at 95% accuracy and has a basic understanding of the story, the text is considered to be at an independent level. Give the student a text to read at the next level to determine the instructional level.

Sometimes a student might read a text quite accurately, but have limited comprehension or little fluency. Even though the accuracy rate might be at an independent level, lack of comprehension and fluency indicate that the student needs more instruction on this level. In this case, you would record this text level as the student's instructional level. There are also occasions when the assessment does not indicate an instructional level. For example, text Level E might be an independent level, but the next level is too difficult. If this happens, report the independent level as the instructional level and work on areas of weakness.

Column 3: Cues Used. Put an *M* if the student's errors are mostly meaning-related. Put an *S* if the student's errors match the structure of the text. Put a *V* if the student tries to sound out an unknown word or makes substitutions that are visually similar. See the Analysis of Running Records in Chapter 2 if you need help identifying and recording this information.

Column 4: Monitors for Meaning (M). Put a plus (+) if the student consistently stops when meaning breaks down and tries to fix the error. Put a check (✔) if the student sometimes monitors for meaning. Put a minus (–) if the student consistently ignores errors that distort meaning.

Column 5: Decodes. Students should learn a variety of decoding strategies during the early levels of reading. Most children develop visual processing skills by first attending to initial letters, then ending letters, and finally the medial letters (Clay, 1991). Put a (+) if the student uses beginning, medial, and final letters when decoding unknown words, including inflectional endings such as –*ed*, –*ing*, and –*s*. Put a check (✓) if the student attends to initial and final letters but tends to ignore medial sounds and some endings. Put a minus (–) if the student uses some letters and sounds but is not consistent in attending to visual information. It is rare for a student reading at Levels D or E to score a plus (+) on decoding.

Column 6: Fluency. Readers at this stage are developing a visual memory for sight words, improving their decoding strategies, and learning to group words together visually. As these processes become automatic, the student reads more fluently. Record the student's fluency rate by using this simple rubric:

1: Reading is very slow, mostly word-by-word.
2: Reading is choppy, mostly two-word phrases.
3: Reading is mostly phrased, but lacks some aspect of fluency, such as
    intonation, expression, or attention to punctuation.
4: Reading is fluent and phrased with appropriate expression and intonation.

Column 7: Retell. Record the child's basic understanding of the text, using the descriptions below as a guide.
Put a plus (+) if the child gives a complete and detailed retelling.
The major plot elements are retold completely, accurately, and in order. All major and minor characters are included. The problem and resolution are clear.
Put a check (✓) if the child gives a partial retelling.
The retelling includes the plot and most major characters. Minor characters and setting may be absent. A few events may be missing or out of sequence.
Put a minus (–) if the child gives a limited retelling.
Central characters are left out, incorrect identification of the problem and/or solution, and essential plot details are absent or out of sequence.

Grouping Students for Instruction

After the assessment information is recorded on the Assessment Summary Chart, group students together who are reading close to the same level (no more than one letter apart) and have similar needs. Most of the students reading at the early levels need more work on decoding skills and fluency, but there may be some who need to focus on retelling or monitoring for meaning. You will likely have students in one group who are reading at about the same level but need to learn different strategies. Although you will still have a single lesson focus, you can meet the diverse needs of the students through your prompting. You might prompt for monitoring with one student and fluency with another. The guided reading lesson provides the opportunity to differentiate your instruction.

At least once a month, reevaluate your guided reading groups by using anecdotal notes taken during the guided reading lessons. Expect your reading groups to change throughout the year.

Materials for Early Guided Reading Lessons

* Timer

* 6 dry-erase boards, markers, and erasers

* 6–8 sets of lowercase magnetic letters

* Pictures for sound sorts (short medial vowels and initial blends)

* Assessment kit

* Leveled books

* Copies of lesson plans

* Sound box template (described in Chapter 3)

* Guided writing journals using lined paper

* High-frequency word chart for each group reading at Levels D–F

I have provided two options for the high-frequency word chart. Option 1 (page 80) allows you to write the words as you introduce them to your group; the second option (pages 81 and 112) lists recommended words for each guided reading level. If the students are reading at an early level (D–I) but do not know how to write the words listed for Levels A, B, and C, teach those words before you teach the words listed at Levels D, E, and F. This is just a recommended list, and the words listed at each level do not need to be taught in any sequence.

Maintain a record of the words students know how to write. You will use this information to select guided reading books, plan your word study, and create your dictated sentence for guided writing.

High-Frequency Word Chart for Levels C–F, Option 2

Check (✓) every time the student writes the word correctly without teacher support. There is no sequence within the level. Teach the words as they appear in the guided reading books.

Level C (3–4)	Student 1	Student 2	Student 3	Student 4	Student 5	Student 6
are						
come						
did						
for						
get						
have						
here						
him						
of						
play						
said						
she						
will						
you						
Adds –s						
Level D (5–6)						
all						
down						
saw						
that						
they						

High-Frequency Word Chart for Levels C–F, Option 2 *(continued)*

Level D (5–6)	Student 1	Student 2	Student 3	Student 4	Student 5	Student 6
this						
was						
went						
what						
when						
where						
with						
Adds –ing						
Level E (7–8)						
day						
get						
give						
her						
new						
out						
over						
she						
then						
want						
were						
your						
Adds –ed						

Early Guided Reading Lesson Plan—Levels D–I

Title: _____   Level: _____   Group: _____

Day 1 Date: _____	Day 2 Date: _____
Sight-Word Review–Writing: (optional after Level E) _____ _____ _____	**Sight-Word Review–Writing:** (optional after Level E) _____ _____ _____
Introduce new book: This book is about _____ _____ New vocabulary: _____	**Continue reading or reread book:** Notes:

Prompts for Early Readers: (Use for Day 1 and Day 2)

- Check the picture. Does it look right and make sense? Reread and think about the story.
- Check the end (or middle) of the word. What would look right and make sense?
- Cover the ending. Is there a part you know? Try that again and think what would make sense.
- Chunk the word and think what would make sense.
- Do you know another word that looks like this one?
- What can you try? What can you do to help yourself?
- Put some words together so it sounds smooth. (fluency)
- Try reading that like the character would say it. (expression)
- What is happening in the story? What is the problem? How might they solve the problem? How does the character feel now? (comprehension)

Teaching Points: Use anecdotal notes to select one or two teaching points each day.

Word-solving strategies:	Fluency & Comprehension:
• Monitor • Reread at difficulty • Attend to endings • Use known parts • Use analogies	• Attend to **bold** words • Reread p. _____ for expression • Recall information • Retell story (beginning–middle–end) • Discuss character's feelings
Discussion Prompt:	**Discussion Prompt:**
Teach Sight Word: (optional after Level E) _____	**Teach Sight Word:** _____
Word Study (Choose one activity): • Picture sorts: _____ • Making words: _____ • Sound boxes: _____ • Analogy Chart: _____	**Guided Writing:**

The Next Step in Guided Reading © 2009 by Jan Richardson, Scholastic Professional

Selecting the Text

Use your Assessment Summary Chart to determine your focus strategy. It might be monitoring and decoding, fluency, or retell. The text you choose will differ according to your focus strategy. If your goal is to teach children to **monitor and decode**, select a text at the students' instructional level (i.e., contains some words the students do not know and need to figure out using strategies). If the students know every word in the book, they won't have an opportunity to use their strategies. If your focus is **fluency**, select an easier text with dialogue. When teaching for fluency, the text should have very few decoding challenges. The students won't be able to practice fluency if there are too many unfamiliar words. Sometimes your focus will be **retelling** because the students are not remembering what they read. For retelling, it is best to choose a fiction text with a clear problem and solution. Retelling information from nonfiction books is too challenging for early readers because the details are usually presented as single items of information. A text with a beginning, middle, and end is best for teaching students to retell.

When selecting texts for students who are learning English as a second language, be sensitive to their limited vocabularies. Choose texts with strong picture support, especially for unfamiliar concepts. Early readers habitually look at the picture and will learn new vocabulary if it is clearly illustrated.

Text Considerations for Early Readers

- Story makes sense and contains a problem and solution.
- Language is natural, with dialogue included.
- Picture and other illustrations provide support for unfamiliar concepts.
- Text provides opportunities for students to problem-solve unknown words.

Description of Early Guided Reading Lesson (Two-Day Plan)

Day 1	Explanation of Procedures: The same book is used for two days. Each lesson takes 20 minutes. If you have more time, you can extend the time for reading, word study, or guided writing.
Sight-Word Review (optional after Level E) (Days 1 & 2) Time: 1 minute Every child writes the word correctly, but some will need your help to do it.	Spend a few <u>seconds</u> at the beginning of the lesson to review sight words from previous guided reading lessons. Distribute whiteboards and dictate 2–3 words for students to write. Writing the word (as opposed to just reading it) helps imprint the word and controls for serial order. If students have difficulty remembering a word, provide a scaffold. For example, if the student cannot remember how to write *want*, you might say, "It's almost like *went* but it has an *a* in it." Provide a visual link with a known word when appropriate. ("*Where* has *here* in it. *They* has *the* in it.") These links give students a visual scaffold for remembering the word. It is best to intervene while the student is writing rather than allow him/her to write the word incorrectly. Every student should write the words accurately, but some will need teacher support. Put a checkmark (✓) on the High-Frequency Word Chart if the student is able to write the word without support. Students should have at least six checkmarks for each word. Just writing it once without help does not mean the student knows the word. **Be sure to teach the words at the lower levels first, even if the students are reading at a higher level.**
Introduction (Day 1 only) Time: 3–4 minutes **Gist Statement** Briefly tell about the story.	**Gist Statement**: Prepare a short introduction that includes the names of the characters and a brief description of the problem. For example, "This book is about a boy named Luke who wants in-line skates but doesn't have the money to buy them. You are going to find out how Luke and his friend Andrew find a way to earn money for the skates."

Day 1	Explanations of Procedures
Preview the text and introduce new vocabulary Explain unfamiliar concepts in the pictures. Make students repeat the word. This helps them remember it when they read. When you introduce a new concept, you are making a deposit in the students' vocabulary bank.	**Text Preview and New Vocabulary**: Before they read, students should look through the book and use the pictures to construct the meaning of the story. I had one teacher who thought this was cheating. Actually, previewing is a prereading strategy that supports comprehension and the use of strategies. You do not need to discuss every page, but you should attend to unfamiliar concepts and new sight words the students cannot decode. When you introduce a new concept, draw attention to the picture. For example, if the new concept is *bulldozer*, explain what a bulldozer is, then have students point to it in the picture and name the concept. This is especially important for those who are learning English. If there are words children would have trouble decoding, write them on a whiteboard so they can see the unusual spelling. For example, *special* may be too difficult for students to decode. You should introduce it before they read. You do not need to explain the unusual phonic elements in the word, just say, "This word may be tricky for you. The word is *special*. What's this word?" (Students say *special*.)
Text Reading (Days 1 & 2) **Day 1: First reading** Time: 8–10 minutes **Day 2: Continue reading the book** Time: 5–8 minutes	**Read and Prompt**: Children should read independently (and softly) while you observe, prompt, coach, and teach individual students. **Do not allow choral or round-robin reading. This inhibits problem-solving behaviors and creates dependent readers.** Also, it is not appropriate for students at this level to read silently. Reading aloud (softly) will help students monitor and recall what they read. Students should read for about ten minutes on the first day. On the second day, the students will have 5–8 minutes to finish the story they began the day before. If students finish reading the book before time is called, they should reread the text to improve their fluency. As you work with individual students, focus on the target strategy for the lesson, but also consider each individual student's needs. The prompts and target strategies for early readers fall under four categories: self-monitoring for meaning, decoding unfamiliar words, fluency, and comprehension. Use the following prompts whenever they are appropriate:

Day 1	Explanations of Procedures
Target Strategies • Self-monitoring • Decoding • Fluency • Comprehension This is your opportunity to differentiate your instruction to meet individual needs. You will prompt some children for decoding strategies and other students for fluency and comprehension.	**Self-monitoring prompts** • *Are you right? Does that make sense and look right?* • *Read that sentence again and see what would make sense.* • *Think about the story and try something that looks right.* **Decoding prompts** • *What can you do to help yourself figure out that word?* • *Can you cover the ending? Is there a part you know that can help?* • *Check the middle (or ending) of that word. What looks right and makes sense?* • *Do you know another word that looks like that?* (Show student a known word that has the same rime. For example, if the student is stuck on the word *fill*, write *will* on a whiteboard and show the student how to use *will* to read *fill*.) **Fluency prompts** • *Put these words together so it sounds smooth* (fluency). • *Try reading that like the character would say it* (expression). **Comprehension prompts** • *Tell me what you just read. What happened at the beginning?* • *How does the character feel now?* • *Why do you think the character did that?* • *What might the character do next?* If the student does not make an error while you listen to him/her, ask if there was a tricky part on another page and work on strategies there. If the student had no difficulty reading the text, you should work on phrasing, expression, or comprehension. (Or you might need to move the student to a higher-level group.) You want to teach every student something in every guided reading lesson. If there is nothing to teach, the book is too easy.

Day 1	Explanations of Procedures
Teaching Points (Days 1 & 2) Time: 1–2 minutes Select one or two examples from the story to demonstrate a specific strategy.	**Teach a strategy**: Each day, after students read the text for 8–10 minutes, spend a few minutes teaching strategies for decoding, fluency, and/or comprehension. Always ask yourself, "What do these students need to learn next?" Usually decoding is a teaching point for early readers, but sometimes fluency and/or comprehension are appropriate teaching points for Day 2. I am often asked the difference between a prompt and a teaching point. A prompt reminds the student to do something you have already taught, whereas a teaching point is a demonstration of a new strategy students need to learn. The following are specific teaching points (demonstrations) for decoding strategies. Regardless of your focus, always emphasize rereading the text to be sure it makes sense. Decoding often gives an approximate pronunciation that must be checked against the meaning of the text. Limit yourself to two teaching points and teach by demonstration (not by talking). The more you talk, the less they listen.
Monitor *I am going to make a mistake as I read. See if you can find it. What would make sense?* *What would look right?*	**Monitor with meaning**: The teacher reads a sentence and makes a mistake. Students find the error. Emphasize the fact that reading must make sense. Prompt students to stop when it doesn't make sense, reread the sentence, and think about the story. **Monitor with letters & sounds (visual)**: Write a tricky word on the whiteboard and say, "Could this word be _____?" For example, if students said *cried* for *cries* during the reading of the book, the teacher would write *cries* (the word from the book) and say, "Can this word be *cried*? Why not?" Students should say it can't be *cried* because there is no *d* at the end of the word. With early readers, you will use this teaching point to help children use visual information to monitor the middle and the end of the word. Other examples might be *said* for *shouted* or *laid* for *landed*. In these examples, the error would make sense, but there would not be a visual match in the middle of the word.

Day 1	Explanations of Procedures
Reread *Try that again and think what would make sense and look right.*	**Reread at difficulty**: Select a page where children had difficulty. Read up to the tricky word and pretend not to know it. Then model how to reread to the beginning of the sentence (not the page) and think what would make sense and look right.
Decode	**Teach a decoding strategy students need to learn.**
Cover the ending. *(standing)*	**Cover the ending**: Write a word with an ending. Tell the students not to say the word, but to share a strategy to use for figuring it out. Students need to learn that *–s –ed, –ing, –er*, and *–ly* can be endings they can cover to help them figure out the word. Covering the ending also draws students' attention to the middle of the word, a part early readers often ignore.
Use known parts. *(for-got)*	**Use known parts**: Write a word that has a known part and say, "What do you know in this word that can help you figure it out?" Some examples are *today*, *stand*, and *forever*.
Chunk big words. *(yes-ter-day)*	**Chunk big words**: Write a big word from the story and show students how to break or chunk that word into smaller units. Efficient readers do not sound out letter by letter. They take big words apart and read in chunks. Examples for this teaching point include *re-mem-ber, be-hind, be-fore, a-round*, and *hap-pens*.
Break down contractions. *I'll = I + will* *They're = they + are*	**Break down contractions**: If students have trouble with contractions, show them how a contraction is a short form for two words. Write the contraction and the two words that make up the contraction on the whiteboard and discuss how this works.

Day 1	Explanations of Procedures

Use analogies
 	
Can you think of a word that has the same part in it? Sh<u>ook</u> is like l<u>ook</u>, s<u>illy</u> is like w<u>ill</u>.
	Use analogies: Write a word from the story that has a familiar rime. The **rime** is the part of the syllable that begins with the vowel. For example in the word *shook*, *sh* is called the **onset** and *ook* is the rime. After you write the word from the story on the whiteboard, underline the rime and ask, "What word do you know that has this part in it?" If the students cannot think of a known word, you should write the known word and discuss how to use a word you know to figure out a word you don't know. Examples for this teaching point:
	
	  j<u>aw</u> is like *s<u>aw</u>*
	  f<u>ound</u> is like *ar<u>ound</u>*
	  wh<u>ile</u> is like *sm<u>ile</u>*
	
	This teaching point is most effective when students already have a large bank of known words.

Fluency **Attend to bold words.** **Read dialogue with expression.**	To teach fluency and expression, select a page that has bold words or dialogue. **Attend to bold words**: First explain that authors use bold words to help the reader know how to say a word. Tell them to read bold words a little louder than the other words in the sentence. Students read the sentence with you so you can support the expression and intonation. Now discuss *why* the word is bold. **Read with expression**: Select a page that has interesting dialogue and have the students read it with you. Emphasize using appropriate expression and inflection.

Day 1	Explanations of Procedures
Comprehension Students retell the story with your support. The following frameworks support early readers as they retell:	**Comprehension** is the most important part of reading and should always be foremost in your mind as you work with your students. However, you will use comprehension as a specific teaching point for the second day of the lesson plan because most of the students will need two days to finish the book. You can select one of the following frameworks for comprehension or design your own.
B-M-E: Retell major events from beginning, middle, and end.	**Beginning-Middle-End (B-M-E)**: Students take turns telling what happened at the beginning, middle, and end of the story. Prompt students for important details. If students forget important events, direct them to use the pictures to help them remember, but don't expect them to remember everything from the story.
S-W-B-S: Summarize the entire story in one "Somebody-Wanted-But-So" sentence.	**Somebody-Wanted-But-So** (Macon, Bewell, and Vogt, 1991): Children are given a framework for **summarizing** the story by recalling the character (Somebody), the character's goal (Wanted), the conflict (But), and finally, the resolution (So). The S-W-B-S does not include all of the details, just the character's problem and solution. After several demonstrations, children should be able to construct a Somebody-Wanted-But-So statement with little teacher support. Here is an example: *The pigs wanted to build their own houses, but the wolf blew their houses down, so they ran to the house of bricks.*
Five-Finger Retell: Include all five story elements: characters, setting, problem, events, solution.	**Five-Finger Retell**: Students use the fingers of one hand to recall and retell five story elements. This activity requires students to include more details from the story as they tell the events. Thumb: *The characters are . . .* 1st finger: *The setting is . . .* Tall finger: *The problem is . . .* Ring finger: *The events are . . . (What did they do first? Next? Then?)* Little finger: *At the end . . .*

Day 1	Explanations of Procedures
More Comprehension Scaffolds: Predictions Problem-Solution Character's feelings	**Make predictions**: Ask students what might happen if there were another page to the story. **Problem-Solution**: Ask students to tell you the problem in the story and how it was solved. **Character's feelings**: Ask how the character felt at the beginning, middle, and end of the story. Only use this teaching point if the character's feelings changed.
Discussion Prompt (Days 1 & 2) Time: 1–2 minutes Strive for deeper understanding.	Each day, prepare one question that requires students to make inferences or draw conclusions from the story. Lean towards open-ended questions such as "Why do you think . . .?" or "What would have happened if . . .?"
Teach One Sight Word (optional) (Days 1 & 2) Time: 1 minute	Spend one or two minutes teaching **one** new sight word with each book. This component is required for students reading at Levels D and E, but it is optional after Level E if students have already learned how to write 50–60 words. It is very important that you keep a record of the sight words students have learned by writing a checkmark on the High-Frequency Word Chart each time the student writes the word without your support. If students are reading at the early levels (D-I) but have not learned the words listed for Levels A, B, or C, teach these first. Once students learn about 50–60 high-frequency sight words, you can eliminate this activity. They have accumulated a large bank of known words and have also developed a way of remembering words. Do **all** the following activities to build visual memory:

Day 1	Explanations of Procedures
Teach One Sight Word (optional) -What's Missing? -Mix & Fix -Table Writing -Whiteboards Do all four steps with each new word. The activities provide a gradual release of responsibility and strengthen visual memory.	**What's Missing?** Write the word on a whiteboard or make it with magnetic letters. Do this in front of the students so they can see the left-to-right construction of the word. Tell students the word and ask them to look at each letter. Have students spell the word as you point to each letter in sequence. This prompts students to study the word by scanning left to right. Some students develop a haphazard approach to looking at print, which can lead to serial order problems. Say: *Boys and girls, this was a word in the story.* (Write the word). *The word is* were. Turn the board towards you and erase (or remove) a letter. Show the board to the students and ask them to tell you what letter is missing. Say: *What's missing?* The students tell you the missing letter, and you put it back in the word. Repeat the procedure two or three more times by erasing a different letter, or two or three letters at a time, until the entire word is erased. Students then spell the word for you as you write (or make) the word on the whiteboard. **Mix & Fix**—Give each student the letters to make the new word. They should check your model to ensure they made the word correctly. Students check the word by sliding their finger under the word and saying the word slowly. Students should now pull each letter down (left to right) to remake the word. Again, prompt for a slow check of the word. Now have students mix the letters and then rearrange (fix) them to remake the word. **Table Writing**—Students use their finger to "write" the word on the table. This finger tracing imprints the word in the children's memory bank. Then they say the word and slide their finger under it to check for accuracy. **Whiteboards**—Students write the word on a whiteboard and say it aloud as they check it with their finger. Discourage spelling the word because you want the child to focus on the entire word, not the individual letters. If you follow these procedures, students will usually learn the word in two days; however, some children have extremely poor visual memory and will need more than two days. Do not introduce a new sight word until students have learned the current one. To do so would only confuse them.

Day 1	Explanations of Procedures
Word Study (Day 1 only) Time: 5–8 minutes Use Appendix A to find activities listed for each level. Four options for word study: picture sorts, magnetic letters, sound boxes, and analogy charts **Target Skills by Level:** **Level D**: digraphs, endings **Level E**: initial blends, onsets/ rimes, contractions **Level F**: final blends, onsets/ rimes, contractions **Level G**: blends, silent *e* rule **Levels H–I**: vowel patterns, endings, compound words **Picture Sorts** **Level D**—short vowels *o* (frog) *u* (duck)	**Activities for teaching phonics and phonemic awareness** Students reading at levels D–I are still learning phonics. Spend the last 5–8 minutes of the lesson on Day 1 doing **one** word study activity that matches their decoding/phonics needs. Use the Summary of Skill Focus and Word Study Activities Levels A–J in Appendix A (pages 271–282) to identify the phonics skill for that level. Although there is a logical sequence for teaching the phonics skill for each level, you should choose the skill the students need, not necessarily the one assigned to a particular text level. Teach the early skills before you teach the ones listed at the higher levels. It is common for struggling readers in second or third grade to be reading at Level E or F but still need to work on short vowel sounds (a target skill for Level C). There are four options for word study: picture sorts, making words, sound boxes, and analogy charts. Choose **one** of these activities for Day 1. I have listed options for teaching the skills most early readers need. **Picture sorts**: This activity is for students who need to learn short vowels, digraphs, or initial blends. It is most commonly used at Levels D and E. Prepare by collecting pictures that begin with digraphs (*th*, *sh*, *ch*) and initial consonant blends. I don't teach the *wh* digraph because I have found that it causes more confusion for children. How often have you seen children write *whent* or *whint*? They were listening when you taught the *wh*, but they didn't understand when to use it. Level D: The skill focus is digraphs, but you may also need to review short medial vowels. Select two or three digraphs and write them on a whiteboard. Distribute pictures that begin with these digraphs (three to four pictures for each student). Students take turns selecting a picture, saying the first part of the word (/sh/, /ch/ or /th/), and saying the letters that make up that digraph. It is important that students actually say the letters of the digraph and not just put the picture under the correct letters. Saying the letter names will help them transfer the skill to writing.

Day 1	Explanations of Procedures
Level E—blends *fr* (frog) *fl* (flag)	<u>Level E</u>: Skill focus is initial blends. Select two or three blends that begin with the same letter (*sl–*, *st–*, *sp–*). Distribute to each student three or four pictures that have these initial blends. Teach them to name the picture (swing), sound the first part (/sw/), say the letters of the blend (*s* and *w*), and put the picture under the correct blend that has been written on the whiteboard. If you sort blends that have the same initial letter, you draw students' attention to the second letter of the blend, which is the sound children have trouble hearing. Once children learn short medial vowels, digraphs, and initial blends, you will not use the picture sort for word study.
Making Words **Level D**: *shot, shop, chop, chip, chin, thin* **Level E:** *slip, slit, spit, spot, spat, scat* **Level F:** *went, west, test, tend, send, sent* **Level G:** *ran, ranch, branch, brunch, crunch, scrunch* **Levels H & I:** *cow, clown, crown, crowd, crowded*	**Making words with magnetic letters**: Use this activity to teach students how to monitor for visual information, control serial order, and break for onset and rime. Distribute the magnetic letters students will need for the word sequence you have planned. The first word they make should be a known word. Tell the students the first word and have them make it with magnetic letters. Students should check each word they make by running their finger under the word and saying it slowly. This helps them control serial order and monitor for a visual/auditory match. Then tell them to change one letter (don't tell them whether it is the first, middle, or last letter) to make a new word. Before students reach for the new letter, they should say the new word slowly and run their finger under the old word. For example, if the first word was *shot*, students should have *s-h-o-t* in front of them. Then you say: *Change a letter to make "shop."* Students should say *shop* slowly and check the magnetic letters in front of them to determine which letter they need to change. Then they remove the *t* in *shot* and replace it with a *p* to make *shop*. This teaches students to monitor with visual information during reading. The students should then break the word *shop* at the onset (*sh*) and rime (*op*). Tell them to point to each part and say it (/sh/, /op/). Finally students put the two parts together and say *shop*.

Day 1	Explanations of Procedures
Sound Boxes Say the word naturally; do not segment the sounds for students. They should say the sounds as they write the corresponding letters in the boxes.	Here is a summary of the procedure for making words: - <u>Check it</u> (run the finger under the word to see what letter needs to be changed) - <u>Make it</u> (replace the wrong letter with the correct letter) - <u>Break it</u> (move the letters apart at the onset and rime) - <u>Say it</u> (say each part as they point to it) and then make the word once more (push the letters together and say the word) **Sound boxes**: Students learn how to segment sounds and write the sounds in sequence using boxes. This activity supports serial order (left-to-right scanning of a word), phonemic segmentation, and linking sounds to letters. Select three or four phonetically regular, one-syllable words. The words should contain the same phonics focus you used with Picture Sorts or Making Words in previous lessons. Use the appendix (pages 274–281) for examples of words to use with sound boxes. You will say each word **naturally**, then ask students to say the word slowly while they segment each sound. The students (not the teacher) should segment each sound. Students then write the word in sound boxes, writing the letter or letters in a box **as** they say the sound. Most boxes will contain one letter with the exception of digraphs (*sh*, *th*, *ch*). A digraph should go in one box because it makes a single sound. Once children write the word in the box, they should check the letters by saying the word naturally and running their finger under the word.
Level D: digraphs **sh** a g m u **ch**	<u>Level D</u>: Use three boxes and dictate words with a digraph (*m-a-sh*; *ch-o-p*; *th-i-n*). You will increase the power of this activity if you select three words with different vowels, consonants, and digraphs. Avoid rhyming families because students will not attend to each sound.
Level E: initial blends **f l** a g **s p** u n	<u>Level E</u>: Use four boxes and dictate words with initial blends (*f-l-i-p*; *s-t-a-b*; *g-r-u-b*). Students should write each letter of a blend in a separate box because each letter represents a distinct phoneme or sound. Avoid using known words such as *stop* and *went* because students will not be forced to segment the sounds. Use different vowel sounds and blends when you select words for students to box.

Day 1	Explanations of Procedures
Level F: final blends f i **s t** m a **s k** **Levels G & H:** initial and final blends **s p** e n t **s p** l i t **Analogy Charts** Always begin with a known word for each pattern. Silent *e* analogy charts have three levels of difficulty. Begin with the easy level and gradually work towards the hardest level.	Level F: Use four boxes and dictate words with final blends (*l-i-s-p*; *l-u-m-p*; *f-e-l-t*; *b-e-n-t*). Levels G & H: Use five boxes and dictate words with initial and final blends (*c-l-a-n-k*; *g-r-a-n-d*; *d-r-i-f-t*). Once students are able to hear and record five phonemes in a word, you can discontinue this activity. They have developed the phonemic awareness they need to sound out words while writing. **Analogy charts**: Use the analogy charts to teach the silent *e* rule and vowel combinations such as *ay*, *ea*, and *ow*. Avoid using the analogy chart until students are reading at Level G. They should first develop the phonemic awareness skills for blends and vowels, and this is best taught with picture sorts, making words, and sound boxes. If you introduce the silent *e* skill too early, you will likely confuse the students. **Procedures for teaching the silent *e* rule:** Each student has a T-chart. I like to put the T-chart template inside a clear, sheet protector and give students a dry-erase marker to write their words. This saves a few seconds since students do not have to draw their T-charts. Students write two known words (dictated by you) at the top. One word has a long vowel with a silent *e* and the other is short (no silent *e*). As you dictate other words, the students decide whether the word has a long vowel and requires a silent *e* or has a short vowel and needs no silent *e*. Students write the word under the key (or known) word that matches the pattern. Avoid using words the students already know how to spell. You want to force them to use the analogy strategy. There are three levels of difficulty for the silent *e* analogy charts. The first uses words that contain the rime from the key words. The next uses words that have the same vowel sounds as the key words (long and short *a*, for example) but do not have the same rime. The third (and hardest) level uses words that have a short or long vowel sound, but the vowel sound varies with each word.

Day 1	Explanations of Procedures

Easy Level

The rime does not change.

hat **make**

chat snake

Harder Level

The rime changes, but the vowel sound remains the same.

hat **make**

snap grape

Hardest Level

The words have a short or long vowel sound. Students apply the silent e rule as appropriate.

short long

hat **make**

chip slope

slot slime

Examples of analogy charts for teaching the silent e rule

easy		harder		hardest	
cap	name	cap	name	cap	name
chap	same	chat	snake	plop	cube
snap	flame	brag	spade	slip	spoke
slap	blame	spam	scrape	stub	spine
hit	like	hit	like	hit	like
pit	hike	chip	spine	spot	grape
slit	spike	spip	gripe	crab	broke
grit	strike	crib	slime	flip	spike

For extra power dictate words that have an initial blend. This helps students review the phonic skills that have been taught in previous lessons.

Day 1	Explanations of Procedures
Analogy Charts for teaching vowel patterns **d<u>ay</u>** **c<u>ow</u>** st<u>ay</u> pl<u>ow</u> spr<u>ay</u> cr<u>ow</u>d pl<u>ay</u>er gr<u>ow</u>ling aw<u>ay</u> dr<u>ow</u>ned	**Using analogy charts to teach vowel patterns** Select two vowel combinations students need to learn (e.g., –*ow* and –*ay*). Begin with distinctly different vowel patterns to reduce confusions. Dictate two **known** words that have these vowel patterns and tell students to write these words on the top of the T-chart. Students underline the vowel patterns in each word. Dictate a word that has one of the vowel patterns. It is best if the students do not already know how to spell it. This forces them to listen the vowel pattern in the word and use an analogy with one of the known words on the T-chart. Students should repeat the word, attending to the vowel pattern, and decide which column they should use to write the word. If students have trouble hearing the vowel sound, teach them how to break the word at the onset and rime. For example, if the new word is "crowd," students would say, "/cr/ - /owd/." This helps them hear the vowel sound. Students write the word under the key word with the same vowel pattern and underline the pattern in the new word. Continue to dictate other unknown words with the target vowel patterns. Use words with digraphs, blends, and endings to increase the power of the task and review skills that have been taught in previous lessons.
Day 2	**Explanations of Procedures**
Sight-Word Review, Reading, and Teaching Points	Follow the same procedures as Day 1 for sight-word review, reading with prompting, and teaching points. Reserve the last ten minutes of your lesson for guided writing.
Guided Writing (Day 2 only) Time: 8–10 minutes	Students write a short response to the book they have read. Writing helps students apply phonetic principles you have taught during your word study. The writing occurs at the guided reading table and is not a seat assignment. Tremendous power is achieved when students write with teacher support. You will prompt individual students during this component, reminding them to apply the skills you have taught them.

Day 2	Explanations of Procedures
Use simple handwriting paper when students control letter formation but need to work on letter size and position.	Make journals using simple lined paper. Fold about ten sheets of paper in half and staple to make a journal. Students write their stories on the bottom half and use the top half to practice letter formation or to work on an unknown word with your help. Do not use whiteboards for this activity because you will want to have a record of what students have been able to write. As students improve with letter formation, you can transition to simple handwriting paper with two lines (top and bottom) and three lines (top, middle, bottom). As you introduce handwriting paper, you will teach children how to form a letter that drops below the line or rises to the middle line.
Dictated Sentence (Levels D & E) *Jack and Billy are playing with the cars. Billy hides a car in the garage.* Students should apply the skills you have taught such as endings, blends, and vowel combinations. Always expect students to apply the skills you have taught them.	**Options for guided writing: Dictated or student-generated response** Choose the written response appropriate for their reading level. At first you will dictate a few sentences, but soon students will take responsibility for crafting their own response. If students finish their response before the lesson is over, they can practice a skill they need (e.g., letter formation or sight-words), or they can add another sentence to their story. **Levels D & E: Dictated or open-ended sentences** At these levels you should dictate a few sentences for students to write. Carefully plan the sentences so they include the new sight word that was taught with this book and other familiar sight words the students need to practice. The sentence should also include unfamiliar words students need to stretch. Be sure students repeat each sentence several times before they begin writing. They need to remember the sentence so you do not have to dictate it word by word. Although the goal is not perfect spelling, the sight words should be spelled correctly. You will prompt students to apply skills you have taught them during guided reading or word study. For example, if you have taught the *er* chunk, expect children to use it in words such as *water, river, mother,* etc. Always expect what you have taught.

Day 2	Explanations of Procedures
B-M-E beginning-middle-end (Levels F–I) **B**: *The lion wanted something to eat.* **M**: *He saw a rabbit but let it go.* **E**: *He saw a deer, but he couldn't catch it.*	**Levels F–I: Beginning-Middle-End (B-M-E).** The students write three to five sentences about the story. The first describes something that happened at the beginning of the book, the next sentence or two describes something that happened in the middle, and the last describes something that happened at the end. This is not dictated. Students must think about the story, sequence the events, and write them down. It may be necessary for some students to orally rehearse the sentences with you before they write. This is especially critical for students who are learning English as a second language.
S-W-B-S (**S**omebody-**W**anted-**B**ut-**S**o) *The lion wanted something to eat, but he couldn't catch the deer, so he had to stay hungry.*	**Levels G–I: Somebody-Wanted-But-So (S-W-B-S)** The students write a one-sentence summary using the S-W-B-S scaffold. At first you will need to help students write this response, but eventually you should be able to say, "Write a 'Somebody-Wanted-But-So' for this story." **Somebody**: Who is the story about? **Wanted**: What did this character want? **But**: But what happened? **So**: So how did it end? What happened next? The response should be written in a complete sentence. As students write independently, you should circulate among the group and scaffold students who need your help.

Day 2	Explanations of Procedures
Teaching Points for Guided Writing: You can diversify your instruction to meet individual needs. • Students forget the sentence. • Students misspell a sight word you have taught the group. • Students need help hearing sounds in words they don't already know how to spell. • Students form letters incorrectly. • Students fail to use capital letters or use them inappropriately. You may also select one of these teaching points to address to the whole group if you see several students with the same problem.	**Teaching points for guided writing** As students write, you have the opportunity to teach students the skills they need. It is likely you will use a different teaching point with each student in the group. Here are some suggestions for teaching points for early writers: **Reread for meaning:** With the dictated sentence, students should always repeat the sentence several times before they begin to write. If they forget the next word to write, prompt them to reread what they have already written and think about what would make sense. Only tell the next word as a last resort. Once students craft their own response, rereading should be automatic. **Spelling sight words:** If students misspell a sight word you have already taught them, erase the wrong letters and say, "What's missing?" Use a visual scaffold such as *"where* has *here* in it" or *"they* has *the* in it." If these prompts are not successful, write the word correctly on the top part of the journal and have the students practice it a few times before they write it correctly in their story. **Spelling unknown words:** Students should say a word slowly as they write the letters they hear. If students have trouble hearing sounds in words, draw a box for each sound on the top half of the journal. The students then segment the word and write the letters for the sounds in the boxes. Avoid saying the word slowly for them. **Incorrect letter formation:** Model the correct formation on the top part of the journal. Students practice writing the letter, paying close attention to formation, size, and position. **Mechanics:** Expect a capital letter at the beginning and a period at the end of each sentence. Do not accept capital letters in the middle of a word.

Rubric for Coaching an Early Guided Reading Lesson Plan (Levels D–I; 5–16)

This rubric can be used for self-evaluation, observation, or coaching.

Observation or Coaching (circle one)	Evident (✓)
Classroom Environment	
Guided reading materials were organized; table was free of clutter.	
Other students were working independently in literacy workstations.	
Teacher was not interrupted by other students in the room.	
Sight-Word Review: (optional after Level E) (1 min.)	
Students <u>wrote</u> three known words.	
Teacher prompted students who had difficulty.	
Teacher used chart to record progress.	
Book Introduction (Day 1 only) (5 min.)	
Teacher gave a short introduction.	
Students looked through book to construct meaning of story.	
Teacher introduced new vocabulary.	
Reading the Book (Days 1 & 2) (8-10 min.)	
Book was at the appropriate level (slightly challenging).	
Students read the book independently (not chorally).	
Students read without pointing.	

    The Next Step in Guided Reading © 2009 by Jan Richardson, Scholastic Professional

Observation or Coaching (circle one)	Evident (✓)
Teacher listened to students read orally and **took anecdotal notes.**	
Teacher prompted **each** student for monitoring, decoding, fluency, or retell.	
Teacher asked a discussion prompt (higher-level question).	
Teacher taught strategies appropriate for the group.	
Teaching of New Sight Word (Optional after Level E) (1-2 min.)	
Followed all **four** procedures: What's Missing?, Mix & Fix, Table Writing, Whiteboards	
New word was in the book.	
Word Study (Day 1 only) (5 min.)	
Circle activity used: Picture sorts, making words, sound boxes, analogy chart. Teacher followed established procedures.	
Students said the words slowly as they worked with magnetic letters or wrote the words in boxes. (Teacher did not say the words slowly for the children!)	
Guided Writing (Day 2 only) (5-8 min.)	
Circle activity used: Dictated or open-ended sentence, B-M-E, S-W-B-S, Other: _____	
Students wrote mostly independently, with teacher prompting at difficulty.	
Practice page may be used for letter formation, sight words, and sound boxes.	
TOTAL LESSON TIME: 20 min.	

Ten-Minute Lesson for Early Readers (Individual Instruction)

If you have an early reader who does not fit into one of your other groups, teach him or her individually for ten minutes a day using the following plan.

Day 1: Ten Minutes

Sight-Word Review (30 seconds): This is an optional activity and is only used if the student is not able to read and write the high-frequency words listed on the chart for levels A–E. Follow the procedures described in the early guided reading lesson plan and discontinue this component when the student has acquired a large bank of sight words.

Read a New Book (8 minutes): When possible, select short texts for these lessons since your time is limited. On Day 1 introduce the book and allow the student to read several pages. Watch the timer and stop the reading when you have one minute left. The student will continue reading the book on Day 2.

Learn a New Sight Word (1 minute): This activity is optional—necessary only if the student does not know how to write the words listed on the high-frequency word chart for levels A–E. Follow the procedures described for the early guided reading lesson.

Day 2: Ten Minutes

Sight-Word Review (30 seconds): Follow same procedure as Day 1 but use different words.

Finish (or continue) Reading Yesterday's New Book (6 minutes): The student begins reading at the point where he or she left off yesterday. If there is time, the student can begin a second reading of the book. Prompt the student to use strategies appropriate for the reading level. Prompts are listed at the bottom of the lesson plan. Watch the timer! **The student should take this book home to practice, or read it with a buddy in the classroom.**

Reteach the Same Sight Word From Day 1 (if appropriate)

Word Study (3 minutes): Select **one** activity appropriate for the student's needs. You will use either a picture sort, making words, sound boxes, or an analogy chart. Your skill focus will determine which activity you use. Use the Summary of Skill Focus and Word Study Activities in Appendix A on pages 271–282 to find the focus strategy for word work. Then use the example provided for that level. Follow the procedures described in this chapter.

Day 3: Ten Minutes

Sight-Word Review (30 seconds): Follow same procedure as Day 1 but practice with different words.

Familiar Reading: At some time outside of the guided reading lesson, the student should read the new book with a buddy. It is best to make guided writing the major focus of Day 3.

Guided Writing (10 minutes): Follow the procedures for guided writing described in this chapter. Since you are working with only one student, you will be able to target the specific skills the student needs.

* *Level D:* Dictate two sentences that include many known sight words and some words the student does not know how to spell. Sight words should be spelled correctly, but encourage invented spelling with other words.

* *Levels E & F. Beginning-Middle-End (B-M-E).* The student generates his or her own retelling of the book by writing one sentence about the beginning, one sentence about the middle, and one sentence about the end. As the student writes, prompt the student to say words slowly, add endings, and use known chunks.

* *Levels G, H, & I:* Gradually expect students to write more during each ten-minute guided writing session. You decide whether the student should write a B-M-E or a Somebody-Wanted-But-So (S-W-B-S). Both responses are explained in the description of early guided reading lessons.

Do not expect an error-free piece. Target the skills the student is ready to learn and let other errors go.

Ten-Minute Lesson Plan for Individual Lessons— Levels D–I

Student: _____ Date: _____

<table>
<tr><td rowspan="3">Day 1</td><td>

Sight-Word Review (optional)

_____   _____   _____
</td></tr>
<tr><td>

Introduction
This book is about _____

New vocabulary: _____
</td></tr>
<tr><td>

Reading and Teaching
Record observations and teaching points:

Discussion Prompt:

New Sight Word: _____
</td></tr>
</table>

<table>
<tr><td rowspan="3">Day 2</td><td>

Sight-Word Review (optional)

_____   _____   _____
</td></tr>
<tr><td>

Reading and Teaching (continue reading book)

Observations and Teaching Points: _____

_____

_____
</td></tr>
<tr><td>

Reteach same sight word: _____
Word study: Do <u>one</u> activity—picture sorts, making words, sound boxes, or analogy chart.
</td></tr>
</table>

Ten-Minute Lesson Plan for Individual Lessons—
Levels D–I *(continued)*

Student: _____ Date: _____

<table>
<tr>
<td rowspan="4">Day 3</td>
<td>Sight-Word Review: _____ _____ _____</td>
</tr>
<tr>
<td>Student rereads book with a buddy outside the lesson.</td>
</tr>
<tr>
<td>Guided Writing:

_____

_____

_____

_____</td>
</tr>
<tr>
<td>*Levels D and E: Dictated sentences; Levels E and F: B-M-E; Levels G–I: B-M-E or S-W-B-S*
Observations and teaching points:

_____

_____

_____

_____

_____

_____</td>
</tr>
</table>

Prompts and Teaching Points to Use During and After Reading, Early Level (D–1)

Decoding Strategies	Fluency & Phrasing	Comprehension (Oral Responses)
❑ Use M, S, & V. *Reread and get your mouth ready. What would make sense and look right?* **Check the ending.** *(−s, −ed, −ing)* ❑ Use known parts. *Is there a part you know?* **Check the middle of the word.** ❑ Look for contractions. ❑ Use analogies with known words. ❑ Do you know another word that looks like this one? ❑ Chunk big words. *Break the word into parts and think what would make sense.*	❑ Read it without your finger. ❑ How would he (the character) say that? ❑ Read these words together. (Teacher frames 2–3 words.) ❑ Teacher slides finger over text as the student reads. (The teacher's finger covers the word the student is reading so the student is forced to move his/her eyes ahead of what is being read.)	❑ Recall—*What did you read?* ❑ Retell—Beginning, Middle, End ❑ Inference—*Why did the character do (or say) that?* ❑ Predict—*What might happen next?* ❑ Problem-solution—*What problem did the character face, and how was it solved?* ❑ Character analysis—*How is the character feeling now? How would you describe the character? How has the character changed in this story?*

The Next Step in Guided Reading © 2009 by Jan Richardson, Scholastic Professional

Questions Teachers Ask About Early Guided Reading

Should I attend to every error the student makes during the reading of the book?

Do not try to fix every mistake. This will only discourage the student and cause him or her to stop taking risks. Attend to one or two errors that are important for constructing meaning or that offer you the opportunity to prompt for a strategy. If you have selected an appropriate book for guided reading, the students will encounter challenges. As you listen to individual students read the book, you should record their errors and your teaching points on the back of the lesson plan. The teaching point should be a strategy the student can use on another book. In other words, don't focus on getting the words right—instead, focus on teaching a problem-solving action. Your goal in guided reading is not reading the book with 100% accuracy; it is using strategies. Think about the book as the vehicle that takes you to your destination. Your destination is helping the student become a more strategic reader, *not* reading the book with 100% accuracy.

What should I do if the student does not make any errors while I am listening to him?

When the students reread the book on Day 2, there may be few or even no errors. You have several choices. You can ask the student if there was a tricky part on another page, or you can work on fluency. You can also prompt for retell or deeper comprehension when you think this is the most important strategy to teach the student. Use the "Prompts and Teaching Points to Use During and After Reading" (page 140) to help you make decisions during the reading of the book. You should have at least one teaching point for each student.

How do I select my teaching points?

After the students read the book on Day 1 and Day 2, you should do one or two teaching points. Usually, you will work on decoding strategies because decoding is the greatest challenge for early readers, but there are other options including fluency and comprehension. As you record student miscues on the back of your lesson plan, circle the miscues that might be helpful for a teaching point. You have only a few seconds to decide the best teaching point for this group. Ask this question, "What strategy can I show these students today that will help them be better readers tomorrow?" Always begin the teaching point by saying, "Let me show you something . . . ." It will automatically shift you into the demonstration mode.

What if a student is not fluent?

Fluency should be taught once the reading is accurate. The first reading is usually not fluent because the student is figuring out challenges in the text. I often teach for fluency and phrasing on Day 2 while the students are rereading the book. If the student is having trouble decoding words, you may need to drop the text level to teach for fluency. If the student is reading accurately but in a choppy manner, it is appropriate to teach phrasing and fluency. Here is a sequence for prompting for fluency:

* Discourage finger pointing. Children should not be pointing with their finger because it will prevent their eyes from tracking quickly across the print.

* Ask the student to read it like the character (or the teacher) would read it.

* Frame two or three words as the student reads. This will help the student focus on two words at a time rather than a single word. Model if necessary and have the child repeat what you read. The student should not frame the words with his finger. This will slow him down.

* Slide your finger over the text to push the student's eye forward. As the student reads, your finger should completely mask the word the student is reading. This will force the child to look ahead and read more fluently.

* You may need to temporarily read with the student to model expression and intonation.

Should I always select a new sight word that matches the text level?

No. Sometimes students are reading books at Levels E and F, but they do not know how to write the sight words at Levels D and E. Always teach the earlier words first because they are usually easier to learn and occur more frequently.

Is it okay to teach the same sight word for more than two days?

Absolutely! In fact children who are slow to accelerate often have poor visual memory. They may take three or four days to learn one sight word. It is very important that you do not introduce a new sight word until the students firmly know the first one. Introducing too many words at one time will only add to their confusion.

Should I do the word work that matches the text level?

Appendix A (pages 271–282) gives you a logical sequence for word work that matches the text level for average readers. Students reading below grade level may need to learn the target skills at a lower level than they are reading. Teach the skills the students need regardless of their level and follow the sequence in the appendix.

What if students are having trouble hearing short vowels?

Use picture sorts and teach students how to say the word slowly and "punch" the vowel sound in the middle of a word. I developed this strategy while observing advanced writers in kindergarten. I noticed they were very noisy as they wrote, pronouncing the word slowly and specifically saying the vowel sound several times. I realized the students were punching the vowel so they could hear it. Once you teach this strategy with picture sorts, encourage children to continue to do it during other word-study activities and during guided writing. Struggling readers in the intermediate grades may have trouble remembering the short vowel sounds. Link the vowel sound to a word they know how to spell—for example, /a/ for *at*, /e/ for *egg*, /i/ for *it*, /o/ for *on*, /u/ for *up*.

What do you do if the student is not applying the phonics skills he or she knows during guided writing?

This is actually quite common and easy to fix. If the students know the letter sounds but do not use them during writing, insist on "noisy writing." Children should say each word as they write it. Saying a word slowly during writing also helps control serial order confusions.

What should I do if I have to put students who read at different levels in the same group?

This is sometimes necessary in order to limit the number of groups. If you have to put students reading at Level 10 with students reading at Level 14, match the texts to the readers and introduce one book each day. For example, on Monday you would introduce a new book to the Level 10 students, but the Level 14 students would not receive a new book. They would spend 8–10 minutes reading familiar books. You still have the opportunity to listen to each child read and prompt for appropriate strategies. The last 8–10 minutes of the lesson would be word study. All students would do the same activity.

On Tuesday, you would introduce a new book to the Level 14 students while the Level 10 students reread Monday's new book and other familiar books. Again, you would work with individual students on the books they are reading. During the final ten minutes of the lesson, all students would do guided writing. The sentences they write should relate to one of the books they read that day. The Level 10 students might write about the problem and solution for the new book you introduced on Monday, while the Level 14 students would write about the new book you introduced to them on Tuesday.

chapter 5

Transitional

GUIDED READING

Transitional readers are able to read text above Level I. They have a large bank of sight words, but they are still learning to decode big words, increase fluency, expand vocabulary, and improve comprehension. Transitional readers can be found in any grade. Strong readers in kindergarten and first grade would be considered transitional readers even if they read fluently because they rarely have the vocabulary and background experiences to comprehend texts above a third-grade level. Average second graders belong to this stage since they are still learning phonics skills, decoding strategies, and comprehension skills. Intermediate students who lag behind their peers are often transitional readers who need to improve decoding skills, vocabulary strategies, and comprehension. It is difficult to assign a specific level range for transitional readers because this changes by grade level. The lesson plans in this chapter are appropriate for kindergarten and first grade students who read above Level I, second grade students reading between Levels J and M, and intermediate students who read between Levels J and P. Once students are able to read and understand text at Level Q, they rarely have decoding and fluency issues, so it would be appropriate to use the Fluent Guided Reading Lesson Plan described in Chapter 6.

General Guideline for Identifying Transitional Readers		
Grade Level	**Transitional Text Levels**	**Instructional Needs**
Kindergarten & first grade	Above Level I	Vocabulary and comprehension
Second grade	J–M	Decoding, fluency, vocabulary, and retell
Third–fifth grades	J–P	Self-monitoring, decoding, fluency, vocabulary, and retell

The strategy focus for the transitional guided reading lesson can be one of these five areas: self-monitoring, decoding, fluency, vocabulary, or retell. After you assess your students and complete the Assessment Summary Chart, you will be able to identify a focus strategy for your transitional reading groups. If you discover a student is strong in all five areas, you should change your instructional focus to deeper comprehension and use the Fluent Guided Reading Lesson Plan in Chapter 6.

Assessments for Transitional Readers

I have found two types of assessments useful for analyzing the strengths and needs of transitional readers: a running record with comprehension questions, and a word study inventory to assess phonics skills. The running record should be an individual assessment, but you can administer the word-study inventory to the entire class at the same time. The running record assessment identifies a student's instructional reading level, reading strategies, and comprehension abilities and is useful in selecting texts and a focus strategy for the lesson. The word study inventory identifies specific skills you should teach during both the word-study and guided writing components.

Using the Running Record With Transitional Readers
To get maximum benefit from the running record, the student should read the passage out loud as you record each miscue, reread, and self-correction. You especially need to consider whether the student monitors for meaning or continues to read when a

mistake changes the meaning of the passage. I have watched many intermediate students mumble or skip words they do not know. It is little wonder these students have trouble recalling what they read. Skipping a word can be a powerful decoding strategy, as long as the student later rereads the sentence to figure out the tricky word.

It is also helpful to listen to the student's phrasing and intonation to evaluate fluency. You can even time the reading to determine the student's reading rate and compare it to grade-level standards. (See page 149.) Always include an oral retell and a few comprehension questions. Transitional readers may be able to read fluently and accurately but lack comprehension. Your goal for the running record is two-fold: you want to determine the student's instructional level so you can select appropriate texts for guided reading, and you want to identify a focus for instruction.

Using the Word Study Inventory to Identify Phonics Needs

This assessment is provided in Chapter 2. After you administer the test, analyze the student's responses and circle the phonics skills the student misses. You can teach these skills during the word-study component in the guided reading lesson. If the student makes few errors on the inventory, no word study is needed.

Using the Assessment Summary Chart for Transitional Readers

Once you have assessed your students, use this summary chart for those reading between Levels I and P. If students are reading above Level P, use the Assessment Summary Chart for Fluent Readers in Chapter 6.

Name	Inst. Level	Monitors for Meaning + ✔ -	Decodes + ✔ -	Fluency (1–4)	Retell + ✔ -		Needs Word Study Check (✔) areas that need to be taught.			
					F	NF				
							vowels	digraphs	blends	endings

Assessment Summary Chart for Transitional Readers

(Fountas & Pinnell Levels J–P)

Monitors for Meaning: (+) always, (✔) sometimes, (−) rarely

Decodes: (+) Uses beginning, medial, and final letters; attends to parts and endings; (✔) Uses beginning and final letters; ignores medial sounds and some endings; (−) Uses some letter sounds; not consistent in attending to visual cues

Fluency: 4 = phrased & fluent with expression; 3 = phrased but without intonation, ignores some punctuation; 2 = mostly two-word phrases; 1 = word by word

Retell: (+) complete, (✔) partial, (−) very limited/weak

Needs Word Study: Use the Word Study Inventory to determine phonics needs.

Columns 1 & 2: Name and Instructional Level. Write the student's name in the first column and record the instructional text level determined by the running record assessment. If you have used both fiction and nonfiction texts for assessment, record the instructional level for both. It is common for students to have a higher instructional level for fiction than nonfiction. The instructional level is the level at which the student reads with at least 90% accuracy and has some comprehension. If the student accurately reads a text but has no recall, the instructional level will be lower. If a student fluently reads the text with at least 95% accuracy and has a strong understanding of the story, then the text is considered to be at an independent level. You should then give the student a more challenging text to determine the instructional level.

Column 3: Monitors for Meaning (M). Put a plus (+) if the student consistently stops and tries to fix the error when meaning breaks down. Put a check (✓) in this column if the student sometimes monitors for meaning. Put a minus (–) if the student consistently ignores errors that change the meaning of the passage.

Column 4: Decodes. Good decoders break words into parts and attend to all inflectional endings. Put a plus (+) if the student uses word parts (chunks) to solve unfamiliar words. A chunk may be a syllable or a known part in a one-syllable word, such as *all* in *small*. Put a check (✓) if the student attends to some word parts but frequently ignores medial chunks and endings. Put minus (–) if the student uses some beginning parts but does not look through the word. Some transitional readers may have strong retell but struggle with decoding due to visual processing problems.

Column 5: Fluency. Readers at the transitional stage may still require fluency instruction. Use the following rubric to evaluate fluency:

1. Reading is very slow, mostly word by word.

2. Reading is choppy, mostly two-word phrases.

3. Reading is mostly phrased, but lacks some aspects of fluency such as speed, intonation, expression, or attention to punctuation.

4. Reading is fluent and phrased with appropriate expression and intonation.

You can also time the student's reading and compare the reading rate (word count per minute, or WCPM) to grade-level standards. Reading speed is not the goal, but it will tell whether fluency needs to be a focus strategy for your lessons.

Average WCPM by grade level and time of year			
	Fall	Winter	Spring
Grade 2	51	72	89
Grade 3	71	92	107
Grade 4	94	112	123
Grade 5	110	127	139
Grade 6	127	140	150

Source: Hasbrouck & Tindal, 2006

Column 6: Retell. Ask the student to retell what he or she read. You should not prompt for specific details, but you can ask the student if he or she remembers anything else. Record the student's basic understanding of the text by rating the retell at complete (+), partial (✓) or weak (–).

Put a plus (+) if the child gives a complete and detailed retelling.

❋ **Fiction (F):** The retelling includes the characters, problem, solution, and important details. The major plot elements are retold completely, accurately and in order. Student shows evidence of inference skills.

❋ **Nonfiction (NF):** Includes every main idea, each supported by at least one or two details. Organization follows the scheme of the book (e.g., chronological, explanatory). The student uses vocabulary in context.

Put a check (✓) if the child gives a partial retelling.

❋ **Fiction (F):** The retelling includes the plot and most major characters. Minor characters and setting may be absent. Student may not show evidence of inference skills.

❋ **Nonfiction (NF):** The retelling includes most of the main ideas. Details may be fragmentary or missing. Vocabulary is included but may not be used correctly. Organization is not as tight, but essential sequences remain in order.

Put a minus (–) if the child gives a limited retelling.

* **Fiction (F)**: The retelling has major holes: central characters left out, incorrect identification of the problem, inability to relate sequence, and/or essential plot points missing.

* **Nonfiction (NF)**: Retelling may include the subject but misses the main ideas. Details are sketchy or not linked with the idea they support. Organization is loose and random, and mistakes occur in essential sequences. Student tells facts incorrectly.

Column 7: Needs Word Study. Use anecdotal notes, running records, writing samples, and the Word Study Inventory to identify phonics skills that need attention. The skills commonly taught at the transitional level include short vowels, digraphs, blends, vowel combinations, silent *e* feature, and endings. Not all transitional readers will require word study, especially if they are fluent decoders and only need to improve in the area of retell. Transitional readers in grades three and above who are weak decoders need word study.

Grouping Students for Guided Reading

Use the columns in this assessment summary chart to group students for guided reading instruction and to select a focus strategy. Students one or two alphabetic levels apart can be included in the same group, but it is very difficult to meet each student's needs if you have a wide spread of reading levels in one guided reading group. Transitional readers can be very diverse. There may be some who have difficulty decoding but are able to recall what they have read. Others may be fluent decoders but need to improve literal recall and retelling. You will likely have students who have different strengths and needs in the same group. Don't worry about this. The transitional lesson format provides for differentiated instruction by offering options for prompting and teaching points. You can use this assessment summary chart to determine which prompts to use with individual students.

At least once a month, reevaluate your guided reading groups by using anecdotal notes taken during the guided reading lessons. Move students into higher text levels when you see them repeatedly experience success in decoding, fluency, and retell. If you find that you did not have anything to teach a group, then the text was probably too easy. You do not need to take a formal running record when you change text levels, but you certainly can if you want to document your decision. The average rate of progress for transitional readers is one alphabetic level every 8–9 weeks. Of course, you want your struggling readers to make more accelerated progress so they can reach grade level standards. Since student learning rates vary, expect your reading groups to change throughout the year.

Materials for Transitional Guided Reading

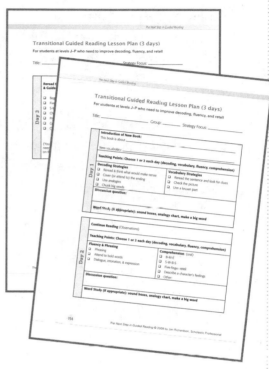

✳ Leveled books, especially short fiction texts written specifically for guided reading. Avoid using novels, as these books take too long to read, and students will lose interest. Encourage students to read novels during self-selected reading. However, you need to monitor their book choices to make sure the texts they choose are at an independent level.

✳ Assessment kit or short, leveled texts that have comprehension questions

✳ Copies of lesson plans

✳ Dry-erase board and marker (for teacher)

✳ 6 sound templates in sheet protectors for word study (see Chapter 3 for the template)

✳ 6 sets of lowercase magnetic letters or letter cards for word study

✳ Guided reading response journals or reading notebooks (see Chapter 1 for description)

✳ Timer (a must!)

✳ 6 copies of the personal word wall (for guided writing) on page 153. The personal word wall has the most frequently misspelled words on one sheet so students can find words quickly. You can personalize the word wall even more by designing it for a specific student. Delete words the student knows how to spell and add others that are not on the list but are challenging for the student.

Using the Personal Word Wall

The goal is for students to locate a word on the list quickly and copy it correctly on their paper. Don't assume the students know how to use a word wall. I have had to teach third- and fourth-grade students how to use the alphabetical framework to locate a word quickly. I have even taught students how to copy a word efficiently from the chart to their paper. This probably sounds elemental, but these are real-life examples from experiences I have had with transitional readers. I observed one student who was copying words one letter at a time. I taught her how to look at the word, say the first three letters aloud, repeat them as she wrote them on her paper, then return to the list and repeat the process with the next three letters.

Emphasize that the words on the list must be spelled correctly every time. No excuses. If you notice that a student misspells a word on the personal word wall, don't circle the misspelled word or point it out. If you do this, you are monitoring for the student. Your goal is for the student to realize when he needs to use the chart. Instead say, "There is a word in this line you need to check because it is on the list. See if you can find it." When I see a student using the word wall, I draw a star on top of the paper and offer a quick praise such as "I am so glad you used the word wall." You will be surprised how other students listen to these "private" conversations and repeat the behavior you just praised. If students need help spelling a word that is not on the list, encourage them to use other spelling strategies such as sounding out or clapping each syllable. If the unknown word is one the student uses frequently, write it on the child's personal word wall and tell him or her you expect them to spell it correctly from now on. If students consistently use this chart, at least 80% of the words they write will be spelled correctly.

You can make additional copies of the personal word wall for students to use during writing workshop. It is much better for students to spell these words correctly the first time than to have fix the spelling during revision.

Personal Word Wall

Includes 100 most frequently misspelled words

A	B	C	D	E	G	H	I	J	L
about	babies	called	decided	ever	get	happy	if	jumped	laugh
after	beautiful	care	didn't	every	getting	happening	I'll		laughed
again	because	carry	different	exciting	girl	have	it's		learn
although	been	caught	does		give	hear			left
always	before	children	doesn't		gone	heard		**K**	let's
animals	beginning	clothes	don't		good	her		kept	little
another	believe	come	dropped	**F**		here		kind	live
any	bought	coming		family		him		knew	long
are	brother	could		father		his		know	
around	brought	course		favorite		home		known	
asked	buy	cousin		felt		house			
		cried		find		how			
				first					
				found					
				four					
				friend					
				frightened					
				from					

M	N	O	P	R	S	T	U	W	Y
made	name	of	people	received	said	than	until	walk	year
many	named	off	perfect	ready	saw	that's	upon	want	young
middle	need	oh	place	really	scared	their	use	wanted	your
money	never	once	put	ride	school	then		was	you're
more	new	one		right	should	there		water	
morning	next	only		room	something	these	**V**	went	
most	nice	other		running	sometimes	they	very	were	
mother	night	ouch			soon	they're		what	
much		our			special	things		when	
			Q		spring	though		where	
			quiet		started	thought		which	
			quick		stared	threw		while	
			quite		still	through		white	
					stopped	together		who	
					summer	too		why	
					suddenly	tried		with	
					surprise	touch		work	
					swimming	two		would	

Transitional Guided Reading Lesson Plan (3 days)

For students at levels J–P who need to improve decoding, fluency, and retell

Title: _____ Group: _____ Strategy Focus: _____

Day 1

Introduction of New Book:

This book is about _____

New vocabulary: _____

Prompts and Teaching Points to Use During Reading: Choose 1 or 2 each day (decoding, vocabulary, fluency, comprehension)

Decoding Strategies	Vocabulary Strategies
❏ Reread & think what would make sense	❏ Reread the sentence and look for clues
❏ Cover (or attend to) the ending	❏ Check the picture
❏ Use analogies	❏ Use a known part
❏ Chunk big words	

Discussion question:

Word Study (if appropriate): sound boxes, analogy chart, make a big word

Day 2

Continue Reading (Observations)

Prompts and Teaching Points to Use During Reading: Choose 1 or 2 each day (decoding, vocabulary, fluency, comprehension)

Fluency & Phrasing	Comprehension: (oral)
❏ Phrasing	❏ B-M-E
❏ Attend to bold words	❏ S-W-B-S
❏ Dialogue, intonation, & expression	❏ Five-finger retell
	❏ Describe a character's feelings
	❏ Other:

Discussion question:

Word Study (if appropriate): sound boxes, analogy chart, make a big word

Transitional Guided Reading Lesson Plan (3 days)

For students at levels J–P who need to improve decoding, fluency, and retell

Title: _____ Group: _____ Strategy Focus: _____.

<table>
<tr>
<td rowspan="2">Day 3</td>
<td>Reread the book for fluency (if necessary)
& Guided Writing

❏ Beginning-Middle-End (3–5 sentences)
❏ Five-finger retell
❏ S-W-B-S
❏ Character analysis (B-M-E)
❏ Problem/solution
❏ Compare/contrast
❏ Other

(You may decide to spend the entire 20 minutes of Day 3 on guided writing. If the students need an extra day to finish reading the book, make this a four-day plan and do guided writing on the fourth day.)</td>
</tr>
</table>

Select a Text

Your primary goal in choosing a text is finding one that supports your focus strategy. If your focus is decoding strategies, select a fiction or informational text with few unknown vocabulary words but with many multisyllabic words that students can problem solve. Usually you will be looking for words with prefixes and endings, since these kinds of words are challenging for transitional readers. It is not helpful to use a book with unfamiliar concepts because students will not be able to check their decoding attempts with meaning. The big words they need to decode should be in their listening vocabulary.

To teach fluency you will probably want to use a fiction text that contains few decoding challenges but interesting dialogue. This affords an opportunity for children to practice reading with appropriate phrasing, expression, and intonation. I don't recommend nonfiction texts for teaching fluency since they are not written to be read with fluency or expression. In fact, most people slow down when they read nonfiction so they can absorb the information and search the illustrations for support.

If students need to practice vocabulary strategies, select a text with some unfamiliar concepts, but one that supports the meaning of those concepts with context clues, illustrations, and a glossary. If you select a nonfiction text, it is best if the students have some experience with the subject matter. For example, if you are just beginning a unit on the rain forest, wait a few days before using a rain forest text in guided reading. If there are too many unfamiliar concepts and words in the book, the children will struggle with comprehension.

Some transitional readers will be fluent decoders who only need to work on retelling. When this is your strategy focus, teach the process with fiction before you expect children to retell nonfiction. Fiction is easier to retell because it has a natural beginning, middle, and end with a problem and solution. Nonfiction texts are more difficult to retell because the information may not follow a specific sequence or organizational pattern. Once students are able to retell fiction, you can begin to use informational text.

Now that you have assessed your students to form needs-based groups and selected your text to match your focus strategy, you are ready to teach with power and purpose. Remember, the transitional lesson plan is designed for three days, but that could vary, depending on the length of the book.

Procedures for Day 1—Guided Reading

Component	Explanations of Procedures
Before Reading Introduce the story. (Day 1 only) Time: 3–4 minutes	Spend the first three or four minutes of the lesson preparing students to read. Tell them a little about the book and invite students to **preview** the text by looking at the illustrations. You do not need to discuss every page, but you should draw the students' attention to important information and unfamiliar concepts in the pictures.
Introduce words students cannot decode. *ancient, although* **Introduce new vocabulary not defined in the text.** Four steps for introducing vocabulary: • Define it. • Connect it to students' experience. • Relate it to the book. • Turn and talk.	Next, introduce the **new words** students are not able to decode or do not know what they mean. If the word is difficult for the group to **decode**, write the word on a whiteboard and pronounce it for the students. Words such as *through, though, enough,* and *precious* can be challenging for transitional readers. When you need to introduce a new word because the students do not know what it **means** and the word is not defined in the text, follow these four steps: 1. Say the new word and a simple definition. Do not ask students if they know the word. Often one student may offer a confusing or erroneous definition that will mislead other students and waste time. I once observed a teacher introduce the word *bandit* by asking if anyone knew what a bandit was. One boy confidently shared that was *when you left your bookbag by the side of the road*. He was confusing "a bandit" with "abandoned." If the new word is *bandit*, say, "A bandit is a thief." 2. Connect the new word to the students' background knowledge and experiences. "For example, if someone steals your bookbag, that person is a bandit, or a thief." Use the new word and the synonym at each step. 3. Relate the new word to the text. Tell the students how the word is used and direct them to an illustration if one is provided. "In this book, you are going to learn about a raccoon that is called a bandit because he is a thief. He likes to steal food from the trash can." 4. Turn and talk. Ask the students to explain the meaning of the word to the person sitting next to them. If an unfamiliar word is defined in the text, the illustration or in the glossary, **do not** introduce the word. Prompt students to use the text clues to help them figure out the meaning of new words. If you introduce words that are defined in the text, you are not teaching students to be independent problem-solvers.

Component	Explanations of Procedures
During Reading **Students read while you conference with other students.** (Days 1 & 2) Time: 10–15 min. Students read softly or silently, depending on your strategy focus. Keep a record of individual teaching points on the back of your lesson plan.	Students will usually need two days to read a book at this level. Once you introduce the book on Day 1, they have about ten minutes to read. Then they mark their place and will continue reading on Day 2. On this day they will have at least fifteen minutes to read, which is long enough to finish most guided reading texts. If students do not finish the book on Day 2, they will continue to read the book on Day 3, and you will extend the lesson to four days. On the back of the lesson plan, take notes on students' reading and record the individual teaching points you make. You will use this information to select your teaching points for the entire group later in the lesson. **Prompt for Strategies** Students should read independently (softly or silently) while you listen, observe, prompt, coach, and teach individual students. Think of these interactions as mini reading conferences. Differentiate your prompting to meet the individual needs of the students. I have identified four focus areas for prompting transitional readers: monitoring, decoding, fluency, and retell.
Prompt students to monitor for meaning. *Are you right?* *Does that make sense?* *Reread that sentence and try to fix it.*	Some transitional readers do not **monitor for meaning**. They make a mistake yet continue to read even though what they are reading does not make sense. Often, the errors are made on **known** words. When this happens, the student is probably not attending to the details of print and not listening to what he or she is reading. To fix this problem, wait until the student finishes the sentence and ask, "Did that make sense?" Then have the student reread and fix the error. When you are prompting students to monitor, ignore errors that make sense. If you attend to every mistake, the student will slow down (to be more accurate) and lose the meaning of the text. **Comprehension**, not total accuracy, is the goal of reading. If the student monitors (stops) but does not correct the error, praise the student for monitoring ("I like the way you noticed it didn't make sense.") and prompt for an appropriate decoding strategy.
Prompt students to use a variety of strategies to decode unknown words. *Can you cover the ending and find a part you know?*	Transitional readers often need strategies for **decoding** long words with multiple syllables and endings. As you prompt students to decode words, remind them to also think about the story. Good readers use phonics to get an approximate pronunciation that is confirmed with meaning. Use one of the following prompts when appropriate for decoding new words:

Component	Explanations of Procedures
	• *What can you try to help yourself figure out that word?* • *Reread that sentence and think about what would make sense and look right. Check all the way to the end of the word.* • *Sound the first part (usually a syllable) and think about what would make sense.* • *Can you cover the ending? Is there a part you know?* DO NOT cover the ending with your own hand. It is important that the student covers the ending. • *Check the middle (or end) of that word.* • *Do you know another word that looks like that?* Help the student use a known word that has a similar part. For example, if the student is stuck on *quite*, show him or her how to use *white* to read *quite*. If the student does not make an error while you are listening, ask if there was a tricky part on another page and work on strategies there. If the student had no difficulty reading the text, you should work on fluency or retell.
Prompt for fluency **First, check the text level.** You should prompt for fluency when the reading is accurate.	Several factors promote **fluency**: (1) text difficulty, (2) automaticity with high-frequency words, (3) efficient decoding strategies, and (4) reading for meaning. If you notice a child is not fluent, first check the text level. If the student is struggling with decoding, it isn't appropriate to work on fluency. Instead, you need to prompt for decoding strategies or switch to an easier text to work on fluency.
Can you pretend you are the character and read it like he would say it? *Read a few words together so it sounds smooth.* Mask the text for the child to push the eye forward.	If the student is not fluent because he or she does not read for meaning, use the prompts for monitoring described in this section. If the student is reading accurately but slowly, it is appropriate (and necessary) to prompt for fluency. Consider using one of the following prompts or techniques: • *How would the character say that? Can you read it like the character?* • *Put the words together so it sounds smooth.* • You (the teacher) can use your fingers to frame two to three words at a time as the student reads. This encourages the student to read in short phrases rather than word by word. • You can also slide your finger over the words to push the student's eye forward. This is a Reading Recovery procedure developed by Marie Clay (1993). It works extremely well with children at the transitional level. By covering the word the student is saying (and possibly even the next word), you are teaching the student to allow her eyes to move

Component	Explanations of Procedures
Read this part with me.	ahead of her mouth. Your goal is to get the student to look at a word one or two words ahead of the ones he is saying. You will need to listen carefully to the student so you do not push your finger too quickly. If the student stops reading, back up and try the procedure again, a little slower. • The teacher reads with the student and models intonation and expression. Some students, especially those learning English as a second language, will need to hear how dialogue should be read. Model and then allow the student to practice reading other conversations.

Prompt for retell.
What did you just read? What happened at the beginning?
 	
Teach STP.
• **Stop**
• **Think**
• **Paraphrase**
	Retell. If students read with accuracy and fluency, check their retell by asking, "What did you read?" If children have difficulty remembering what they have just read, teach them the STP strategy.
	    After students read each page, they **stop**, cover the text with their hand, **think** about what they just read, and **paraphrase** (softly tell what was read as they look at the picture). Using the picture as they retell helps them visualize what they read—a critical process for remembering. If students have trouble retelling at the end of a page, have them stop at the end of each paragraph. If this does not work, select an easier text.
	    As students read independently and softly use STP, you can circulate among them to listen and prompt for important details they may omit. Once students can retell with picture support, ask them to use STP without looking at the picture. Your goal is for them to create their own pictures in their heads to help them recall what they read.

Who was on this page, and **what** did s/he do? **Beginning-Middle-End** (B-M-E) Students stop three times to summarize what they have read.	**Who and What**: Another strategy for improving retell is to have the student summarize each page by saying **who** this page was about and **what** the character did. You can insert a few sticky notes in the book and have students write the Who and What for those pages. Once students are able to tell you what they have read on a page, you can use the **Beginning-Middle-End (B-M-E)** strategy. Now insert a 3″ sticky note at three places in the text. Children read up to each sticky note and write what happened in that section. They are required to summarize several pages. After students complete the story, they take the sticky notes out of the book, mix them up, and reorder them in sequence.

Component	Explanations of Procedures
As you conference with students, use the following prompts: *What did you read on this page?* *What's the problem?* *How does the character feel now?*	**Sticky note #1** Claire and Abby went to ride horses.　　**Sticky note #2** Claire's pony would jump, but Abby's pony was stubborn.　　**Sticky note #3** Abby taught her pony how to do what she asked. **Track the character's feelings:** This technique is appropriate to use once children can remember what they have read. Now you will ask them to think about the character and write a word that describes the character's feelings. Before students read, insert 1" sticky notes on pages where the character's feelings change. On a whiteboard, list a few words students should use to describe the character in the book. Use words like *excited*, *depressed*, and *upset*. If you don't do this, students will only be able to think of *happy, sad,* and *mad*. Be sure to discuss the meaning of these words prior to reading. As students come to a sticky note, they write a word from the list that describes how the character is feeling on that page. 　　During the discussion portion of the lesson, have students take out their sticky notes, scramble them, and sequence them. Students take turns sharing how the character felt at the beginning, middle, and end of the story. Be sure you tell students they must explain why the character felt that way. An easy scaffold to use is, "At the beginning of the story, Jack felt _____ because . . . ." Encourage students to use complete sentences as they retell the story by tracking the changes in the character's feelings. The following example shows the feeling words students wrote on sticky notes, and how they retold the story during the discussion. Sticky notes: 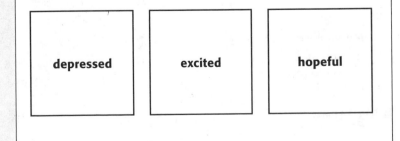

Component	Explanations of Procedures
	Discussion: *In the beginning, Luis feels depressed because he can't play basketball in his wheelchair. In the middle he is excited because he got a ticket to see a basketball game. At the end he feels hopeful because he believes he may be able to play basketball in a wheelchair some day.* Do not require students to do a lot of writing as they read; this will take time away from reading. They will do more writing on Day 3 after they finish the story. As you work with individual students, use the following prompts to support retelling: • *Look at the picture and tell me what you read.* (retell with picture support) • *What did you read on this page?* (cover picture & retell without support) • *Who was on this page, and what did he or she do?* • *How is the character feeling now? Why?* • *What happened at the beginning of the story? Then what happened?* When five minutes are left in the lesson, tell students to stop reading and mark their place. They will begin reading where they stopped when you meet with them again on Day 2.
Teaching Points (Days 1 & 2) Time: 1–2 minutes **Demonstrate a decoding strategy.**	Each day, after students read the text, use your anecdotal notes to select one or two teaching points that match the needs of the students. • To teach **monitoring for meaning**, ask the students to follow along in their books as you read a sentence out loud. Deliberately make an error that does not make sense. Say, "Did you notice my mistake? Did it make sense? What should I do?" • To teach **decoding**, write a tricky word from the story that gives you the opportunity to demonstrate one of the following strategies:
Reread and think.	**Reread and think: What makes sense?** This is, by far, the most important (and effective) decoding strategy. If children encounter a difficult word (but one they have heard before), and they reread the sentence up to the first few letters of the difficult word, the correct word will often pop out of their mouths. If there is a picture on the page, be sure to direct the child's attention to use that clue, too. Rereading and sounding the first part will work if the unknown word is in the child's listening vocabulary AND the student is thinking about what would make sense.

Component	Explanations of Procedures
Cover the ending. e.g., *carefully*	**Cover the ending** and look for a part you know in that word. Sometimes just sounding the first part is not enough to figure out the word. Transitional readers at Levels J, K, and L often struggle on long words with inflectional endings. Teach the students to put their hand over the ending and see if there is a known part. Covering the ending has an additional benefit—it directs the student's attention to the middle of the word. Many transitional readers who have decoding problems say miscues that match the beginning and ending letters, but do not match the middle letters in the word.
Chunk the word. e.g., *comfortable* *conversation*	**Chunk** (or break) the word into parts. Write a long word on a whiteboard and ask students to help you break it into parts (e.g., *disappointed, unusually, uncomfortable*). Remind students to always think about the meaning of the sentence when they chunk words.
Use an analogy. The *eigh* in *neighbor* is like *eight*.	**Use an analogy.** Poor decoders commonly have trouble remembering the rules of phonics. Instead of asking students to recite a phonics rule, prompt them to think of a known word that looks similar. For example, the students may have stopped at the word *shawl*. It probably won't help if you ask for the *aw* sound. If the students knew the *aw* sound, they probably would have decoded the word. Instead ask, "Do you know a word that has this part in it?" as you write __*aw* on a whiteboard. Usually the students will respond with "saw." Then you say, "Good. Now use *saw* to help you figure out the new word." The analogy strategy is powerful because the students can apply it to other difficult words they encounter. Whichever decoding strategy you teach, always emphasize rereading the text to be sure it makes sense. Decoding often gives an approximate pronunciation that must be checked against the meaning.
Demonstrate a vocabulary strategy. Reread for clues. Check the picture.	Most transitional readers have trouble decoding words that are in their listening vocabulary. They know what the word means, but they just don't know how to read it. Second language learners, however, may encounter words they can decode, but the words are not in their listening vocabulary—they don't know what they mean. To teach **vocabulary** strategies, select one or two unfamiliar words that were defined in the text. Direct students to read for context clues or use illustrations to determine the meaning of these words. Additional vocabulary strategies for fluent guided reading are described in Chapter 6 on page 200–203.

Component	Explanations of Procedures
Demonstrate appropriate intonation. **Use the five-finger retell strategy.**	• To teach **phrasing and expression**, select one page from the story that contains interesting dialogue. Have the students chorally read the text with you, using appropriate phrasing, intonation, and expression. • Have students **orally** retell the story. If necessary, encourage them to use the pictures in the book. **B-M-E**—*What happened at the beginning, the middle, and the end?* **Track the character's feelings**—*How did the character feel at the beginning, middle, and end? Why did the character feel that way?* **Five-finger retell**—Students take turns describing one of the following story elements: Thumb: The characters are . . . Pointer: The setting is . . . Tall finger: The problem is . . . Ring finger: The events are (beginning, middle, end) . . . Little finger: At the end . . . (See page 172.)
Discussion Prompt (Day 1 or 2) Time: 1–2 minutes	Prepare a question that requires students to make inferences or draw conclusions. Even though your primary focus for transitional guided reading is literal retell, you should take this opportunity to prompt for deeper comprehension.
Word Study (Days 1 & 2) Time: 3–5 minutes	**Word Study Activities for Teaching Phonemic Awareness and Phonics** If your transitional readers are fluent decoders with excellent phonics skills, you do not need to do this component. If the students have difficulty reading or writing words with blends, vowel patterns, and multiple syllables, do an appropriate word study activity for three to five minutes on Day 1 and Day 2. The Word Study Inventory on page 48 of Chapter 2 can help you identify specific skills you need to teach.

Component	Explanations of Procedures
Not all transitional readers will need word study. Use the Word Study Inventory and observations to determine your focus. Use your skill focus to plan the word study activity.	Use Appendix A to find specific word study activities that match each skill focus. Even though these students are reading above Level I, they may need the word study activities listed for levels C–G. It is not unusual to find intermediate students who still do not apply the silent *e* rule or who struggle with words that end in a blend. Three word study activities are efficient and effective for teaching skills to transitional readers. They are engaging and purposeful and can be completed in less than five minutes. The activities are **Sound Boxes, Analogy Charts,** and **Making a Big Word**. Each activity is appropriate for teaching a specific phonic focus. For example, if the students need help hearing blends, short vowels, and digraphs, students should use sound boxes. If they have difficulty with endings, applying the silent *e* rule, or understanding vowel combinations, use analogy charts. Students who struggle with decoding multisyllabic words can use magnetic letters or letter cards to make and break a big word. Appendix A has specific words to use for each focus skill.

Phonics Focus	Activity	Appendix A Resource
Short vowels	Sound boxes	Level C
Digraphs	Sound boxes	Level D
Blends	Sound boxes	Levels E–G
Silent *e* rule	Analogy charts	Level G
Vowel patterns	Analogy charts	Levels G–I
Endings	Analogy charts Making a big word	Levels G–I

Component	Explanations of Procedures

Sound boxes

w	e	p	t

s	p	l	i	t

Silent e

easy

c**ap**	n**ame**
cl**ap**	s**ame**
ch**ap**	sh**ame**
sl**ap**	bl**ame**
sn**ap**	fl**ame**

harder

c**ap**	n**ame**
chat	snake
mash	grape
brag	spade
snap	scrape

hardest

c**ap**	n**ame**
slip	stoke
stub	spine
twin	huge
plop	flame

Sound boxes (4 or 5 boxes to teach short vowels, digraphs, and blends)

Distribute dry-erase markers and the Sound Box Template (see page 83) that has been placed inside a sheet protector. Dictate a phonetic word with a blend and a short vowel. Students repeat the word slowly, segmenting the sounds on their fingers. (Do not segment the sounds for the students.) Then students say the word slowly again and write one letter in each box. Blends should have separate boxes for each letter, but digraphs (*ch, th, sh*) go in one box because they are one sound. Examples of words with blends include *plant, stump, clasp, strap, shrink, twist, chest, slump,* and *chomp.* Note that *shrink, chest,* and *champ* also contain digraphs. Encourage "noisy" writing. Students must say the word slowly **as** they write the letters in the boxes. This helps them write phonetically.

Analogy charts (to teach silent *e* rule, vowel patterns, & endings)

Students have their own T-chart and write the words as you dictate them. I like to place a T-chart inside a plastic sheet protector and give students a dry-erase marker to write the words. It saves a few seconds since students do not have to draw the T-chart.

Procedures for teaching the silent e rule

The key words students write at the top of their T-chart should always be known words. The other words you will dictate should be words students do not automatically know how to write. This forces them to use the analogy strategy.

There are three levels of difficulty for the silent *e* analogy charts. The first uses words that have the same rime as the key words. The next uses words that have the same vowel sounds as the key words (long and short *a*, for example), but do not have the same rime. The hardest level uses words that have a short or long vowel sound, but the vowel sound will vary with each word.

For extra power dictate words that have an initial blend. This helps students review the phonic skills that have been taught in previous lessons.

Component	Explanations of Procedures

Here are some examples of analogy charts for teaching the silent e rule. Notice how the pattern changes with the activities at the harder levels. Always begin with the easy examples, but you need to take students to the harder levels to make sure they have internalized the silent e feature.

EASY		HARDER		HARDEST	
sick	line	hot	note	cat	came
slick	swine	spot	strode	slip	slide
prick	twine	drop	slope	chap	choke
stick	shrine	plop	spoke	stub	prune

Vowel patterns

car	ball
star	small
charm	calling
march	stalled
darker	taller

day	cow
stay	plow
spray	crowd
player	howling
away	drowned

Procedures for teaching vowel patterns using an analogy chart

Choose two vowel patterns. Dictate two **known** words that have those vowel patterns and ask students to write the two words on the top of the T-chart, underlining the vowel patterns in each word.

Now dictate other words (preferably ones the students **do not know** how to spell) that contain the same vowel pattern. Appendix B has examples of words to use for each vowel pattern. After you say the word, students should repeat the word and listen for the vowel pattern. Then they decide which key word has the same vowel sound as the word they need to write. Students write the new word under the key word with the same vowel pattern and underline the pattern in the new word. Use words with digraphs, blends, and endings to increase the difficulty of the task and to review skills that have been taught in previous lessons.

Three levels of challenge

Easy: Change the onset by using different blends.
Harder: Use words with endings.
Hardest: Use words with multiple syllables.

Component	Explanations of Procedures
More examples of analogy charts	**Examples of Analogy Charts to Teach Vowel Patterns** **z<u>oo</u>** **r<u>ai</u>n** **f<u>or</u>** **l<u>oo</u>k** **s<u>aw</u>** **b<u>oy</u>** sh<u>oo</u>t st<u>ai</u>n c<u>or</u>d br<u>oo</u>k j<u>aw</u> j<u>oy</u> sm<u>oo</u>th cl<u>ai</u>m n<u>or</u>th st<u>oo</u>d l<u>aw</u>n enj<u>oy</u> w<u>oo</u>lly p<u>ai</u>nful sc<u>or</u>ched cr<u>oo</u>ked dr<u>aw</u>n r<u>oy</u>al **n<u>ee</u>d** **n<u>igh</u>t** **<u>ou</u>t** **n<u>ew</u>** **<u>ea</u>t** **b<u>oa</u>t** sp<u>ee</u>d fl<u>igh</u>t sp<u>ou</u>t gr<u>ew</u> tr<u>ea</u>t fl<u>oa</u>t sw<u>ee</u>p f<u>igh</u>ter gr<u>ou</u>nd st<u>ew</u> dr<u>ea</u>m c<u>oa</u>ch w<u>ee</u>kend fr<u>igh</u>ten surr<u>ou</u>nd n<u>ew</u>lywed ch<u>ew</u>ing f<u>oa</u>my **n<u>igh</u>t** **<u>oi</u>l** **c<u>are</u>** **<u>eigh</u>t** **c<u>au</u>se** **h<u>ow</u>** f<u>igh</u>t t<u>oi</u>l sh<u>are</u> w<u>eigh</u> cl<u>au</u>se pl<u>ow</u> fl<u>igh</u>t sp<u>oi</u>l b<u>are</u>ly w<u>eigh</u>t bec<u>au</u>se cr<u>ow</u>d l<u>igh</u>tly b<u>oi</u>ling c<u>are</u>ful n<u>eigh</u>bor h<u>au</u>nted dr<u>ow</u>ning t<u>igh</u>ter av<u>oi</u>ded
Making a big word out of magnetic letters helps students decode multisyllabic words.	**Making a big word**. Use this activity if students are having difficulty breaking multisyllabic words into parts. Give each student the magnetic letters or letter cards to make a multisyllabic word that was in the book. Say the word and have the students clap the syllables. The students use the letters to make the word. Then they break it into parts and remake it.

Procedures for Day 2—Guided Reading

Component	Explanations of Procedures
Reading and teaching Time: 15 minutes	Students **continue reading** from where they left off on Day 1. If students finish the book before time is called, they should reread the story. You should prompt individual students based upon need, following the same procedures as described in Day 1. After about 15 minutes, stop the reading and teach one or two strategies. Don't forget to ask a discussion question that focuses on deeper comprehension.
Word study Time: 3–5 minutes	Select an activity that meets the needs of the students, following the same procedures as listed in Day 1.

Procedures for Day 3—Guided Writing

Component	Explanations of Procedures
Rereading text for fluency (Optional) Time: 5 minutes	If students need to improve **fluency**, allocate five minutes of Day 3 for rereading the book as you prompt individual students for fluency. When teaching for fluency, ignore errors that make sense. Focusing on accuracy will cause the student to read slower. Students should also read familiar and easy books outside of guided reading to improve fluency. If some students have difficulty staying focused, they can reread the book with a buddy from their guided reading group.
Guided writing Time: 15–20 minutes Guided writing is assisted writing, not assigned writing.	**Guided writing** occurs the day after students finish reading the book. Usually this occurs on Day 3, but sometimes it may take three days to read a book, and Day 4 would be for guided writing. The purpose of using this activity during the transitional guided reading lesson is twofold: it helps students retell what they read, and it improves writing skills. The writing is completed during the guided reading lesson with your support. It is assisted writing, not assigned writing.

Component	Explanations of Procedures
	During guided writing, support students as they write a one- or two-paragraph response to the text. The task should be short enough to be completed during one guided reading lesson. The guided writing response will vary according to the text structure of the guided reading book and the comprehension strategy they used during reading. Although the students are not expected to revise or edit these pieces, you should expect a readable, organized response. A perfect, error-free piece is not the goal.
Help students plan by writing key words from the story.	**Planning:** Spend about two to three minutes helping students plan their response by briefly discussing the story and listing key words on sticky notes or a whiteboard. Listing the key words is essential for these students because it helps them stay focused and jogs their memory for the text.
As students write at the table, have mini-conferences with individual students. Ask yourself, "What can I teach today that will help this child be a better writer?" **Individual teaching points for guided writing:** *Spelling:* Use the personal word wall or teach other spelling strategies. *Organization:* Use the key words on the plan.	**Writing (with your support):** As the students write their ideas (not dictated sentences), you circulate among the group and assist individual students as appropriate. As you read what students have written, you will make on-the-spot decisions based upon the strengths and needs of individual students. Think of these interactions as mini writing conferences. The goal of each interaction is not to fix the writing but to teach something that will make the student a better writer. You will attend to some errors and issues and let others go, depending on the individual needs of the students. Here are some possible teaching points for guided writing: • **Spelling:** Students learn to use a variety of strategies to spell unknown words. These strategies include using the Personal Word Wall, clapping a big word and sounding out each syllable, using the book as a resource, and using spelling patterns from known words to write a new word. • **Organization:** Students learn to use a simple plan with key words listed under the part of the story in which they occurred: Beginning-Middle-End. Prompt students to use transition phrases such as "At the beginning of the story . . . ," "In the middle . . . ," and "Later on . . ." • **Complete Sentences:** Prompt students to orally rehearse each sentence before they write it. This also reminds them to put a period at the end of each sentence.

Component	Explanations of Procedures
Mechanics: Prompt for capital letters and periods. *Sentence variety:* Combine two sentences or use a transition word.	• **Mechanics**: Although perfect grammar, punctuation, and capitalization are not the focus of guided writing, you should expect students to capitalize the first word in a sentence and put a period or another punctuation mark at the end of each sentence. • **Sentence variety**: If you notice some students always begin a sentence with *I* or *the*, teach them to vary sentence structure by combining two sentences or adding a transition such as *then*, *next*, *after a while*, etc.
Possible Guided Writing Responses **Retelling using B-M-E**	**Beginning-Middle-End (B-M-E):** Students write three paragraphs summarizing important events that occurred at the beginning (paragraph 1), middle (paragraph 2), and end (paragraph 3) of the story. If students have trouble recalling events from the story, prompt them to use their sticky notes or an illustration from the book.
Summarizing with a Five-Finger Retell	**Five-Finger Retell**: Students use the five-finger-retell to write three paragraphs about the story. Paragraph one includes the characters (thumb), setting (index finger), and problem (tall finger). Paragraph two describes the two major events (ring finger) that led to solving the problem. Paragraph three includes the solution to the problem and other events that happened at the end (little finger) of the story. (See Five-Finger Retell, page 172.)
Summarizing using S-W-B-S	**Somebody-Wanted-But-So** (Macon, Bewell, & Vogt, 1991): Students can use the S-W-B-S framework to write their own summary of the story. This should be written in sentence form. Somebody: Who is the story about? Wanted: What did this character want? But: But what happened? So: So how did it end? What happened next? Example of a S-W-B-S: *Jack and Emilio wanted to go surfing, but a shark attacked Jack, so Emilio saved his life.*

Component	Explanations of Procedures
Retelling using events and details	**Events and Details** Students identify an event in the story and write a paragraph that includes several details related to that event. You could have one student write an event-detail paragraph for the beginning of the story, another write about the end, and the others could write about the middle. The students sequence their paragraphs to create a retelling of the story.
Describing a character's feelings	**Problem/Feelings and Solution/Feelings** Students write a short paragraph describing the problem, the character's feelings at that point in the story, the solution to the problem, and the character's feelings at the end of the story.

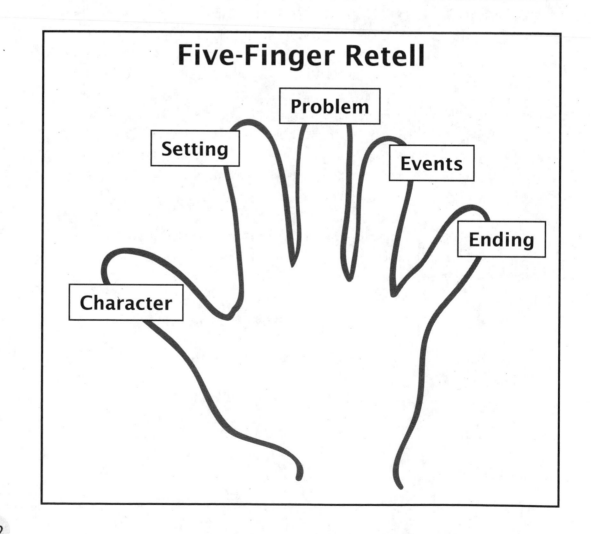

Rubric for Coaching a Transitional Guided Reading Lesson (Levels J–P)

This rubric can be used for self-evaluation, observation, or coaching.

Observation or Coaching (circle one) Record comments on reverse side.	Evident (✓)
Classroom Environment	
Guided reading materials were organized; table was free of clutter.	
Other students were working independently (reading, writing, or literacy stations).	
Teacher was not interrupted by other students in the room.	
Book Introduction (Day 1) (not more than 5 min.)	
Teacher gave short introduction (gist statement).	
Students quickly previewed the text.	
Teacher introduced new vocabulary (no more than five words).	
Reading the Book With Teacher Prompting (10–15 min.)	
Students read softly and independently (not chorally).	
Book was at the appropriate level (slightly challenging).	
Teacher listened to individual students and took anecdotal notes.	
Teacher appropriately prompted each student for monitoring, decoding, fluency, or comprehension.	
Teaching Points (circle two items taught) (2–3 min.)	
Decoding (reread, endings, analogies, chunk big words)	
Fluency (phrasing, bold words, dialogue)	
Vocabulary strategies (reread & check pictures, use known parts)	
Comprehension (B-M-E, five-finger retell, S-W-B-S, character's feelings)	
Discussion Prompt: Higher-level thinking question	
Word Study—Optional, if students are good decoders. (3–5 min.)	
Sound boxes, analogy chart, make a big word. Used correct procedures.	
GUIDED WRITING (10–20 min.)	
After students reread for fluency, they wrote a response at the guided reading table. (usually Day 3 of the book)	
Students used a personal word wall for spelling support.	
Students wrote mostly independently with teacher prompting at difficulty.	
Total Lesson: 20 minutes	

Ten-Minute Lesson Plan for Individual Lessons

Title: _____   Level: _____   Lesson #: _____   Dates: _____

<table>
<tr><td rowspan="2">Day 1</td><td colspan="2">New Book Introduction:
This book is about _____

New vocabulary: _____</td></tr>
<tr><td colspan="2">Observations and Teaching Points:
Discussion Prompt:</td></tr>
</table>

<table>
<tr><td rowspan="2">Day 2</td><td>Finish reading the book.
Observations and Teaching Points:

Discussion Prompt:</td><td>Word Study: Do one of the activities below.
Sound Boxes:

Analogy Chart:</td></tr>
</table>

<table>
<tr><td>Day 3</td><td>Guided Writing: Record observations and teaching points
• B-M-E
• Five-finger retell
• S-W-B-S
• Events and details
• Problem and character's feeling about it; solution and character's feeling about it</td></tr>
</table>

	Prompts for Monitoring and Decoding	**Prompts for Fluency**	**Prompts for Retelling**
Teaching Points	• *Does that make sense? Reread and think about what would make sense & look right.* • *Check the middle (or end) of the word.* • *Cover the ending and find a part you know.* • *Chunk the word.* • *Is there another word you know that looks like this part?*	• *Read it without your finger.* • *How would the character say that?* • *Can you make it sound like talking?* • *Read these words together.* (Teacher frames 2–3 words.) • Teacher slides finger over text to push the student's eye forward.	• STP—Student **stops**, covers the page, and **thinks** about the story. • Student **paraphrases** the text. • If a student has trouble, prompt him/her to look at the picture. • *Who was on this page and what did s/he do?* • Predict: *What might happen next?*

Ten-Minute Lesson for Transitional Readers (Individual Instruction)

If you have a transitional reader who does not fit into any group, teach him or her individually for ten minutes each day until the student accelerates and is able to join one of your guided reading groups.

Natalie (not her real name) was coded as a special education student with a learning disability when she moved to a new school at the beginning of fourth grade. Her teacher assessed her reading at Level I (end of first grade), which was significantly lower than every other student in the class. Natalie's teacher used the ten-minute lesson plan to teach her the skills and strategies she was lacking. At the end of fourth grade, Natalie was reading Level N, which is beginning third grade.

In fifth grade, Natalie again received the ten-minute lesson from her new classroom teacher. She made progress, and after eight weeks, she was able to join one of the guided reading groups. At the end of the year, Natalie was reading fifth grade material with fairly good comprehension (75% on the QRI). Although she still has challenges with spelling and making inferences, Natalie should be successful in middle school. The following individual lesson plan is appropriate for struggling readers like Natalie.

Day 1: Reading

Introduce the book, inviting the student to make one or two predictions from the illustrations. Introduce new vocabulary the student could not decode or could not figure out the meaning. As the student reads to you, prompt for self-monitoring, decoding, fluency, or retell as appropriate. Follow the prompts and teaching points described in this chapter.

Day 2: Reading and Word Study

The student reads for the first five minutes while you listen and prompt for strategies. Then spend a few minutes discussing the story, giving the student the opportunity to retell the book and respond to a deeper comprehension question.

> **Word Work (3 minutes):** If a student is still learning blends, short vowels, and vowel patterns, select one word work activity described in this chapter. Refer to Appendix A for words to use with each of the following activities.
>
> * **Sound boxes**: If the student needs to work on blends and short vowels, use the sound box activity. Dictate three or four phonetically regular words for the student to segment and write in the boxes.
>
> * **Analogy charts**: Use this activity if the student needs practice with the silent *e* rule or vowel patterns.

If the student is a good speller and decoder, you do not need to do word study.

Day 3: Guided Writing

Help the student write a response to the story. If the student has trouble with spelling, show him or her how to use a personal word wall as a resource.

* ✳ Write five sentences that retell the beginning, middle, and end (B-M-E).

* ✳ Write a five-finger retell.

* ✳ Write a Somebody-Wanted-But-So sentence.

* ✳ Describe how the character's feelings changed.

* ✳ What did the character learn?

The student does not read the book with the teacher on Day 3. However, the student should reread the book for fluency with a buddy, on a tape recorder, or individually at some time during the day.

Questions Teachers Ask About Transitional Guided Reading

When should I use the transitional lesson plan?

The transitional lesson plan is for students reading between Levels J and P who need to work on decoding, fluency, and retelling.

Do students always need to reread for fluency on Day 3?

No. If the students are fluent on Day 2, then you can spend Day 3 on guided writing.

What if students need help spelling a word during guided writing? Should I tell them how to spell it?

Always give the students the personal word wall to use during guided writing. It contains the 100 most frequently misspelled words, and you can add other words they commonly misspell. If the students need a word that is not on the list, you can direct them to use their book as a resource or teach them how to use a spelling feature from a word they already know. For example, if they need help spelling the *ou* part in *cloud*, have them write *out* and show them how the /ou/ sound in *out* is the same as the /ou/ sound in *cloud*. The final product may have some spelling errors, but it should be organized and readable.

How can I help students who have trouble with retelling?

Teach students how to softly Stop, Think, and Paraphrase (STP) on each page even when you are not working with them. If students have trouble retelling after each page, tell them to use the picture as they STP. If they cannot retell using the picture, select an easier book. After students have read the whole book, help them retell the story by using the pictures in the book. Eventually, wean them from actually using the pictures by saying, "Think about the first picture in the book. What happened on that page?"

What should I do while the students read at the table?

If students have decoding and fluency issues, you should listen to children read and prompt them accordingly. If the students do not have decoding or fluency issues, you should ask them to retell the page they just read. If the students make no errors, read fluently, and can retell, the book is too easy. If the student is ready to work on deeper comprehension strategies, use the fluent lesson plan.

Should I ever use nonfiction texts with transitional readers?

Yes, especially when your strategy focus is vocabulary or retell. When you are trying to teach decoding strategies and fluency, fiction texts are a better choice because it is easier for students to access meaning. Fiction texts also give students the opportunity to read with expression and intonation. We don't want children to read informational texts quickly; we want them to read these texts thoughtfully. (Consider how you read informational texts—such as instructions for completing your income tax!)

Does every transitional group need guided writing?

Most transitional readers need to improve writing skills. Guided writing is an excellent format for extending comprehension and teaching students how to become better writers. Additionally, reading and writing are reciprocal processes. What children learn in one area can be practiced and applied in the other.

chapter 6

Fluent

GUIDED READING

Several years ago I taught a guided reading group that was learning to clarify and visualize a challenging poem by Emily Dickinson. I was both amused and delighted when one of the students pushed up his sleeves and exclaimed, "Well, I can see I am going to have to work at this!" As a fluent, advanced reader, he had rarely encountered a difficult text, but guided reading lifted his processing level by forcing him to apply comprehension strategies.

Comprehension instruction is part of every guided reading lesson, even with emergent readers, but it plays an especially important role in the fluent lesson. Because fluent readers have few decoding problems, they are able to explore the process of comprehension on challenging texts. As students read, they write short responses that teachers use to assess comprehension. Then the teacher has mini-conferences to identify any confusions and to scaffold students who need support. The most important factor at the fluent level is using a text that offers just the right amount of challenge to force students to "work at it."

The comprehension scaffolds described in this chapter help students think as they read so comprehension can improve. Each guided reading lesson has a specific strategy focus, but the ultimate goal is for students to use a variety of strategies flexibly and independently to understand what they read.

Using Assessments to Form Small Groups

A leveled assessment kit such as the Qualitative Reading Inventory (Leslie & Caldwell, 2005) or the Fountas and Pinnell Benchmark Assessment System, A–Z (2008) is a good first step in determining each student's instructional level and comprehension needs in order to form guided reading groups for fluent readers. Additionally, you may choose to use the Comprehension Interview (Keene, 1997) described in Chapter 2 to provide a deeper analysis of specific strategies the student needs to learn. Standardized reading tests, anecdotal records, and individual conferences may also help you identify individual strengths and needs. The following assessment summary chart is useful for compiling assessment information to form guided reading groups and identify a teaching focus. The most common comprehension strategies are listed, but you may decide to include others based upon the reading standards you are required to teach.

Directions for Using the Assessment Summary Chart for Fluent Readers

This chart is for students reading fluently at or above Level N (DRA 30). If you have students who are reading above Level N but need to improve decoding, fluency, or retell, you should use the lesson plan and strategies described in Chapter 5 for transitional guided reading.

Columns 1 and 2: Name and Instructional Level

Write the student's name in the first column and record the instructional text level. This is the level at which the student reads with at least 90% accuracy and has some comprehension and fluency. If the student reads the text with at least 95% accuracy and has a strong understanding of the story, then the text is considered to be at an independent level. You should give the student a more difficult text to determine the instructional level. To save time, it is appropriate to have the student read the text silently and then ask the student to retell and answer the comprehension questions. Running records are not useful for analyzing fluent readers because fluent readers do not make many errors.

Notice that there are two columns (*F* and *NF*) under "Instructional Level." One is for fiction, the other for nonfiction. Since students often have different instructional levels for fiction and nonfiction texts, it is best to assess them on both.

Column 3: Retell

Put a plus (+) if the child gives a complete and detailed retelling.

Fiction (F): The major plot elements are retold completely, accurately, and in order. All major characters are included. The problem and resolution are clear. The retelling includes details, minor characters, and nonessential events, but not at the expense of the story. Student shows evidence of inference skills.

Nonfiction (NF): Includes every main idea, each supported by at least one or two details. Organization follows the scheme of the book (e.g., chronological, explanatory). The student uses vocabulary correctly and in context.

Put a check (✓) if the child gives a partial retelling.

Fiction (F): The retelling includes the plot and most major characters. Minor characters and setting may be absent. Events not essential to the plot are missing or out of order. Student may not show evidence of inference skills.

Nonfiction (NF): The retelling includes most of the main ideas. Details may be fragmentary or missing. Vocabulary is included but may not be used correctly. Organization is looser, but essential sequences, processes, and explanations remain in order.

Put a minus (−) if the child gives a limited retelling.

Fiction (F): The retelling has major holes: omission of central characters, incorrect identification of the problem, inability to relate sequence, and/or absence of essential plot points.

Nonfiction (NF): Retelling may include the subject but misses many of the main ideas. Details are sketchy or not linked with the idea they support. Organization is loose and random, and mistakes occur in essential sequences. Student tells facts incorrectly.

Columns 4–11: Comprehension Strategies

Students reading at fluent levels need instruction in a variety of comprehension strategies with both fiction and nonfiction texts. These columns are used to identify specific strategies the student needs to learn. Under each strategy put a (+) if the student is proficient in the strategy, a (✓) if the student is partially proficient, and a (−) if the student is not proficient.

Assessment Summary Chart for Fluent Readers

Name	Instr. Text Level		Retell		Visualize		Predict		Connect		Question		Determine Importance		Summarize		Infer		Evaluate	
	F	NF	F	NF	F	NF	F	NF	F	NF	F	NF	F	NF	F	NF	F	NF	F	NF

You will use a variety of assessments and anecdotal notes to complete the chart. To assess a student's ability to summarize, ask him or her to tell you in one sentence what the passage was about. The first comprehension question on the Qualitative Reading Inventory (QRI) asks students to summarize. Teachers can also use the implicit questions from the QRI to evaluate a student's inferencing abilities. Additional information for completing the chart can come from teacher observations, reading conferences, and the Comprehension Interview (Keene, 1997) included in Chapter 2. It is possible for a student to be proficient in a comprehension strategy on fiction but not on nonfiction. The completed chart will indicate which strategies you need to teach and which genre you need to use for guided reading.

Group Students for Guided Reading

The chart makes it easy for you to group students flexibly, based on the strategy focus. Perhaps several students need more help with interpretive or evaluative comprehension. Or maybe a group has difficulty reading visual information from charts or graphs. Students may be placed with one group when using a fiction text and another group when an informational text is used. **The bottom line is this: Know your students and teach them what they need to learn to become better readers**. About once a month, reevaluate your guided reading groups by using anecdotal notes taken during the guided reading lessons. I recommend you limit your groups to six students so you have time to conference with each student and so that all students have an opportunity to share in the discussion.

Select a Focus Strategy

A powerful guided reading lesson at the fluent level has a strategy focus. After you model the strategy, the students silently and independently read a short text as you work with individuals to help them construct meaning by using the target strategy. Consider these interactions to be mini reading conferences. Assistance or scaffolding occurs in the form of your prompts and the comprehension strategy cards and organizers found in this chapter. Students use the cards and organizers to respond to the text. Remember: The strategy is not the goal; constructing meaning is the goal. Each strategy you teach in guided reading should be put in the context of comprehending text. As you teach a lesson, always explain how the strategy students are learning helps them understand what they read.

The following chart describes many of the strategies proficient readers use to comprehend (Pearson, Rohler, Duffy & Dole, 1992; Keene & Zimmerman, 1997). The first column lists the strategy and a scaffold for students to use as they respond to the text. The second describes the strategy and includes prompts you can use with students who have difficulty understanding what they read.

Comprehension Strategies, Scaffolds, and Prompts

Strategy & Scaffold	Description and Teacher Prompts
Clarify Vocabulary *I didn't understand . . .*	Students identify a word or concept that was unclear. *What words or ideas were new or confusing to you?* *What strategies can you use to figure it out?*
Retell *I read . . .*	Students remember and retell what they read. *Tell me what you just read.*
Visualize *I see . . .*	Students create a mental picture of an event, character, setting, etc., and draw it. *What are you picturing in your head?*
Predict *I predict . . .*	Students predict what will happen next in the story. *What do you think will happen next? What makes you think that?*
Make Connections *This reminds me of . . .*	Students think of personal experiences or other texts that relate to the story. *What did this remind you of?* *Does this remind you of another story we've read?*
Ask Questions *Why . . .* *I wonder . . .*	Students ask a question about the story. *What questions are you asking yourself? What are you wondering?*
Determine Importance *The most important part is . . .*	Students identify the most important elements in the passage. *What is the most important part of the story?* *What are the most important words you just read?*
Summarize *The main idea is . . .*	Students synthesize the passage and write a short summary of the main events. *Tell me in one or two sentences what you just read.*
Infer *I think . . .*	Students read between the lines and make inferences that are not stated in the text. *What do you think the character is thinking here?* *What are you thinking now?*
Evaluate *I agree (or disagree) with the author because . . .*	Students determine biases, form opinions, and make judgments based on information gathered from the text. *How do you feel about this passage?* *What is your opinion? Do you agree or disagree with the author?* *How is the author trying to influence you?*

Select the Guided Reading Text

You have formed your groups and identified a focus strategy for each. Now you need to select a text that provides a slight challenge for the group and fits your focus strategy. It is common for intermediate teachers to be uncomfortable selecting texts for guided reading because they are not accustomed to matching texts to readers. Don't worry about that. You will get better at it as you work with your students and understand their strengths and needs. If you find the students did not need your help during the guided reading lesson, then the text was too easy. Your students' body language and facial expressions usually let you know when the text you selected is too difficult. If your students cry (or you want to cry), it was too hard!

The guided reading text is a vehicle that will transport your students toward becoming better readers. Any relatively short text can be used—poetry, short stories, newspaper articles, magazine articles, short chapter books, and informational books. I do not recommend using a novel for guided reading. Longer texts are better suited for literature circles and self-selected reading. You can, however, have students read a chapter from a novel to teach a particular strategy such as foreshadowing, mood, or inferencing.

Read the text to make sure it gives students an opportunity to practice the focus strategy. It is not necessary to finish the entire book during guided reading, especially if you achieve your instructional objective before the students reach the end of the text.

Due to the increased popularity of guided reading, many publishing companies offer leveled texts for small-group instruction. Some are leveled by the A–Z system developed by Fountas and Pinnell (2008), and others by a graded reading level (e.g., 2.5). I have learned not to rely solely on the publisher's text level when determining if a book will be appropriate. You have to consider the vocabulary level and background experiences of your students. An otherwise easy, decodable passage could be challenging if it deals with content and vocabulary unfamiliar to the students.

Using Fiction

If you decide to use fiction, select short stories or short chapter books. When possible use those that have been specifically written for guided reading. These books almost always contain clear character development, conflict, plot, climax, and resolution. Plus, your students will be able to read them in three or four days. You can teach almost any comprehension strategy with a fiction text. However, when you want to teach inferring, you need to read the book. To make the book interesting, most authors write fiction expecting the reader to make inferences. Some series written especially for struggling readers or second language learners, however, do not give the reader an opportunity to make inferences. When selecting a text for the inferencing strategy, simply read it and ask yourself, "Am I making inferences as I read?" If the answer is "no," get another book.

Using Nonfiction

Publishing companies have recognized the need for nonfiction texts and now offer a variety of leveled texts appropriate for guided reading. Informational text should fit your purpose (focus strategy) and offer some challenge to the students. The best way to determine if a nonfiction text fits the strategy focus is to read it and ask, "What do I do to help myself understand this text?" Informational texts appropriate for guided reading include, but are not limited to, the following:

* Informational books written for guided reading (Scholastic Leveled Library, Nonfiction Focus)

* Short passages (such as those found in Harvey & Goudvis's *Toolkit Texts: Short Nonfiction for Guided and Independent Practice*)

* Biographies

* Articles from children's magazines (e.g., *Time for Kids*, *Scholastic News*)

* Letters to the editor and opinion columns (from newspapers)

Using Poetry

For the following reasons, poems are excellent for fluent guided reading lessons.

* A poem is usually short, making it possible to complete the lesson in one or two days.

* Poetry is often challenging to understand and thereby forces the reader to slow down and think, exactly the process desired for teaching comprehension strategies.

* Poetry provides the opportunity to teach a variety of literary elements, such as simile, metaphor, and personification.

* Poets commonly use figurative language that requires readers to visualize, make inferences, and make connections.

No matter how advanced the readers, you can always find a poem that is challenging and appropriate for guided reading.

Materials for Fluent Guided Reading

* Assessment kit

* Texts in a variety of genres

* Copies of the lesson plan

* Dry-erase board and marker (for the teacher)

* Reading Notebooks (for student responses and new vocabulary—See Chapter 1, page 23)

* Comprehension scaffold cards—There are numerous comprehension cards in this chapter that help students learn the comprehension strategy. Make six sets of each card and laminate them.

* 6 laminated copies of the vocabulary strategies cards (Appendix C)

* Sticky notes (1" and 3") and sticky flags

* Timer

Guided Writing (if appropriate): After students finish reading the book, help them extend their understanding of the text by writing with teacher support for 20 minutes. Recommended for struggling writers.

Fluent Guided Reading Lesson Plan (Day 1)

Title: _____ Level: _____ Strategy Focus: _____

Date: _____ Pages: _____

Before Reading (5 minutes)	Read & Respond (10 minutes)	After Reading (5 minutes)
Introduction _____ _____ _____ _____ **Preview & Predict** **New Vocabulary for Day 1** _____ _____ _____ _____	**Model Strategy** _____ _____ _____ **Observations** _____ _____ _____ _____ _____ _____	**Discussion and teaching points** _____ _____ _____ _____ _____ **Words for the New Word List** 1. _____ 2. _____

Possible Teaching Points for Fluent Guided Reading

Decoding	Comprehension–fiction	Comprehension–nonfiction	Comprehension–poetry
❑ Reread & think ❑ Cover the ending ❑ Use known parts ❑ Chunk big words ❑ Connect	❑ Retell–STP, VIP ❑ Visualize ❑ Predict & support ❑ Make connections ❑ Character traits ❑ Ask questions ❑ Determine importance ❑ Summarize by chapter ❑ Cause and effect ❑ Character analysis ❑ Make inferences– (from dialogue, action, or physical description)	❑ Retell–STP ❑ Ask questions ❑ Summarize with key words ❑ Main Idea/Details ❑ Important/Interesting ❑ Interpreting visual information (maps, charts) ❑ Contrast or Compare ❑ Cause/Effect ❑ Evaluate–fact/opinion, author's point of view ❑ Reciprocal teaching ❑ Other:_____	❑ Clarify ❑ Visualize ❑ Make connections ❑ Ask literal questions ❑ Summarize ❑ Ask inferential questions ❑ Make inferences ❑ Draw conclusions ❑ Interpret author's purpose ❑ Figurative language (simile, metaphor, personification, etc.) ❑ Reciprocal teaching
Vocabulary ❑ Use context clues ❑ Use pictures or visualize ❑ Use a known part ❑ Make a connection ❑ Use the glossary			

Fluent Guided Reading Lesson Plan (Continued)

Date: _____ Pages: _____ Strategy Focus: _____

Before Reading (5 minutes)	Read & Respond (10 minutes)	After Reading (5 minutes)
Introduction _____ _____ _____ **New Vocabulary** _____ _____ _____ _____ _____	**Observations** _____ _____ _____ _____ _____ _____ _____ _____ _____ _____ _____	**Discussion and teaching points** _____ _____ _____ _____ **Words for the New Word List** 1. _____ 2. _____

Date: _____ Pages: _____ Strategy Focus: _____

Before Reading (5 minutes)	Read & Respond (10 minutes)	After Reading (5 minutes)
Introduction _____ _____ _____ **New Vocabulary** _____ _____ _____ _____ _____	**Observations** _____ _____ _____ _____ _____ _____ _____ _____ _____ _____ _____	**Discussion and teaching points** _____ _____ _____ _____ **Words for the New Word List** 1. _____ 2. _____

Description of the Fluent Guided Reading Lesson

Component	Explanation
Text Introduction	**Introduce** the text with a one-or-two-sentence gist statement. Avoid asking, "What do you think this book is about?" That will waste precious time and not be very productive. (I don't see a lot of value in having students make predictions based solely on the cover of a book.) Here is an example of a simple gist statement: "This book is about different types of mummies that are found around the world. You are going to learn how scientists discover more about a culture by studying mummies."
Preview & Predict (3–4 minutes) This occurs only on the first day with the book.	Now invite the students to **preview** the book and share their **predictions** about what they will learn. Direct them to use the table of contents or illustrations. When introducing nonfiction texts, I ask each student to find an interesting picture and share a prediction. It might be like this, "I think we are going to learn how ancient Egyptians preserved the mummies." You can spend a few seconds activating students' background knowledge—but watch the clock. Your introduction should not last more than three or four minutes. **The primary focus of guided reading is <u>reading</u>.** Don't spend 20 minutes just talking *about* the book.
Introduce new vocabulary. (1–2 minutes) Each day you will introduce the new words for that section of text.	Introduce **unfamiliar** words students will encounter *during today's guided reading lesson.* **Which words should you introduce?** It is not necessary to introduce every new word the students will encounter. Only introduce a word if . . . • Students lack the decoding skills to read it (foreign words, proper names). • Students have never heard the word before but should learn it. • There are no clues about its meaning in the text. • The word is essential to understanding the passage. • Students will encounter this word in other contexts. • The word has a common root you want to emphasize.

Component	Explanation
Make students responsible for using context clues and the glossary to define unfamiliar words as they encounter them. Note: If there are more than five words to introduce that day, the text is probably too difficult. Use the four steps to introduce new words.	**Do <u>not</u> pre-teach new vocabulary if there is support in the text for determining its meaning**. You want to empower students to figure out words they do not know. You do not want them to depend on you to define every new word. If your lesson focus is on learning vocabulary strategies, draw the students' attention to the particular strategy you want them to practice. It might be to look at the bold words and use the glossary. Or it might be to look for context clues to determine the meaning of the word. Informational texts will have illustrations or diagrams that support new vocabulary. **How should I introduce a new word?** The following four steps are efficient and effective ways to introduce new vocabulary. **Step 1**: Provide students with a kid-friendly **definition**. Do not ask them if they know the word. This wastes time and may mislead students. For example, if the new word is *maneuver*, say, "*Maneuver* means to move around." **Step 2**: **Connect** the new word to the students' background knowledge and experiences. For example, "A soccer player <u>maneuvers</u> or <u>moves</u> the ball around the opponents to get to the goal." Be sure to use the new word with a kid-friendly definition during your explanation. **Step 3**: **Relate** the new word **to the text**. Tell the students how the word is used and direct them to an illustration if one is provided. "In this text, you will read how ancient workers maneuvered, or moved, large stones without machinery."
Tape a world map to your guided reading table to introduce the setting for the text.	**Step 4**: **Turn and talk**. Ask the students to explain the new word to a student who is sitting next to them. "Talk to your partner about something you can maneuver." I suggest you tape a world map to your guided reading table. Informational texts often refer to countries or places new to the students. The map is a quick way to show them where these places are located. Example: "Today our story takes place in the Andes Mountains. Look on this map of South America. Here are the Andes Mountains."

Component	Explanation
Introduce the Focus Strategy (1 minute)	**Before students read**, they need to know the **focus strategy**. It will save time if students have seen the strategy demonstrated in a whole-class mini-lesson before they try it during guided reading. On the first day of the lesson, model the comprehension strategy students will be learning. Think aloud and SHOW (not tell) them how the strategy works. Then decide how you will scaffold students as they practice the strategy. Usually the scaffold will change as students read through the book. As students become more proficient in using the strategy, decrease your support. Later in this chapter you will find comprehension cards and suggestions for scaffolding students as they practice a particular strategy. Always remember, the goal of a guided reading lesson is to support students as they construct meaning. Tell students how learning to apply the focus strategy will help them be better readers.
Read & Respond (10 minutes) Students write **as** they read. **No round-robin reading!**	Students **read** the text **independently** and silently for about ten minutes and **write short responses** that match the comprehension or vocabulary strategy. If you want to improve comprehension, have students write as they read. I usually have students write a sentence after they read a page or two. Then they read another page and respond. Writing during reading helps the students organize their thoughts and keeps them focused on the task. Students' written responses help you, too, for you can monitor their comprehension and know when to scaffold and support. As you work with each student, you can read his/her written responses, help the student clarify confusions, and probe for deeper understanding. **Should the students read out loud to the teacher?** Because fluent readers are good decoders and read with appropriate phrasing and fluency, they should read silently. If during your conferencing, you are puzzled by a student's response, you can invite that student to softly read a paragraph and discuss it so you can help clarify a misunderstanding.

Component	Explanation
Prompt for vocabulary or comprehension based upon each student's needs.	While students read and respond, circulate among the group and work with individual students. Your goal is to have a short (two-minute) reading conference with each student. Since most fluent readers have strong decoding strategies, you will prompt for vocabulary and comprehension during your conferences. For example, if you suspect that a student is not using **vocabulary strategies**, you might ask one of the following questions: • *Is there a word you don't understand?* • *Are there clues in the sentence to help you?* • *Can you think of another word you could substitute for this word?* • *Does the picture help you figure out what the word means?* • *Where could you look when it is a bold word?* If there is no vocabulary to clarify, read the student's response and either clarify confusion or prompt for deeper understanding. Usually your prompts will match the strategy focus for the lesson.
Discussion and Teaching Points (5 minutes) **Comprehension teaching point** **Vocabulary teaching point**	After students read for about 10–12 minutes, you should have five to seven minutes left for **discussion and teaching**. Students share their written responses while you facilitate the discussion. The lesson plan has a place to write a few thought-provoking questions aimed at lifting the processing level of the students. During the discussion, think about the level of support that will be needed at the next guided reading session. At the close of every lesson ask two questions: 1) *What did I teach these students today?* and 2) *What should I teach them next to help them become better readers?* You may also use some of the discussion time to ask students about a challenging word in the text, especially if it provides an opportunity to teach a specific vocabulary strategy. Perhaps it was a bold word, and you noticed students did not use the glossary for help. Or it might have been a word that could be defined using context clues or known parts. Have students find the word in the book and share strategies they could use to define it.

Component	Explanation
New Word List (1 minute) Target useful words that appear regularly across a variety of contexts.	Close each lesson by having students **add two words** to the New Word List in their reading notebooks. (Pages 27–29 of Chapter 1 have specific instructions for using the New Word List.) These words could be ones you defined during the introduction or words you used as a teaching point at the end of the lesson. Select high-utility words or words that provide opportunities to teach word analysis strategies (common affixes and roots). Beck (2002) refers to these as Tier Two words. They are important and useful to mature readers. Give your students an opportunity to use the words during reading workshop. I have listed practice activities on page 28 of Chapter 1. Periodically (every few weeks), test the students on these words. To save time, write the two new words and their definitions on a whiteboard and send the students away from the table to write the words on the New Word List in their notebooks. This gives you a minute to review your lesson plan for your next group.
Guided Writing (Optional activity done at the end of a book) (20 minutes) **Guided writing occurs *at* the table with teacher support.**	During guided reading students should always write a short response that matches the comprehension focus; however, if students need more help with writing, you may decide to do a guided writing lesson the day after students finish the book or article. **Purpose**: Guided writing helps students improve writing skills and solidify or extend their understanding of the text. The writing is completed during the guided reading lesson with the teacher's support. It is not an assignment they complete at their desks. It is not unusual to find fluent readers who are struggling writers. Use this opportunity to prompt and encourage students to apply the principles of good writing you taught them during writing workshop.

Component	Explanation
Fluent readers who struggle with writing benefit from guided writing. An error-free piece is not the goal of first-draft writing.	**Procedures**: Guided writing occurs the day **after** students finish reading the text. The guided writing response will vary according to the text structure of the guided reading book and your strategy focus. In most responses, students will use the text as a resource, but they should not copy sentences from the book. As students write, circulate among the group and assist individual students as appropriate. Make on-the-spot decisions based upon the strengths and needs of individual students. The goal is teaching whatever the student is ready to learn next; therefore, you will attend to some errors and let others go.
Responses to Fiction **Describe one of the characters by giving examples of a character trait s/he exhibits.** **Write a poem from the character's point of view.**	**Possible Guided Writing Responses to Fiction** **Character Analysis**—Students select one of the main characters in the story and identify a character trait such as *generous*, *brave*, *thoughtful*, *determined*, *cunning*, etc. Then students write a paragraph about the character, using examples from the story. **I Poems** (Kucan, 2007)—Students select a character from the story and write a poem from that character's point of view. If students need support, you can provide a simple framework by selecting *a few* of the following sentence stems: *I am . . .* *I wonder . . .* *I hear . . .* *I see . . .* *I want . . .* *I pretend . . .* *I feel . . .* *I worry . . .* *I cry . . .* *I understand . . .* *I say . . .* *I dream . . .*

Component	Explanation
Explain a microtheme from the story. *What was the author's message? What did the character learn that you can apply to your life?* **Choose your own ending.**	**Microthemes**—Students select one of the themes and write a paragraph that explains how the theme was illustrated in the book. A theme is a message the author wants to communicate or a lesson the character learns. Themes are generic statements that have wide applications and are not specific to one story. For example, a microtheme of the folktale "Three Little Pigs" is "Be prepared for adversity," not "Always build a house of bricks." **Alternate Ending**—Students think of a different way the story could have ended. They write a paragraph that describes what could have happened and what the consequences would have been.
Responses to Informational Text **Use information about a famous person to write a biopoem.**	**Possible Guided Writing Responses to Informational Text** Teachers should consider the text structure when designing guided writing activities for informational texts. If the text compares ideas, then it would be logical for students to write a comparison. If the text describes cause-and-effect relationships, students should write a paragraph about causes and effects. **Biopoems**—Students follow a predetermined structure to write a poem about a famous person. Here is one type of structure, but teachers can make adjustments to fit the text. Line 1: First name Line 2: Four traits that describe the person Line 3: Lover of . . . (three things or people) Line 4: Who needs . . . (three items) Line 5: Who fears . . . (three items) Line 6: Who gives . . . (three items) Line 7: Resident of . . . Line 8: Last name <center>Martin Courageous, caring, persistent, intelligent Lover of peace, equality, and children Who needs to be heard, and seen, and understood Who fears violence, anger, and war Who gives speeches, encouragement, and solutions Resident of Alabama King</center>

Component	Explanation
Summarize one chapter from the book.	**Chapter Summaries**—Each student selects one chapter from the table of contents and writes a paragraph that describes the most important information s/he learned in that chapter. Encourage students to use the illustrations in the chapter to capture important ideas.
Use the index to find key ideas.	**Key-Idea Poem**—Students use important ideas from the text to write a non-rhyming poem. If students have trouble recalling key ideas, direct them to the index. Here is an example of a key-idea poem written about the book *Twisters* by Sarah Feldman. Line 1: Title of the book Line 2: Verbs (*–ing* words) Line 3: Where are they found? Line 4: What do they look like? Line 5: What do they do? Line 6: Other nouns for the topic Line 7: Three adjectives for the topic Lines 8, 9, & 10: How to protect yourself Line 11: One word to close the poem <div align="center">Twisters roaring, rumbling, growling, swirling down Tornado Alley in Oklahoma or Kansas whirling tongues of devastating destruction vacuuming everything in their path funnels, waterspouts, tornadoes, violent, fast, dangerous hide in a basement, or bathroom, or closet. Safe!</div>

Component	Explanation
Students scan the index to find two concepts they can compare and contrast.	**Compare/Contrast**—If the text structure is description, students could select two topics and write a paragraph that compares the ideas and one that contrasts them. They could compare and contrast two animals, two landforms, two cloud formations . . . whatever matches the information in the text. One interesting way to do this is to direct students to select two concepts from the index. As they search the index, students must think, "What concepts can be compared or contrasted?" Look over their selections to make sure the topics work for the task.
Write about the causes and effects of an historical event.	**Cause/Effect**—This response works well with historical texts. Students select one important event (such as the Boston Tea Party, the Underground Railroad, or the Great Depression). They write one paragraph that describes the events or feelings that caused or led to the important event. Then they write another paragraph that describes the effect(s) of that important event. Example: Paragraph 1 (causes) *One important event from this book is the Battle of Gettysburg. Several factors caused this event to happen . . .* Paragraph 2 (effects) *One effect of this important battle was . . .* *Another effect this event had on history was . . .*
Use chapter titles and headings to write a paragraph explaining the main idea of the chapter.	**Main Idea/Details**—Students select one main idea from the text and write a paragraph that uses details and examples from the text to describe or explain the main idea. Main ideas are usually found in chapter titles and headings. Students could also select an important graph or chart and explain it by using the details in the text.

Component	Explanation
Response to Poetry	**Possible Guided Writing Responses to Poetry**
Make connections to the poem.	**Connections**—Students write one to three paragraphs that describe connections they were able to make to the poem. Whether the students write one, two, or three paragraphs depends on their writing skills. Remember, you want to complete the writing in one 20-minute session.
This poem reminds me of . . .	Paragraph 1: Text-to-Self connections. This poem reminds me of the time I . . .

Paragraph 2: Text-to-Text connections. This poem reminds me of another poem or story I have read. They both . . . |
What is the poet's message?	Paragraph 3: Text-to-World connections. This poem reminds me of something in real life . . .
What did the poet say? What does the poem mean to you?	**Author's Purpose**—Students identify a theme of the poem and write a paragraph that explains how the theme is developed or supported.
Explain a literary element the poet used.	**Literal/Figurative Meaning**—Students write two paragraphs about the poem. The first paragraph summarizes the literal interpretation of the poem, "What did the poet actually say?" The second summarizes the figurative interpretation of the poem, "What does this poem mean to you?"
What did the author mean?	**Figurative Language**—Students identify figurative language and explain what the author meant.

Example of a figurative language paragraph about "Casey at the Bat":

In "Casey at the Bat" the author uses figurative language to communicate his message. When the poem says, "The batter was dead at second," he didn't mean that the batter actually died. He meant that the batter was tagged out at second. |

Rubric for Fluent Guided Reading Lesson (Levels N+)

This rubric can be used for self-evaluation, observation, or coaching.

Observation or Coaching (circle one) Record comments on bottom of page.	Evident (✓)
Classroom Environment	
Materials were organized and handy; table was free of clutter.	
Other students were working independently in reading, writing, or literacy activities.	
Teacher was not interrupted by other students in the room.	
Introduction (Not more than 5 minutes)	
Teacher gave a short introduction or gist statement. *Today you will read. . . .*	
Students quickly previewed the book or portion of text being read that day.	
Teacher introduced new vocabulary (no more than 5 words).	
Teacher used the four steps to efficiently define the new words: 1) Teacher gave a definition. 2) Teacher connected the word to the students. 3) Teacher related the word to the book. 4) Students talked to each other and related the word to personal experiences.	
Teacher modeled strategy (if necessary).	
Reading With Teacher Prompting (At least 10 minutes)	
Students read silently unless teacher was working with them.	
Book was at the appropriate level (slightly challenging).	
Students wrote while they read (according to the strategy focus).	
Teacher may have listened to some students read orally, if appropriate.	
Teacher prompted individual students for vocabulary and/or comprehension.	
Teacher monitored individual students' comprehension by reading written responses and asking questions.	
Teacher took anecdotal notes on students.	
Sharing and Discussion (5 minutes)	
Students shared written responses while teacher facilitated the discussion.	
Discussion lifted students' understanding of the text.	
New vocabulary defined in the text was discussed.	
Students added two words to their New Word Lists.	
Total Lesson Time: 20 minutes	

Comments:

> **"**One of the greatest resources for comprehension is a good vocabulary."
>
> Dorn et al. (2005), *Teaching for Deep Comprehension*, p. 62

Teaching Vocabulary

Research on vocabulary instruction reveals that (1) most vocabulary is learned indirectly through everyday experiences with oral and written language, and (2) students benefit from direct instruction in new words and vocabulary strategies (Cunningham, 2009).

Indirect Vocabulary Learning

Students learn vocabulary indirectly when they are read to (Beck, McKeown, & Kucan, 2002; Elley, 1989), when they read on their own (Nagy, Anderson, & Herman, 1987), and when they converse with adults. Hart and Risley (1995) learned that children from professional families generally have richer speaking and listening vocabularies than working-class families because they have more conversations in the home. To close the gap in listening vocabulary, teachers need to provide opportunities for learning vocabulary through read-alouds and sustained independent reading (Cunningham, 2009).

Direct Vocabulary Instruction

Students can also increase their vocabularies when they are explicitly taught both individual words and word-learning strategies. Direct instruction of vocabulary is most effective when these elements are present:

* Students have multiple and varied encounters with the new words.

* Pictures are included.

* Students are taught strategies for learning new words.

* Vocabulary is imbedded in the text.

Although new vocabulary can and should be taught during whole group experiences (such as with a read-aloud), the varied backgrounds and reading levels in any classroom challenge teachers to select the right words. It is safe to assume whole-group vocabulary instruction will be appropriate for some children but too easy or too difficult for others.

Guided reading provides one context for teaching vocabulary that targets the needs of all students. Each guided reading group learns vocabulary appropriate for their reading level and experiences. Additionally, the essential elements of effective vocabulary instruction are met:

✳   Students will encounter the words in text they can read.

✳   Pictures are often included, especially with nonfiction texts.

✳   Students are prompted to use vocabulary strategies during reading.

During the first minutes of the guided reading lesson, you should introduce a few new words students would not be able to figure out on their own. Guided reading teachers should not attend to words that have context or other clues because students should be expected (and prompted) to use strategies if they encounter unfamiliar words. At the end of each lesson, select one or two useful words for students to add to their New Word Lists. Repeated exposure to new vocabulary in many contexts aids word learning; consequently, students should be encouraged to use the new words they learn in guided reading when they speak and write. By using the procedures for the New Word List, described on pages 27-29 of Chapter 1, you hold students accountable for learning these words. If students do not know how to use strategies to define unfamiliar words, make that the focus for your guided reading lesson and use the following scaffolds.

Teaching Vocabulary Strategies During Guided Reading

1. Prepare the guided reading texts by inserting small sticky notes on pages where students will encounter unfamiliar words that are defined with context clues. If you write the first letter of the new words on the sticky note, students will have a clue for finding the tricky word.

2. Distribute the vocabulary strategies cards (Appendix C) and model the first strategy (using context clues).

3. Tell the students that as they read, they will find new words that can be defined with context clues. Students should write the new word on the sticky note and write their definition for that word (using context clues).

4. At the end of the lesson, students share the new vocabulary they learned that day.

5. Repeat the procedure with the other vocabulary strategies on the card.

Once children have learned all the vocabulary strategies, they should be able to locate new vocabulary (without the first letter clue), write their own definition, and identify the vocabulary strategy they used.

Vocabulary Strategies (also in Appendix C)

1. **Reread (or read ahead) and look for clues in the text.** Teachers often assume students are able to use context clues, but some students need to be taught **how** to use this strategy. As students read, ask them to show you the clues in the sentence that tell them what a word means.

2. **Check the picture/illustrations or visualize the sentence.** Authors commonly use diagrams, illustrations, or charts to explain vocabulary, but not all students know how to use these text features to discover the meaning of new words. Recently, I worked with a group that was reading about the layers of the earth. As the students read, I watched their eyes to see if they would use the diagram to help them understand the passage. Not one student looked at the illustration. I was not surprised they had a weak understanding of what they had just read. When I modeled how to stop, use your finger to mark your place, and search the illustrations for help, the students made a dramatic improvement in their comprehension.

3. **Use a known part.** Students will encounter new words that contain a familiar part. Compound words are obvious examples of this strategy, but known parts also include prefixes, suffixes, and root words. In "The sun was *knifing* through the cloudless sky," *knifing* may be an unfamiliar word, but students can use what they know about *knife* to deduce what *knifing* means.

4. **Make a connection to words that are similar.** This strategy requires students to think about words they know that are similar to the new word. For example, if the text says, "The man was teetering on the edge," students who know what a teeter totter is can make a connection to *teetering*. Many new words students encounter during reading are connected to words they already know. Linguists estimate that every word you know is connected to seven other words you know (Cunningham, 2009). As students make connections to words they already know, they will learn more than you can directly teach.

5. **Use text features such as the glossary or footnotes.** I frequently see good readers sail past bold words without referring to the glossary for help. Encourage students to turn to the glossary *as* they read if they do not know the meaning of a word.

Students can complete this chart in their reading notebooks to identify new words, create a kid-friendly definition, and share the strategies they used for determining the meaning of the word.

Page	New word	My definition	Strategies I used
6	undergrowth	bushes or short plants	2 (pictures) & 3 (known part)
8	commence	begin	1 (context)

Comprehension Scaffolds for Guided Reading

The following pages contain scaffolding steps for teaching a variety of comprehension strategies. Use your assessments to determine which strategies you need to teach and in what order. Many of the strategies have scaffolding cards students can use to help themselves apply it. The goal for every strategy is that the students will internalize the process and be able to apply it independently to construct meaning on any text.

Literal, Interpretive, and Evaluative Comprehension Scaffolds

A useful way to discriminate among comprehension strategies is to classify them as requiring literal, interpretive, or evaluative thinking (Stead, 2006). **Literal** comprehension requires students to recall information that is explicitly stated in the text. When readers make an inference or draw a conclusion, they are using **interpretive** comprehension. **Evaluative** responses challenge the reader to make judgments, form an opinion, or weigh evidence from the text that either supports or opposes a position. When readers engage in evaluative comprehension, they bring personal experiences to the process. Teach a strategy at the literal level before moving to the interpretive or evaluative.

Visualize

Good readers create mental images as they read. Visualization helps the reader remember and understand what was read. This strategy can be used with fiction, nonfiction, and poetry.

Fiction

Students read a portion of the text and sketch what they are seeing in their head. If students are having difficulty with this strategy, try the following prompts:

    ❋   *What are you seeing in your mind?*

    ❋   *Draw the character's face. How is he or she feeling now?*

> **"**...creating vivid images during reading correlates highly with overall comprehension."
>
> Keene & Zimmermann (1997), *Mosaic of Thought,* p. 129

Nonfiction

Instruct students to read a section, close their book, and illustrate what they just read. With nonfiction, visualization may take the form of a diagram with labels. For example, if the students read a text about the parts of a volcano, they could close their book and draw a volcano, labeling its parts.

Poetry

Poems are usually rich with imagery, so visualization is a great strategy to use with poetry. Students should read and illustrate each stanza in a poem. You are then able to evaluate student understanding through each student's drawing.

Instructional Scaffolds

Visualization can be taught at the literal, interpretive, or evaluative levels. Always begin with the literal level and increase the challenge as appropriate.

Literal Level—Be the Illustrator: Students draw a picture or diagram that explains some idea *stated* in the text. If the text already has pictures, cover them with a large sticky note. As students read, they stop and sketch their mental images on the sticky note. Remind students that illustrators try to capture the most important information in their illustrations.

Interpretive Level: Students draw a picture or diagram that explains some idea *not stated* in the text, one that must be inferred. For fiction, you might ask students to sketch what a character might be thinking. For nonfiction, you could have students sketch an idea they must interpret from the text, diagram, or chart.

Evaluative Level: Students draw a picture or diagram that illustrates their *opinion* about the text. After reading, they have the opportunity to explain and defend their ideas to the group.

For Advanced Readers: Visualization is an appropriate strategy to use with advanced readers, especially when they read informational texts that challenge them. Give students a magazine or newspaper article and ask them to create a drawing that demonstrates how important elements in the text are related. They might use a flow chart to illustrate environmental issues or a concept map to show the two sides of an argument, the sequence of a battle, or the causes of political tensions.

Predict, Support, and Confirm

The prediction cycle begins when readers anticipate what they will read in the text. Good readers monitor their comprehension, gather evidence to support their predictions and, when necessary, abandon earlier predictions and make new ones. Proficient readers constantly move through this prediction cycle.

Readers make predictions using information from the text and their prior knowledge. If students have trouble making predictions, they either don't understand what they read or they lack background experiences that relate to the story. When reading nonfiction, prediction plays a slightly different role. Rather than predicting what will happen next, students should use text headings, illustrations, and features such as maps, captions, and tables to make logical predictions about what they will learn in the next section.

Because this strategy has been taught since kindergarten, most intermediate students are good at making predictions. Some, however, may need more instruction. They may hesitate to share their predictions because they are afraid they will be wrong. Although predictions do not need to be accurate, they need to be logical.

> **"**Predicting involves readers in books because they feel compelled to read on and confirm their hunches."
>
> Laura Robb (2000), *Teaching Reading in Middle School*, p. 119

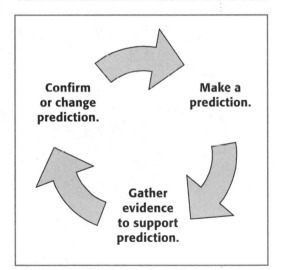

Fig. 6-1, prediction cycle

Literal Level (fiction):
Write one or two predictions.

Mark a place in the text where the author expects the reader to make a prediction. It is best to paperclip this page to the back of the book so the students resist the urge to read ahead. Be sure to emphasize that predictions do not have to be "right," but that they should be logical and supported in the text. One way to encourage risk is to ask students to write two predictions. During the discussion, students share one of their predictions and tell "why" they thought that might happen. Praise students for making predictions, especially those that are logical but are not confirmed in the text. Explain that good writers often lead their readers one way and surprise them with an outcome they did not expect.

Interpretive Level (fiction): Predict and Support

Again, mark a place where you want students to write a prediction. To make the discussion interesting, you may have students write predictions in different places rather than on the same page. Have students construct the following two-column chart in their reading notebooks. In the first column they write their predictions, and in the second they write evidence from the text that supports their predictions ("I think this will happen because . . . ").

Prediction	Support

Evaluative Level (fiction): Predict, Support, and Confirm or Change

Students replicate the following three-column chart in their reading notebooks.

Prediction	Support	Confirmed (✔) Changed (▲)

After students complete columns one and two, they read on until they either confirm their prediction by putting a check mark in column three (✔) or decide to change their prediction by putting a delta (▲). Value all logical predictions and especially praise the student for changing a prediction. You will notice children eagerly making predictions and no longer concerned about predicting exactly what is in the text.

Instructional Scaffolds for Nonfiction

Students preview the text and share words they think are important. The teacher writes these words on a whiteboard. Students use the words to write their own predictions. For example, if they are preparing to read a text about earthquakes, they may write, "I think I will learn that scientists are able to predict where earthquakes will occur and how strong they will be." During and after reading, students underline the ideas from their predictions that were confirmed in the text and add new information they did not predict.

For Advanced Readers: Students preview the text and record key words or ideas in their notebooks. Students use these ideas to write a few questions. During and after reading, students answer their own questions and share the questions not answered in the text. The unanswered questions could be assigned as research.

Make Connections

When readers make connections, they enhance their comprehension as long as they do not "bird walk," or get carried away with their connections and fail to realize their thinking is leading them away from the text rather than deeper into it. Expect fluent readers to analyze their connections to determine how the connection helped them understand the text.

Literal Level (fiction or nonfiction)

STEP 1: Insert a sticky note where students should be able to make a connection. Students write their connection on the sticky note. Accept any connection the students make. If children have trouble making a connection, prompt by saying, "Does this remind you of something you have done?" or "Can you remember a time when you felt the same as this character?"

> "In fact, deep comprehension is greatly impaired—if not impossible—if the reader is unable to construct mental bridges between the author's message and the reader's experiences."
>
> Dorn et al. (2005), *Teaching for Deep Comprehension*, p. 9

If students have difficulty making connections, it is usually because they have not shared the same experiences. I once worked with a boy who was reading a story about flying a kite. He couldn't make a connection because he had never flown a kite. I asked him if he had ever flown a paper airplane. He smiled at me and was able to use his paper airplane experience to make a connection to how the character in the story felt when he was successful in getting his kite to fly.

STEP 2: Do not flag the text for the students. Students should mark the place where they make a connection and record the page number and connection on a chart in their reading notebooks.

Scaffold #1 (literal level)

Page #	Connection: This reminds me of . . .

Interpretive Level (fiction or nonfiction)

As students read, they record their connections in their reading notebook and classify the connection as one of the following:

❋ **Text-to-Self** (T-S) reminds the reader of an experience he or she has had.

❋ **Text-to-Text** (T-T) reminds the reader of another text he or she has read.

❋ **Text-to-World** (T-W) reminds the reader of knowledge he or she has about the subject through movies, videos, conversations, experience, classroom instruction, etc. (Keene, 1997)

Scaffold #2 (interpretive level)

Page #	My connection	Type T-S, T-T, T-W

Evaluative Level (fiction or nonfiction)

Students now evaluate their connections and share how the connection helped them understand the story. Connections should enhance comprehension and not distract the reader. For example, a book about saving whales might remind them of the movie *Free Willy*. That is a connection that will likely enhance their understanding. However, if they start to think about the popcorn they had when they watched the movie, they are straying from the text.

Connections commonly help a reader visualize. For example, if I am reading a text about Washington, D.C., I'll immediately make connections to the monuments I have visited and the traffic I have experienced. I'll be able to visualize the scene. Connections also help readers understand how a character feels. If the story has a character who is embarrassed about being chubby, I would connect to the character's feelings because I was chubby as a child. A third way connections enhance comprehension is through prediction. As I am reading historical fiction, I make connections that help me predict upcoming events. Also, I may predict how a romance novel might end because the story reminds me of other novels I have read with similar story lines.

Scaffold #3 (evaluative level)

Page #	My Connection	How it enhanced my understanding: Visualize (V) Predict (P) Understand character's feelings (F)

For Advanced Readers: Ask students to make four columns in their notebooks. In the first they write the page where they made a connection. In the second, they write their connection. In the third, they should code their connection (T-S, T-T, or T-W). In the last column they reflect on their connection and write how it enhanced their comprehension.

Scaffold #4 (for advanced readers)

Page #	My connection	Type T-S, T-T, T-W	How it enhanced my understanding: Visualize (V), Predict (P) Understand character's Feelings (F)

Ask Questions

Questioning is a critical comprehension strategy that helps readers construct and extend meaning. It is one of the most powerful strategies students can learn, and one of the easiest for you to teach. Questions can be asked and answered before, during, and after guided reading. Before students read, they can ask questions as they preview the text. During guided reading, students jot down their questions to clarify and extend their comprehension. After they read, students share their questions with their group and call on other group members to answer them.

All the following scaffolds can be used with either fiction or nonfiction, but it is best to introduce this strategy with fiction. Some of the ideas have been adapted from the Question-Answer-Response questions developed by Raphael (1982). By classifying the types of questions as green, yellow, and red, students—even first graders—are able to distinguish between questions that are literal and interpretive. I often use a stop light to explain the differences among the questions.

> **"A reader with no questions might just as well abandon the book."**
>
> Harvey and Goudvis (2000), *Strategies That Work*, p. 82

Green questions are answered in one place in the book. The reader can go directly to the text and find the answer. Yellow questions require more thought to construct. The answer is still in the text but can't be found in just one place, instead the reader must use several paragraphs or pages to answer the question. Examples of yellow questions are those that ask the reader to compare, contrast, or give examples. Finally, the red questions are interpretive and evaluative. The answers to these questions are not found in the text. The reader uses personal experiences and background knowledge to interpret and infer.

Teachers are used to asking questions. In fact, we are quite good at it. Students, however, are used to answering questions, not asking them. At first, students may be challenged by this strategy, but with guided practice and scaffolding, they will eventually ask and answer their own questions and thereby significantly enhance their comprehension.

Teach the Syntax for Writing a Question

You may have to teach some children *how* to ask a question, especially if they are learning English as a second language. On a whiteboard, copy a simple sentence from the text. Show the students how to rearrange the words in the sentence to make a question. Then give students some sticky flags and have them mark interesting sentences as they read their guided reading books. After reading, have students share the interesting ideas they flagged and support them as they reword the sentence to ask a question. This is an *oral* task. You are trying to teach the English syntax for asking questions. Most students will not need this step.

Literal Level (fiction or nonfiction)
STEP 1: Turning Facts Into Questions

Use the green question cards (page 215) and the information on the following pages to teach students how to write a question that is answered "right there" in the text. Students make two columns in their notebook, one for "Facts" and one for "Questions." As students read the text, they write a fact from the story in the first column. Then they turn the fact into a question and write it in the second column. After reading, students close their books and take turns asking their questions and calling on other members of the group to answer them. If no one in the group can answer the question, the children are permitted to look back in the text for the answer. The purpose of this activity is to help children see that asking questions helps them recall information. It is the same procedure we use when studying for an exam. We create questions to prepare for the test.

The text below is from page 11 of *Sounds of the Night* (People's Education).

Night Flyers

Shadow Hunters
Although they may look sweet with their heart-shaped faces, barn owls are some of nature's finest hunters. These owls are experts at grabbing their prey at night. Their bodies are built for hunting. To find their dinner, owls have to have good hearing. In addition, they have to be able to sneak up on their prey. The barn owl can handle this too!

Amazing Owl Ears
Like other birds, owls hear through ears. A bird's ears are made to cut down on wind noise when the bird flies. However, a barn owl's ears are designed especially for hunting. They detect even the faintest sound. They can hear the tiniest mouse squeak half a mile away!

Example of Fact-Question Response:

Fact	Questions
These owls are experts at grabbing their prey at night.	When do barn owls eat?
To find their dinner, owls have to have good hearing.	What do owls use to find their food?

STEP 2: Ask Green Questions (literal)

Students should know how to do Step 1 before you try this step. Students make two columns in their notebooks, one for "Question" and one for "Answer." This time as students read, they stop and write a green question (column 1) that is answered in the text. They no longer need to write the fact. Then they close their books and write the answer to their question (column 2). Requiring students to close their books to write their answer prevents students from copying directly from the text. During the sharing and discussion, children take turns asking their questions to the group. They should first try to answer the question with their books closed. Only allow them to look back in the text if no one can answer the question (or to confirm an answer). You are sending the message that comprehension is understanding what you read, not finding answers.

> ### Green Questions
> The answer is found in one place in the text. I can GO directly to the text and find the answer to this kind of question.
>
> Who . . .   When . . .
> What . . .   How . . .
> Where . . .

Example of Green Question - Answer Response

Question (green)	Answer
How do barn owls find their prey?	They use their good sense of hearing.

Red Questions

The question is not answered directly in the text. I must stop and think about the passage and what I know to help me answer this question.

I wonder why . . .   Why would . . .
How could . . .   What if . . .
What would have happened if . . .

Interpretive Level (fiction or nonfiction)
STEP 3: Ask Red Questions (inferential)

The answers to these questions are not found in the text. The reader needs to infer the answer using text clues and prior knowledge. As students read, they use the text to ask questions that begin with the words "I wonder why . . ." or "How would . . . ." Since the answer is not explicitly stated in the text, there can be more than one logical answer. Guide students to ask questions that *could be* answered using background knowledge and the information in the text. When students share their questions, encourage them to think of more than one logical answer to the question. At first students only need to write a red question without writing the answer. After spending a couple of days praising students for writing red questions, you should require them to write an answer to their question in their notebooks. Encourage risks by valuing divergent thinking and different answers. Here is an example of Red Question/Answer for the same passage, "Night Flyers."

Question (red)	Answer
Why do barn owls hunt at night?	Student 1: *They are nocturnal animals so they sleep during the day.* (The answer is not in the text so students must use prior knowledge to make an inference.) Student 2: *Maybe the animals they like to eat only come out at night.* (This child did not know owls were nocturnal so he made a different inference.)
How are barn owls especially built for hunting?	*I think they are good at hunting because they can glide without flapping their wings. Their prey can't hear the owl coming. Plus they have big, sharp claws to grab their food.*

STEP 4: Ask Yellow Questions (complex)

The yellow questions require the reader to use different portions of text to ask and then answer questions. These questions include cause/effect, compare/contrast, and idea-to-examples. This is a challenging task for most students and should only be introduced when children are proficient at asking green and red questions. Be sure to model *how* to ask these kinds of questions. Then consider the steps you should take to scaffold this strategy. If students have trouble asking cause-and-effect questions, use the scaffolds described later in this chapter for teaching cause-and-effect relationships.

Yellow Question

Compare: How are ___ and ___ alike?

Contrast: How are ___ & ___ different?

What were the differences . . .?

Cause/Effect: What caused . . .?

What were the effects . . .?

Example of Yellow Question-Answer Response

Question (yellow)	Answer
How are the barn owl's ears different from a bird's ears?	The bird's ears are designed to reduce wind noise, but the owl's ears are designed to hear every sound.

STEP 5: Combine Questions

Once students know how to ask at least two kinds of questions, expand the comprehension process by requiring them to think of different kinds of questions. To increase the challenge, you can include other comprehension strategies you have already taught. By combining strategies you are replicating the reading process of proficient readers. Proficient readers don't solely ask questions as they read; they use a variety of strategies to help them construct meaning.

Ask Green and Red Questions: Students make two columns in their notebooks. As they read, they must think of a green question (column 1) and a red question (column 2). If students finish reading the text before the time is up, they should think of more questions to ask the group. During share time, students can choose one of their questions to ask the group. Before the group answers the question, the students must first decide if it is a red question or a green question. This reinforces the fact that green questions need to be answered with the information in the book and red questions require the reader to think and use background knowledge.

Question-Answer & Connection or Prediction: Using a three-column framework, students write a question (either red, green, or yellow) in column 1, their answer in column 2, and a connection or prediction in column three. You can use this framework in a variety of ways to encourage students to combine asking questions with other reading strategies you have already taught them. Students might write a question, write their answer, and then offer an opinion about the text they read. The chart that follows shows only a few of the possibilities.

Green Question	Answer	Connection/Prediction
Red Question	Answer	Connection/Prediction
Question	Answer	Summary
Question	Answer	Opinion

Evaluative Level (fiction or nonfiction)

At the evaluative level, students use the text to think of a question that asks for an opinion or judgment. Questions might begin with "Why do you think . . .? Do you agree (or disagree) that . . .? Do you think it was right for . . .?"

Question Cards

Adapted from QAR strategy, Raphael (1982)

Directions: Distribute a question card to each student. Begin with green questions and gradually work towards red and yellow questions.

Green Questions

The answer is found in one place in the text. I can **GO** directly to the text and find the answer to this kind of question.

Who . . . ?	*When . . . ?*
What . . . ?	*How . . . ?*
Where . . . ?	

Yellow Questions

The answer is found by searching several places in the text. I must **slow down** and **look** in more than one place in the text to answer this kind of question.

Compare: How are _____ & _____ similar?
Contrast: How are _____ & _____ different?
What are the differences between _____ & _____?
Cause & Effect: What caused . . . ? What was the effect of . . . ?
Main idea/details: What are some examples of . . . ?

Red Questions

The question is not answered directly in the text. I must **stop** and think about the passage and what I know to help me answer this question.

I wonder why . . .	*Why would . . . ?*
Why do you think . . . ?	*How could . . . ?*
What would have happened if . . . ?	*What if . . . ?*
Do you think it was right for . . . ?	

The Next Step in Guided Reading © 2009 by Jan Richardson, Scholastic Professional

Determine Importance

This strategy is important when reading any genre or texts from any subject area. Students cannot possibly remember every single word they read. Instead they must learn to distinguish between important ideas that need to be remembered and information that may be interesting but isn't critical to understanding the overall meaning.

Determining Importance With Fiction

When you identify this as your focus strategy, I suggest you teach it first with fiction. The following scaffolds help students identify important actions, events, feelings, and themes. Students should understand the process at the literal level before you expect them to do it at the interpretive or evaluative levels.

> " Simply put, readers of nonfiction have to decide and remember what is important in the texts they read if they are going to learn anything from them."
>
> Harvey & Goudvis (2000). *Strategies That Work*, p. 118

VIP Strategy (Very Important Part)

Sometimes children are able to recall what they have read, but they have trouble identifying the important parts. By trying to recall every single event or detail, they miss the primary message of the text. The VIP strategy is a scaffold that helps students identify the Very Important Part. I have listed scaffolds for teaching it at the literal, interpretive, and evaluative levels.

Literal Level

STEP 1: Distribute small sticky notes or flags and tell students to mark the most important sentence after they read one or two pages. Explain that it is not necessary to remember every single word they read, but they do need to remember the important parts. Usually, the important part contains an action that a character takes in the story. Be prepared for differing opinions on what each student thinks in the most important part. As long as students can support their reasoning, accept the response.

STEP 2: Instead of identifying the VIP after one or two pages, extend the task to include a short chapter. Students flag the VIP sentence in each chapter and then paraphrase the action or idea in their notebooks.

If you use a short chapter book designed for guided reading, prompt students to consider the title of the chapter and the illustrations to determine the Very Important Part. During individual conferences, clarify confusions by asking why the student marked a particular sentence. You might say, "Why did you pick that part as the VIP?

What you were thinking?" Sometimes children miss the important part because they misunderstand the action or draw faulty conclusions. When their response is not what you were expecting, always prompt students to tell you what they were thinking so you can analyze their thought process and provide appropriate support.

Interpretive Level—Analyze the internal story.

STEP 1: Students read a chapter and decide the VIP of the *internal* story. The internal story involves the feelings and relationships of the characters. The student must make inferences to determine the internal VIP. The prompt would be, "What is the Very Important Part of the character's feelings in this chapter? What are you thinking?"

STEP 2: Students identify a VIP for both the internal and external story. This encourages thoughtful reading. Students should ask themselves, "What is the most important action (external) and the most important relationship or feeling (internal) in this chapter?" If a student does not identify the same VIP you did, it does not mean the student is wrong. Ask students to explain their reasoning and encourage different responses. The goal is deeper comprehension, not imitation of the teacher's thinking.

Evaluative Level—Evaluate both the internal and external stories.

Once students finish reading the story, they consider the VIPs they have identified for each chapter and select one external and one internal VIP for the entire book. Now they must make a judgment as to the most important event (external) and the most important character change or feeling (internal) and explain their reasoning.

Other Scaffolds for Determining Importance

There are a variety of ways to help students determine importance when reading fiction. Some of the following scaffolds target the literal level of comprehension; others focus on the interpretive or evaluative level. Choose the approach that best meets your students' needs.

* **Who and What? (Literal):** This scaffold helps students focus on important characters and their actions. As students read a page or two, they stop and write "Who" was the most important character in this section and "What" was the most important action or event.

* **Be the Illustrator (Interpretive):** Students play the role of the illustrator. Select a book with few illustrations (or cover the illustrations with large sticky notes). As students read a short chapter, they stop and sketch what they think was most

important.

✳ **Create Your Own Title (Interpretive):** Select a short chapter book that does not have titles (or cover the titles with sticky notes). After children read a chapter, they must write their own title. Prompt students to think about the illustrations and the "who and what" from the chapter to create an appropriate title. It is not important for students to think of the exact title the author used. Often I find the student titles to be as good as the ones in the book.

✳ **Important/Interesting (Evaluative):** Students use two-column notes to record facts that are important and facts that are interesting but not important. This activity requires they evaluate the chapter and formulate personal opinions. Of course, the goal is not for students to agree but for students to think as they read. Expect a lively discussion during the last five minutes of the lesson as students share their opinions and try to convince other members of the group that their ideas are right. Divergent thinking leads to interesting discussions.

✳ **Identify the Theme (Evaluative):** Students read a poem, a short story, or a chapter of a novel and identify the theme. A theme is a general message that is communicated through the characters, their actions, and events. Often a theme in fiction is a lesson to be learned, such as "always tell the truth" or "friends can help people cope with tragedy." The theme may be stated or implied, but the clues to the theme tend to recur in the book. Classical literature often has a rich theme and provides an appropriate challenge for advanced readers.

The following prompts lead children to understand and discover themes in fiction:

♦ How does the title of the passage relate to the theme?

♦ What do you want to remember about this passage?

♦ What moral or lesson does the text teach?

♦ What is the main idea of the text?

♦ Why did the author write this story? What point is author trying to make?

Determining Importance With Nonfiction

Once students understand how to determine importance with fiction, it is appropriate to introduce the strategy using nonfiction texts. Students will learn to use text clues such as headings, repeated words, and illustrations to identify main ideas and important details. At the literal level students find the main idea that is stated in the passage. When the text does not have headings or the main idea is not clearly stated, students must use interpretive and evaluative skills to determine importance.

VIP (Literal)

Choose books with headings and demonstrate how to use the heading to determine the Very Important Part. Distribute flags and have students mark the most important sentence in the section. Prompt students to find the sentence that includes important words from the heading, repeated words, and possibly words in boldface type.

Main Idea Question/Details (Literal)

Use books with headings and show students how to turn a heading into a question. Students write this "main idea" question on the left side of the T-chart. As they read each sentence, they should reread their question and decide whether they learned any information that answers that question. If so, students write the detail (in bullet form) under the right side of the T-chart. Teaching children how to bullet ideas helps them capture the most important ideas without copying from the text.

Example of a Main Idea/Details chart

Text: *Oceans and Seas* by Catherine Chambers, pp. 10–11 (Heinemann)

Looking Below the Surface

The ocean basin

The ocean **basin** goes down in steps. The steps get deeper as they get further from the continents. The first step is called the **continental shelf**. It runs from the shores or continents and into the oceans for an average of 43 miles (75 kilometers). In some places though, there is hardly any shelf at all. The waters plunge almost straight down from the continents to a great depth. In other places, the continental shelf stretches out 930 miles (1,500 kilometers).

The second step is called the continental **slope**. It goes down about 8,200 feet (2,500 meters).

The third part is the continental rise. This is a slope of thick sediment made of rock, soil, **minerals**, and the remains of plants and animals.

The fourth part of the ocean is a very deep area of flat plains with many mountains. Most mountains lie in chains that form ridges running nearly 4,000 miles (6,500 kilometers) along the ocean floor. Deep trenches plunge from the ridges. The deepest part of the oceans is the Mariana Trench in the Pacific, which plunges 35,840 feet (10,924 meters). Trenches separate the ocean floor into **plates**, which are slowly moving apart. Earthquakes and volcanoes are common in many of the areas where plates meet.

Main-Idea Question	Details
What makes up the ocean basin?	Continental shelf, continental slope, continental rise, and ocean floor

Since this text is rich in facts about the parts of the ocean basin, you can ask students to write a question about each part of the basin and record important details. Teach students how to write in bullets. This is a valuable note-taking skill they will use throughout their educational career. During the last five minutes of your lesson, students take turns retelling a section by using the bullets to create complete sentences.

Main-Idea Question	Details
What is the continental shelf?	• Meets the shores of continents • Can stretch for miles or plunge quickly
What is the continental slope?	• Second step of the ocean • 8,200 feet deep
What is the continental rise?	• Thick sediment • Rock, soil, and minerals
What is the ocean floor?	• Plains and mountains • Deep trenches separate plates • Earthquakes and volcanoes

Main-Idea Question-Details (Interpretive)

To encourage deeper thinking, use a text without headings or cover the headings with sticky note tape. Students write their own main idea questions using clues from the text such as bold and repeated words. Then they add details (in bullet form) that answer the main-idea question.

Evaluative Level Discussion

As students read, they use sticky note flags to mark important sentences. After reading, they share the points they marked and justify their answers. "I think this is the most important part because . . . " Students are encouraged to challenge each other.

For Advanced Readers: Use three-column notes to combine this strategy with others you have taught. The goal is to prompt students to think about the text in a variety of ways to deepen their understanding.

Main Idea	Details	Question
Main Idea	Details	Summary
Main Idea	Details	Connection

> " Deep comprehension is the result of the mind's analyzing and synthesizing multiple sources of information, thus lifting a reader's comprehension to new levels of meaning."
>
> Dorn et al. (2005), *Teaching for Deep Comprehension*, p. 14.

Summarize

Beware! Summarizing is one of the toughest strategies for students to learn, and one of the most difficult to teach. You must repeatedly model it, provide scaffolds, and gradually release your support until the students can summarize independently.

One of the following usually happens when you ask students to summarize:

* They write too much.

* They do not capture the most important ideas.

* They do not write enough.

* They copy word for word.

What should *students do when they summarize?*

* Identify key words and phrases.

* Pull out main ideas.

* Write enough to convey the gist of the passage.

* Write succinctly.

A summary is a higher-level response than a retelling because the reader must synthesize information and prepare a condensed account that covers the main points. The goal is for students to write a summary that is clear, complete, and concise. Teaching children how to summarize is perhaps one of the most important (and complex) strategies. Proficient readers use many comprehension strategies to construct a summary. They ask questions, make inferences, and determine the important words. Therefore, it is best to teach children how to retell and determine importance **before** you teach them how to summarize.

Summarize Fiction

It is harder to summarize than it is to retell. Students must analyze all the events and select only those that are essential to the story. One scaffold that helps students identify the main character, the problem, and the resolution is the Somebody-Wanted-But-So scaffold (Macon, Bewell, & Vogt, 1991). Although this strategy is included with early and transitional guided reading, it is still appropriate to use it with fluent readers when they read a short story.

Somebody-Wanted-But-So

After reading a short text or chapter, students write a single sentence telling who was the main character (**somebody**), what the character **wanted** (goal), **but** there was a problem, **so** this is how the problem was solved (solution). As the students continue reading, they extend their summary by adding "then" and writing a second Somebody-Wanted-But-So statement. Here is an example for the story of Rumpelstiltskin:

> The King wanted the miller's daughter to spin straw into gold, but she didn't know how, so Rumpelstiltskin spun the straw into gold in return for her firstborn child.
> Then, The King married the girl, and they had a baby. Rumpelstiltskin wanted the baby, but the Queen didn't want to give it to him, so Rumpelstiltskin agreed that she could keep the baby if she could guess his name. Then the queen wanted to keep her baby, but she couldn't guess his name, so she sent a spy to trick him and learned his real name.

Synthesize (Interpretive)

Although summaries are confined to the information stated in the text, you can push summarizing to an interpretive level by teaching students how to add their thoughts to the important information to form a synthesis. When readers synthesize fiction, they summarize the story and add what the story means to them. This response chart will help students synthesize each chapter as they read a short text for guided reading.

Chapter	**Summary:** What was the most important thing that happened?	**What does this chapter mean to you?**
1		
2		

Summarizing Nonfiction

Because this is such a difficult strategy for most students, I have listed specific steps that provide for a gradual release of your support. As you take students through the four steps, they will learn how to identify key words and use them to create a clear, complete, and concise summary. At the interpretive level, students learn how to draw conclusions by adding prior knowledge to their summaries.

Key Word/Summary (Literal)

As students read a text, they record key words and use them to compose a summary. This is the best scaffold for teaching students how to summarize nonfiction, but it should be taught after they have learned how to determine importance. The following steps provide for a gradual release of support—how long you stay at each step depends upon the group.

STEP 1: Write the key words (with initial letters provided). Select a text that clearly states key words (they may even be bold). Give students the initial letters for the key words. Tell them to read the text and write the key words that begin with those letters. Remind them the key words are related to the heading and may be supported by illustrations. During the discussion portion of the lesson, discuss why the words are important and create a summary using the key words.

STEP 2: Write the key words (without initial letter support). Now tell students they must find the key words in the passage without knowing the initial letter. Prompt them to think about words that are repeated, words that are bold, and words from the title to determine the key words of the passage. As you work with individual students, you will probably need to help some of them by providing the first letter for the key word. After reading, students take turns sharing one of the key words they selected. They do not have to agree on the key words, but they should be able to support their choices. Create the summary together as a group.

STEP 3: Write the key words and a summary. Students read the text, write three to five key words or phrases, and use the key words to compose their own summaries. They have already been exposed to several models by this time. As students prepare their summaries, have them underline the key words and remind them to use all the key words in their summaries. You will probably spend several days at this scaffold level. It is imperative that children write their summaries in their own words. This is the level at which you work on clarity and completeness. The summaries need to make sense (be clear) while including all the key words/ideas (be complete). Do not worry about length. That comes with Step 4.

STEP 4: Revise the summary to make it concise. Students continue to identify key words and write their summaries, but now the focus is on revising their first draft and eliminating unnecessary words. Aim for fewer than 20 words per summary.

Scaffold for Summarizing

Directions: As you read the passage, record three or four key words/phrases. Use the key words/phrases to write a sentence that succinctly summarizes the passage. Use one box for each section of text.

Key Words:

_____   _____

_____   _____

Summary:

Key Words:

_____   _____

_____   _____

Summary:

Key Words:

_____   _____

_____   _____

Summary:

Draw Conclusions (Interpretive)

When readers draw a conclusion, they use information in the text and add background knowledge to stretch their thinking and deepen their understanding. The chart below is one example of how students can organize what they've read and what they know to draw conclusions. In the first column, students summarize the most important ideas in a text. In the second, students write background information that relates to the text. In the third, they apply their prior knowledge to the summary to create a new generalization or inference.

I taught this strategy to a group of fifth graders who were advanced readers. They read a short informational text from *Aliens and UFOs* (McGraw-Hill/Jamestown Education, 2002). I asked them to stop three times as they read the story to summarize, record their background knowledge (connections), and draw their own conclusions. This was the first part of the text they read:

UFOs Over Washington

It was a hot July evening in 1952. Air traffic was slow at Washington National Airport. Only one radar operator was on duty. At 11:40 P.M., he stifled a yawn and stared at his nearly empty radar screen. Suddenly, his eyes grew wide. A group of seven blips—targets had appeared, moving across the skies at 100-130 miles per hour. By looking at their position on the radar screen, he could tell they were southwest of Andrews Air Force Base in nearby Maryland. In a way they looked like slow airplanes flying in formation. But no planes were due in the area. Suddenly, two of the blips shot across the screen, and out of range. The radar operator, blinked in amazement. No airplane he knew about could move that fast! "Hey, come look at this!" he called to his supervisor. The senior controller took one look at the radar screen and called over two more men. Everyone agreed that the targets were not airplanes. But if they weren't airplanes, what could they possibly be?

Summary I read. . .	Background knowledge I know . . .	Conclusion Now I'm thinking . . .
A radar operator reported strange blips on his radar screen that resembled airplanes flying at 100–130 mph.	I know helicopters travel slower than airplanes.	The blips weren't airplanes. Perhaps they were helicopters or solid parts of an explosion.

Another framework for teaching students how to draw inferences is "If . . . Then . . . " At first, you could provide the "I" part of the statement and the students would read the text and add their conclusion (Then . . .). Eventually, you should expect students to create their own "If . . . Then . . . " statements. When selecting a text for this activity, consider your students' background knowledge and experiences. If they do not have prior knowledge about the topic, they will have difficulty drawing conclusions.

Cause-and-Effect Relationships

The purpose of the following activities is to teach students how to search for cause-and-effect relationships that are stated or implied in a text. The following steps provide for a gradual release of teacher support and foster independence.

Model: As with every reading strategy, you should always model the *process* you use to think of a cause or effect question. Basically, you locate an effect in the text and turn it into a question. Here are a few paragraphs from "War: What happens when nations don't work it out?" (Harvey & Goudvis, 2007).

> War is the worst kind of conflict of all. It's bad enough when a few people fight. But when entire countries can't get along, the results are horrible. The weapons of war are frightening—tanks, bombs, missiles, jet fighters. In wartime, people are killed. Homes, businesses, and schools are destroyed. The countryside may be ruined. In the 20th century alone, wars killed more than 160 million people. And countless others were wounded or left homeless. Why can't nations work out their conflicts before they turn to war? Despite the horrors, people have always fought wars. They have fought for many different reasons. Nations fight to defend themselves or other nations from attack. They fight because they want something another nation has, such as land. They fight because they believe they are right and the other nation is wrong. Sometimes groups within a nation fight against each other. This is called a civil war.

This is the process you want to teach your students: Find a sentence that has an effect such as "*They have fought for many different reasons.*" Then turn the sentence into a question such as "*What causes nations to fight each other?*"

Text selection: Most historical and scientific texts are ideal for teaching this strategy, but it is always important to read the text to ensure it contains cause-and-effect relationships.

Literal Level: Students find a cause-and-effect relationship stated in the text.

STEP 1: The teacher flags the effect. Before students read the text, insert sticky flags directly on sentences that contain the effect. Students can have the same or different effects flagged in their books. Whenever the students come to a sticky flag, they must write a "What caused . . ." question using the effect flagged in the text. After the students write their question in their notebooks, they should write the answer. The answer, which is the cause, is in the book. After students write their "What caused . . ." questions, they continue to read the entire section of text to prepare for the discussion. During the last five minutes of the lesson, students take turns asking their "What caused . . ." questions and calling on members of the group to answer the question. Tell students to raise their thumbs if they remember the answer. If they don't remember, they should look back in the text and find the answer.

STEP 2: The teacher flags the paragraph that contains a cause/effect relationship. Before reading, insert sticky flags in the margin of a paragraph that contains a cause-and-effect relationship. The discussion is richer if each student has a different paragraph flagged in his or her text; however, the students are responsible for reading the entire passage, not just the paragraph flagged in their books. Whenever the students come to a paragraph that is flagged, they know to read for a cause-and-effect relationship. Basically, they read each sentence and determine whether they can ask a "What caused . . ." question from that sentence. If they can, they write the question in their notebooks and answer it. During the discussion, students take turns asking their "What caused . . ." questions and calling on other members of the group to answer the questions.

STEP 3: The teacher flags a page that contains a cause/effect relationship. Prepare for the lesson by flagging a different page for each student. Tell students they must read the entire selection, but they are responsible for writing a "What caused . . ." question for the page that is flagged in their book. Students must read each sentence critically to decide whether it could be turned into a "What caused . . ." question. Even though the students only write a "What caused . . ." question for one page, they are responsible for reading the entire chapter or section to prepare for the discussion. As before, students take turns asking their question during the discussion portion of the lesson (last five minutes).

As you work with individuals, ask them to tell you about the passage. Then ask them to show you a sentence that contains an effect. If necessary, help them identify the effect or turn it into a question. Remind students they must always write the answer to their question using their own words. Students who copy answers from the book are not extending their comprehension.

Interpretive Level: Students find cause-and-effect relationships implied in the text.

At this level, students must make connections to their prior knowledge to find a cause-and-effect relationship that is not clearly stated but needs to be inferred. Here is an example from the text about war. One sentence reads, "The countryside may be ruined."

This is an effect that can be turned into a question: "What causes the countryside to be ruined during war?" The text doesn't directly answer this, but we infer that bombs or missiles contaminate the land and destroy crops.

Here is a second example: The text says, "Sometimes groups within a nation fight against each other." The cause question would be "What causes groups within a nation to fight against each other?" Again the text doesn't say, but we use our background knowledge about civil wars to answer.

To teach this process, flag a specific paragraph for each student. Explain they are to write a "What caused . . ." question that is not answered in the text but can be inferred using their background knowledge. As before, students take turns asking their "What caused . . ." questions during the discussion portion of the lesson. Students will have a variety of answers for these questions since the cause is not stated and they bring different experiences to the process. Value all responses and praise students for taking risks.

Evaluative Level: Students share cause-and-effect relationships and determine whether they are literal (in the book) or inferred (in one's head).

Now that students understand how to identify cause-and-effect relationships, they record these relationships on a three-column chart. They write the cause in the first column and the effect in the second. In the third column they identify whether the relationship is stated (in the book) or inferred (in one's head). This is the most challenging level, so you will probably need to prompt and scaffold students. You might point to a specific paragraph and say, "There is a cause-and-effect relationship in this paragraph—see if you can find it." During the discussion, students turn their cause/effect relationship into a question to ask their peers. After students answer the question, they discuss whether the answer was in the book (literal) or in their heads (inferred).

Cause	Effect	**In the book** or **In my head**

Character Analysis

There are many levels of character analysis. Kindergarten and first-grade students can discuss the hen's feelings when reading "The Little Red Hen," and advanced readers in fifth grade can analyze Jim's motivation for selling his gold watch in O. Henry's "The Gift of the Magi." Most fluent readers have little trouble discerning a character's feelings, but they may need support in identifying character traits.

> **"A book's characters are at the center of multiple relationships; this suggests that deep comprehension is dependent on the reader's ability to infer and analyze characters."**
>
> Dorn et al. (2005), *Teaching for Deep Comprehension*, p. 22

Explain the difference between a feeling and a trait. A feeling is an emotion that changes, but a trait describes what the character is like on the inside. The trait does not usually change in a story. Before students are ready to try this strategy during guided reading, they will need many whole-group experiences learning the definitions for a variety of character traits. One effective way to teach character traits and increase vocabulary is to introduce one trait a week and connect the trait to familiar people in current events, well-known fiction, and fairy tales, or to famous people discussed in the content areas.

Manyak (2007) recommends a schoolwide approach to teaching character trait vocabulary. Each grade level is responsible for teaching about 20 traits. These traits should be explained during read-alouds, shared reading, and guided reading. If a school follows this plan, students will leave fifth grade knowing 120 character traits. If this is your first year implementing this plan, each grade will likely have to introduce traits at the lower grades before they can effectively teach the ones assigned to their grade level.

To teach these traits in kindergarten and first grade, connect the trait to a well-known person or familiar storybook character. For example, use a picture of Curious George to teach "curious," the Selfish Giant to teach "selfish," and Abraham Lincoln to teach "honest." For grades 2–5, create a character-trait chart and add a new trait and example each week. The following chart was developed by fourth graders:

Character Trait	Synonyms	Example
Tolerant	Understanding	Louis Armstrong
Mischievous	Naughty	White Witch of Narnia
Optimistic	Positive	Dr. Martin Luther King, Jr.
Malicious	Evil	Lord Voldemort
Admirable	Praiseworthy	Roberto Clemente
Persistent	Determined	Nancy Drew
Spiteful	Hateful	Nazi soldier

Recommended Character Traits by Grade Level (Manyak, 2007)	
Grade	**Recommended character-trait vocabulary**
K	brave, careful, cheerful, clever, confident, considerate, curious, dishonest, foolish, gloomy, grumpy, honest, intelligent, impatient, irresponsible, patient, reliable, selfish, ungrateful, wicked
First	arrogant, calm, cautious, considerate, cowardly, courageous, cruel, dependable, fearless, ferocious, gullible, humble, inconsiderate, loyal, mischievous, miserable, optimistic, pessimistic, undependable, wise
Second	argumentative, bold, careless, conceited, envious, faithful, independent, insensitive, irritable, modest, predictable, self-assured, sensible, stern, sympathetic, supportive, timid, unpredictable
Third	admirable, appreciative, carefree, demanding, indecisive, egotistical, innocent, insensitive, irritable, modest, persistent, prudent, rambunctious, rash, sensitive, spiteful, sympathetic, tolerant, trustworthy, unsympathetic
Fourth	assertive, cordial, cunning, defiant, fickle, haughty, hesitant, indifferent, meek, menacing, noble, perceptive, pompous, reckless, ruthless, skeptical, submissive, surly, unassuming, uncompromising
Fifth	apprehensive, compliant, corrupt, cross, depraved, dignified, discreet, docile, ethical, frank, glum, ingenious, lackadaisical, malicious, plucky, prudent, rebellious, selfless, sheepish, sullen
Sixth	abrupt, amiable, callous, candid, cantankerous, capricious, confrontational, cynical, devoted, eloquent, erratic, forlorn, gallant, impish, incredulous, pitiless, uncooperative, unflappable, unyielding, whimsical

Action-Character Trait Link (Interpretive)

Once students understand a variety of words that define characters, they can do the following activity during guided reading. As they read a story, they list a character's action in the first column and list a character trait that those actions reveal in the second. Most students will need a list of possible traits from which to choose. Keep a list of traits you have taught near the guided reading table for students to use as a reference.

Action	Character Trait
Jim secretly sold his watch to buy a present for his wife.	Discreet, selfless

Character-Trait Web (Interpretive)

Students put a character's name inside a circle. As they read a short story, they list traits for the character and write examples (with page numbers) from the story to support each trait. If necessary, give each student a list of character traits you have taught the class to use as a reference. Otherwise students will write common words such as *good*, *nice*, or *kind*. Challenge your students to use words that are not common. If the story has several main characters, students can choose different characters to analyze.

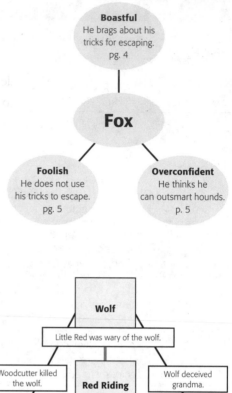

Sociogram (Interpretive)

Students use a simple graphic organizer to analyze and summarize the relationships between characters. Each square represents a character. As students read, they evaluate actions and dialogue to infer the important relationships.

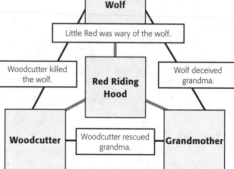

Character's Motivation (Evaluative)

This strategy is an excellent challenge for advanced readers because they must make inferences to determine why a character acts a certain way. To prepare for the lesson, use sticky flags to mark specific actions of characters in the text. As students read the story and come to the flag, they stop and list the action that occurred in the text. Then they reflect on the character's action and write what motivated the character to act in that way. It is not unusual for students to list different motivations for the same action.

Character's Action What did s/he do?	Motivation Why did s/he do it?

Make Inferences

Authors often expect the reader to draw a conclusion not clearly stated in the text. The writer gives hints or clues that lead the reader to make an inference about a character or an event. The reader needs to use these clues and personal connections to construct a deeper understanding of the text. This process is called *inferring*. When you **infer**, you go beyond the surface details to see other meanings the details suggest or *imply* but are not stated in the text. The clues are in the text, but the connections and the final inferences are in the reader's mind.

For years I struggled with how to teach inference. Even after multiple demonstrations and think-alouds, some of my students still struggled with this strategy. I remember telling them they had to "read between the lines." They didn't have a clue about what that meant. I finally had a breakthrough while reading *Teaching Reading in Middle School* (Robb, 2000). Robb explains how readers must access a variety of clues authors give us to imply information. By drawing attention to these text clues, I was finally able to help my students understand the process of inferring. Authors leave clues that help us discover implied meanings in the following four ways:

* Dialogue between characters

* Actions a character decides to take

* Physical descriptions of characters

* Inner thoughts of characters that are not spoken as dialogue

> " . . . quoting the great writer Umberto Eco, 'Reading is the taking of inferential walks. The text offers point A and point E, and the reader must walk points B, C, and D to reach point E.' Reading of all kinds requires continual inference-making, because so much of what an author communicates is not directly stated."
>
> Jeff Wilhelm (2001), *Improving Comprehension with Think-Aloud Strategies*, p. 25

Make Inferences From Dialogue (including speaker tags)

Background: The reader should consider the dialogue between two characters in a story and ask, "*What is the character thinking?*" or "*How did the character say those words?*" or "*How did the character feel when she said that?*" The reader uses the dialogue and personal connections to make inferences about the character. There are several ways a teacher can scaffold a student to make an inference from dialogue.

STEP 1: Understand Speaker Tags. Prompt: *How did the character say that?*
A speaker tag is the phrase that tells the reader *how* something was said. Sometimes students do not infer because they do not read the speaker tag, or they do not know the vocabulary used in the speaker tag.

Explain that speaker tags tell the reader how a character says something. The speaker tag often leads the reader into making an inference from dialogue. For example, the following dialogue draws different inferences from the speaker tag.

Example 1: "I'm not going to the mall," she giggled.

Example 2: "I'm n-n-not going to the mall?" she wailed.

Example 3: "I'm not going to the mall!" she declared in defiance.

Since it is difficult for children to read with expression if they read silently, they should whisper-read the story. Tell them to read dialogue the way the character would have said it. As you circulate among the students, listen for appropriate intonation and expression and ask, "How would the character say that? What does *whined* mean? If the character whined when she said that, how would it sound?" Students might be asked to demonstrate verbs like this (after they've had a chance to consider the definition and practice privately). Another clue to reading dialogue with expression is often found in the adverbs. Phrases such as *she said crisply* (or *savagely*, or *curiously*), give text clues that help readers make inferences from dialogue. If a student is not making an inference from a speaker tag, check to see if the tag includes an unfamiliar word.

STEP 2: Visualize Facial Expressions. Prompt: *How did the character feel when he said that? How did the character's face look when he said that?*

Use a small sticky note or flag to mark dialogue where the author expects the reader to draw an inference. Students use the dialogue to make an inference about the character's feelings by drawing the character's face on a sticky note placed next to the dialogue. As you circulate among the students, ask individual students to talk about the character's feelings. Students may need a brief lesson on how to draw various expressions such as *scared*, *angry*, *surprised*, etc.

STEP 3: Create Speech Bubbles/Thought Bubbles. Prompt: *What was the character thinking when she said that?*

Flag some dialogue in the book. Students draw a face and write something the character says in a speech bubble and what the character might be thinking in the thought bubble. If you find that students are not challenged with this strategy, you might have chosen a text that is too easy. I did this activity with ninth graders reading *Macbeth*. It was excellent for helping the students discover implied meanings in Shakespeare's plays.

STEP 4: Speech Bubbles/Thought Bubbles. Prompt:
What was the character thinking when she said that?

This time, the students flag a significant dialogue in
the book and find dialogic clues for making inferences.
They write what the character says in the speech
bubble and what the character might be thinking in
the thought bubble.

STEP 5: Two-Column Notes. Prompt: *In the book (the character said . . .) / In my head
(I think . . .)*

Students flag a line of dialogue in the book where they made an inference, record the
page number of the dialogue under the column "In the Book," and write their inference
under the column "In My Head." This is the last scaffolding step. Once students are able
to do this without your help, they understand how to make inferences from dialogue and
are ready to learn how to use other text clues.

In the Book	In My Head
p. 7	I think the character is afraid the other kids will make fun of him.

Make Inferences From a Character's Actions

Background: Often an author has a character do something in the story to help the
reader make an inference. The reader must use the text clues (actions in this case) and
personal experience (background knowledge) to make inferences. The reader should
consider specific adjectives, adverbs, or phrases that describe the character's behavior.

STEP 1: Visualize facial expressions from a character's action. Prompt: *How is the
character feeling when he does that? Describe the character's facial expressions.*

The **teacher flags** some action in the book where the reader is expected to draw an
inference. Students use the action or event to make an inference about the character's
feelings by drawing the character's face on a sticky note or on a blank sheet of paper.

STEP 2: Create thought bubbles. Prompt: *What is the **character thinking** when she
does that?*

Now the **students flag** an action in the book and write what the character is thinking
in a thought bubble.

STEP 3: Make two-column notes (In the Book/In My Head). Prompt: *What am I thinking about the character now?*

The students flag an action in the book where they made an inference from a character's actions. They write the page number under "In the Book" and their inference under "In My Head." This is the final scaffolding step for this text clue. Students are now able to make inferences from a character's actions.

Make Inferences From Physical Descriptions

Background: Sometimes authors help the reader make an inference about a character by describing what the character looks like. Words that describe a character's facial expression, body size, clothing, hair, etc., are text clues that help readers make an inference about the character.

Read Washington Irving's description of Ichabod Crane from *The Legend of Sleepy Hollow*. Notice the inferences you make about Ichabod based solely upon the author's description.

> *He was tall, but exceedingly lank, with narrow shoulders, long arms and legs, hands that dangled a mile out of his sleeves, feet that might have served for shovels, and his whole frame most loosely hung together. His head was small, and flat at top, with huge ears, large green glassy eyes, and a long snipe nose, so that it looked like a weather-cock, perched upon his spindle neck, to tell which way the wind blew.*

STEP 1: Create Two-Column Notes (In the Book/In My Head). Prompt: *What do I infer about a character as a result of the character's physical description?*

Flag a character's physical description where the reader is expected to draw an inference. Students write the page number in the left column (In the Book), and they write what they are thinking about the character in the right column (In My Head).

STEP 2: Two-Column Notes (In the Book/In My Head). Prompt: *What do I infer about a character as a result of the author's physical description of him or her?*

Now **students** flag a place where the author describes a character's physical traits. They write the page number under the column labeled "In the Book," and their inference under the column labeled, "In My Head."

Make Inferences From a Character's Inner Thoughts

Background: Authors leave clues about a character's thoughts that help readers infer. These words are not spoken in dialogue, but they let the reader know what the character is thinking. Students should study these thoughts and reflect on what they show about the character's mood, feelings, and personality.

STEP 1: Make Two-Column Notes (In the Book/In My Head). Prompt: *What do I infer about a character as a result of the character's inner thoughts?*

Flag a character's inner thoughts where the reader is expected to draw an inference. Students write the page number of the flag in the left column (In the Book), and they write their inference about the character in the right column (In My Head).

STEP 2: Make Two-Column Notes (In the Book/In My Head). Prompt: *What do I infer about a character as a result of the character's inner thoughts?*

After you've identified a passage that reflects a character's thoughts, now **students** assume responsibility for flagging a place in the book where the author describes a character's inner thoughts. They write the page number under the column labeled "In the Book" and their inference under the column labeled, "In My Head."

The following cards help students use text clues to make inferences. When you teach each text clue, distribute that card to the students to use during reading. Once you have taught students all four text clues, distribute a different card to each student. As they read, students make inferences from the text clue on the card. After reading, students discuss inferences they made.

Physical Traits	**Dialogue**
What does the character look like? How does the author describe a character's facial expression, looks, and gestures? *The character is . . .* *So I think . . .*	Why did the character say that? What is the character thinking? Visualize the character's expression and gestures. What are you thinking about the character? *When the character says . . .* *I think . . .*
Action	**Inner Thoughts**
Why did the character do that? *What might the character do next?* *I think the character does this because . . .*	What is the character thinking? Why didn't the character say this out loud? *What do the character's thoughts show you?* *The text says the character thinks . . .* *So I think . . .*

Evaluative Level: Classifying Inferences.
"At this point, students should be able not only to make an inference, but also to classify the inference. They need to be able to explain what led to that inference (dialogue, action, physical traits, inner thoughts).

STEP 1: Make Modified Two-Column Notes for Inference Classification (see chart below). Prompt: Where do I make an inference? What text clues did the author give to help me make that inference? Flag a place in the text where the reader is expected to make an inference. The students classify the inference (dialogue, action, physical traits, inner thoughts), write the page number in the left column (In the Book), and then write their inference in the right column (In My Head).

STEP 2: Now students flag a place in the text where the reader is expected to make an inference. The students identify the source of their inferences (dialogue, action, physical traits, inner thoughts), write the page number in the left column (In the Book), and then write their inference in the right column (In My Head). The following chart can be used as a scaffold for this activity.

Evaluative Scaffold for Making Inferences

Inferences from **Dialogue** (including speaker tags)	
In the Book (page #)	In My Head (I think . . .)
Inferences from **Action**	
In the Book (page #)	In My Head (I think . . .)
Inferences from **Physical Descriptions**	
In the Book (page #)	In My Head (I think . . .)
Inferences from a Character's **Inner Thoughts**	
In the Book (page #)	In My Head (I think . . .)

Comprehending Visual Information

Visual information includes pictures, diagrams, figures, maps, legends, scales, charts, graphs, time lines, etc. These text features are found in informational text because they enhance comprehension, yet most children need explicit instruction on how to read them. In *Reality Checks*, Tony Stead devotes an entire chapter to visual literacy and offers suggestions on how to teach this strategy with whole-class demonstrations.

Literal Level: What does the chart say?

The first step in teaching visual comprehension is showing students how to read a graph or chart. If students are proficient with this skill, you can skip these activities and do those described for the interpretive level.

Just the Facts

Students record facts they learn from the chart or diagram. Simply stated, they are reading the map. Students may need explicit demonstrations on how to use a scale, key, compass, and legend. During discussion, students share one of their facts, and the other members of the group refer to the diagram to confirm it.

> **"**It is assumed that when information is presented in a visual format, children are naturally able to understand it, because there are no strings of words to decode and comprehend. If anything, I find that children struggle even more with visual information than with words."
>
> Tony Stead (2006) *Reality Checks,* pp. 149–150

Green Questions (answered in the diagram, chart, or other visual)

As students read a text with a map (or chart or graph), they write "green" questions in their notebooks that can be answered from the chart. During the discussion, students take turns asking their questions to the group. Students are encouraged to use the map to answer these questions.

Interpretive Level: What can I infer from the diagram?

At this level, students are expected to draw conclusions from visual information. They read the chart and write statements that are implied rather than stated. Students can create If . . . Then . . . statements to support this process.

Inferred Facts

Students read a chart or map and record facts that can be inferred (not clearly stated) from the chart. It is critical that students already know how to make inferences from text before they try to make inferences from visual information. Often students can write an inferred fact by comparing or combining visual information. As students share their inferred facts, they should explain how they used the chart to make their conclusion.

Red Questions (not answered in the diagram, chart, or other visual)

Students read the text and write "red" questions that ask for inferences or judgments. For example, a diagram may indicate there are more kangaroos in one part of Australia than in other parts. A red question would be, "Why are there more kangaroos in that part of Australia?" The chart does not give this information, but students can use background knowledge to make an inference. Students should record their own answers in their notebooks, but they should understand that red questions may not have one correct answer. After reading, share and discuss the questions to clear up any misconceptions.

Yellow Questions

Distribute the "yellow" question cards and support students as they consider a question that requires them to compare, contrast, or identify a cause and effect relationship using the visual information. For example, "Compare kangaroo populations in Queensland and in Western Australia."

Evaluative Level: What opinion do I have about the information?

Students write a question about the diagram that requires an opinion or judgment. You may give students one of the following questions as a scaffold:

* ✳ Why do you think . . .?

* ✳ Do you agree that . . .?

* ✳ Do you think it was right for . . .?

* ✳ Why do you agree or disagree with the author's position on . . .?

Note: Not every diagram or chart can be analyzed at the evaluative level. Information that invites comparison, contrast, or cause-and-effect judgments works best.

Poetry Analysis

Using poetry during guided reading provides one of the best contexts for teaching the process of comprehension because poems force readers to slow down, reread for meaning, and think deeply. Poets use sensory images that help readers visualize, and they use figurative language that requires readers to make inferences and connections. In addition, most poetry selections are short enough to be completed in one or two days.

Select a Text

Select a poem that is at an instructional level for the group. The challenge usually comes from the text structure, new vocabulary, and figurative language. If the students can easily understand the poem on the first reading, it is not appropriate for guided reading. A good source of poetry for elementary students is the Poetry for Young People Series (Sterling Publishing Company). Each book contains child-appropriate poems written by famous poets.

Identify a Focus Strategy for the Group

To determine an appropriate strategy focus, read the poem and reflect on your own comprehension process. What did you do to help yourself understand the author's message? Did you visualize? Did you reread to clarify confusions? Did you make connections? What questions did you ask as you read? Also consider the needs of the students. What strategies do they need to explore and practice? Just about any comprehension strategy can be taught using poetry. At first you should focus on only one strategy, but understanding poetry almost always requires the reader to use several at the same time. Whatever your comprehension focus, it is best to teach it on a fiction text before you introduce it with poetry.

Introduce the Poem

Before the students read the poem, you should give some background information on the poet, especially if the poem has an historical context. Clarify any time-period vocabulary and discuss unfamiliar words unless context clues are provided.

Read and Respond

Your lesson will be more powerful if you have students write as they read each stanza rather than after they finish the entire poem. You want to capture the comprehension process *as* the students read, not after they have read.

Literal Comprehension Strategies

The following strategies help students grasp the literal meaning of a poem. It is important that students clearly understand what the poet said before they can interpret what the poet means.

Clarify: Students identify words or phrases they did not understand and write the strategies they used to clarify the text: *I didn't understand this part so I . . . reread the text . . . thought about an experience I had . . . visualized the setting . . . related it to the time period . . . ,* and so on.

Visualize: As students read the poem, they illustrate each stanza. I almost always have students visualize poetry because it lets me know if they understand what they are reading. Have crayons or markers available so students can include color words from the poem in their illustrations.

Make Connections: As students read the poem, they write the connections they are making to life experiences and other texts. To push their thinking, ask students to write how their connections helped their understanding. Connections help readers visualize, identify with a character's feelings, or predict.

Ask Literal Questions (green): Students stop after each stanza and write the questions that are answered in the poem. Green questions begin with *Who, What, Where, When,* and *How.* Asking literal questions while reading a poem helps the reader understand what the author is saying. It may be necessary for students to ask some literal questions before they are able to summarize.

Summarize: Students should always summarize each stanza to paraphrase what the author is saying. Do not expect the students to interpret each stanza (*"What does the author mean?"*). Interpretation is best done after the students read the entire poem.

Figurative Language: Students circle or highlight examples of similes, metaphors, and/or personification.

Interpretive Comprehension Strategies

Now that students understand the literal message, it is appropriate to boost their comprehension by asking them to make inferences and interpret the poem. Be cautious of expecting every student to come to the same conclusion. The goal is to lift the processing level of the students, not to agree on one interpretation.

Ask Inferential Questions (red): Distribute the red question cards (page 215) to scaffold students to make inferences or clarify confusions: *I wonder why . . . What does the author mean when s/he says . . . ? What do the two roads represent?*

Make Inferences: Most poems contain implied meanings that must be inferred by the reader. When students respond with "I'm thinking . . . ," they are making an inference. Affirm the students when they make an inference that is different from those made by their peers. When you value their interpretation and ideas, students will be willing to take more risks and share their inferences. For advanced readers, challenge them to underline the exact words from the poem that triggered their inference: *I'm thinking this because in the poem it says . . .*

Interpretation: When you ask students to share their interpretations of a poem, be sure to value every response. You want students to make a personal interpretation and support it with the text: *I think the author is telling us . . .* or *I think the author means . . . because he says . . . .*

Figurative Language: Students interpret similes, metaphors, and personification by describing the comparisons. For example, *The author compares trees to time because they both change.* Students can also think about the mood the poet was trying to create through the use of figurative language.

Evaluative Comprehension Strategies

After students read and analyze the poem (using some of the strategies listed above), ask them to share (in writing) why they think the author wrote the poem. I always have students write their responses before we share because I don't want them to forget what they were thinking or to discount their opinion because of what another student says. Also, if every student first writes his or her opinion, you can read the students response and assess areas that need more teaching and support.

Combine Strategies

Once students are proficient with individual strategies, ask them to respond to the poem. Good readers use a variety of strategies to comprehend challenging text. By using the following examples, you are replicating the process of comprehension. Each strategy on the chart is completed for each stanza.

Example 1

Clarify	Visualize	Summarize
Students write down words or ideas that confused them and what they did to help their understanding.	Students draw the details in the stanza.	Students summarize the most important ideas in the stanza.

Example 2

Visualize	Question	Summarize
Students illustrate the stanza.	Students write questions that come to mind as they read.	Students summarize the most important ideas in the stanza.

Example 3

Visualize	Connect	Summarize
Students illustrate the stanza.	Students write the connections they make as they read the stanza.	Students summarize the most important ideas in the stanza.

Example 4

Visualize	Literal Analysis	Interpretative Analysis
Students illustrate the stanza.	What did the author say?	What did the author mean?

Individual Prompting

As your students read silently and write a short response to each stanza, you should work with individuals. If some are having trouble writing a response, work with them first and scaffold their comprehension. Ask them questions that uncover their confusions: "Was there a tricky part for you? Was there something you didn't understand? Is there a word you don't know?" Prompt them to share their thinking: "What are you thinking now? What questions are you asking yourself?" Even though you are working with these students in the same group, and they are reading at about the same level, you will have to differentiate your prompting to meet their individual needs.

Share and Discuss

It is usually best if students share and discuss after each stanza. That way you can clarify confusions before they continue reading. I have students read and write for about 10–15 minutes while I circulate among the group and coach individual students. Students should spend the final five minutes of the lesson discussing the poem and the focus strategy you selected for their response. If all the students are working on the same strategy, you can encourage risk-taking by saying, "Did anyone have a different way of saying that?" I prefer to read each student's response prior to the sharing so no one is embarrassed. It isn't helpful for students to share a response that is totally off the mark. It is your job as the teacher to guide and support the students during the individual prompting so they are successful when they share their responses. Do not get so caught up in the strategy that you lose sight of the poem. The goal of every guided reading lesson is to construct meaning and extend understanding.

Continue the Poem the Next Day

If you are unable to complete the poem during one guided reading lesson, it is appropriate to continue it when you meet with the group again.

Evaluative Comprehension

I have included evaluative levels with each strategy, but it is also important to consider ways to teach this strategy on texts specifically written to evoke opinion and emotions. Evaluative comprehension requires students to identify and understand an author's bias, assumptions, persuasions, facts, and opinions in order to make a personal judgment.

Thesis-Proof

The purpose of this activity is to help students gather support and opposition for a thesis statement (or argument). It works with either fiction or nonfiction. Sometimes the thesis is clearly stated in the heading or title of the article. If not, the teacher should give students the thesis to write across the top of their paper. Underneath this, students make two columns, and label one SUPPORT and the other OPPOSITION. Then, as students read the text, they will jot down the key ideas, making certain they fall either under supporting or opposing the thesis. After students evaluate the thesis for support and opposition, they can identify the side they agree with or they can develop a different position.

> **"**Evaluative understandings are an important branch of comprehension that often gets overlooked in nonfiction because of our focus on getting children to simply find the facts."
>
> Tony Stead (2005), *Reality Checks*, p. 114

For example: Students can read an article about hurricanes and flood insurance. The thesis might be "The federal government should provide flood insurance for people who live along the Gulf Coast." As students read the article, they record facts that support and oppose the thesis statement.

Thesis: The federal government should subsidize flood insurance for Gulf Coast residents.

Support	Opposition
Not all insurance companies provide flood insurance.	People who live in Tennessee shouldn't have to pay for the flood insurance of people who choose to live in hurricane prone regions.
Flood insurance is too expensive.	People don't have to live on the coast. They can choose to live other places that don't flood.

Backtalks (Wilhelm, 2001)

After students read a text, they get to talk back to the author or to a specific character, person, or group. Students should write down their ideas and take turns reading them to the group. To lift the discussion, assume the role of the person (or author) the student is talking back to.

There are a variety of response formats you can use when teaching evaluative comprehension. Here are a few:

My opinion	Proof from the text
Facts from the text	Opinions from the text
Quote (direct from the text)	Personal response: *What does this mean to me?*
Author's opinion (from the text)	My opinion: *What do I think about this topic?*

Reciprocal Teaching (Palincsar & Brown, 1984)

Reciprocal teaching is an interactive instructional method that was developed to improve reading comprehension. Although it was originally designed to be used with nonfiction texts, it works with fiction as well. Students first receive modeling and guided practice with four reading strategies: clarify, question, summarize, and predict. Once students learn how to respond to these strategies, they take turns leading discussions of a text.

* *Clarify*: Students identify a place in the text where they were confused and share the steps they took to repair meaning.

* *Question*: Students use key information in the text to form a question.

* *Summary*: Students summarize the text.

* *Predict*: Students make a prediction about what they think will happen in the text.

Steps to Reciprocal Teaching

STEP 1: During a read-aloud or shared reading, introduce the reciprocal teaching strategies to the entire class. Do a different strategy each day and have students practice the strategies in small heterogeneous groups.

STEP 2: During guided reading, students practice *one* of the strategies on an instructional level text. As students read, they write their response while you circulate and support individual students. After reading, students share their responses. Repeat this step with all four strategies.

STEP 3: Each student receives a different strategy card. As students read a text, they write a response for their strategy. You should work with individual students as needed. During the discussion, students take the lead and teach their strategy to the group. Your role is to facilitate the discussion, lift the students' understanding, and provide feedback. The goal of reciprocal teaching is for students to apply these strategies automatically when they encounter difficulties while reading independently.

Strategy Cards

Distribute the following cards to the students as you teach each strategy. Students use the response starter on the card to help them apply the strategy to text. The original reciprocal teaching strategies include *summarize, clarify, predict,* and *question.* I have added the *make a connection* and *visualize* cards to accommodate six students in a group and provide additional practice in those strategies.

Reciprocal Teaching Strategy Cards

PREDICT	SUMMARIZE	QUESTION
Fiction: What will happen next? How did you make that prediction? *I predict that . . .* *because . . .* Nonfiction: What will you learn next? What helped you make that prediction? *I predict I will learn . . .* *because. . .*	In one or two sentences, use key ideas to tell what you have read. Be clear and concise. *This passage is about . . .*	What question did you ask yourself as you read? What were you wondering as you were reading? *I'm curious about . . .* *I wonder why . . .* *How . . .* *What would happen if . . .*
CLARIFY	**MAKE A CONNECTION**	**VISUALIZE**
What confused you as you read the passage? Were there any words you didn't understand? How did you figure them out? *At first, I didn't understand this word (or idea) so I . . .* • reread and looked for clues • used unknown parts in the word • tried to put myself in the character's place	*This reminds me of another book I've read . . .* *This reminds me of a time I . . .* *This reminds me of something I've learned . . .*	What did you see in your mind as you read the text? Draw a picture that helps you remember and understand what you read. Share your picture with the group and explain it.

The following chart lists each strategy explained in this chapter. Next to the strategy are scaffolds or tips for teaching it at the literal, interpretive, or evaluative level. The final column lists the pages where you can find a complete description of the procedures.

Scaffolds for Literal, Interpretive, and Evaluative Comprehension Strategies

Strategy	Literal scaffolds	Interpretive scaffolds	Evaluative scaffolds	Page
Retell	• STP • Beginning-Middle-End (B-M-E) • Five-Finger retell • S-W-B-S • Who? What? • Green questions • VIP (external)	• VIP (internal) • Red questions	• VIP (internal and external)	160, 164, 171, 172, 211–214
Visualize	• Be the illustrator	• Picture explains implicit ideas	• Picture explains opinion or conclusion	203, 204
Predict	• Write predictions	• Predict & Support	• Predict-Support-Adjust	205–206
Connect	• Make connections	• Interpret connections	• Evaluate connections	207–209
Ask Questions	• Fact-Question • Green questions	• Yellow questions • Red questions	• Evaluative questions	209–214
Determine Importance	• VIP (external) • Who and What?	• VIP (internal) • Be the illustrator • Create titles	• VIP (internal and external) • Important/Interesting • Identify theme	215–217
Main Idea & Details	• Flag main idea • Turn heading into a main-idea question	• Infer the main idea • VIP (internal)	• Evaluate and defend inferred main ideas • VIP (internal and external)	218–219
Summarize	• Use key words • S-W-B-S	• Synthesize • Draw conclusions	• Evaluate summaries	220–222

Strategy	Literal scaffolds	Interpretive scaffolds	Evaluative scaffolds	Page
Cause/Effect	• Identify explicit cause/effect relationships	• Identify implied cause/effect relationships	• Evaluate cause/effect relationships	225–227
Character Analysis		• Action-Trait • Character Trait Web • Sociogram	• Action-Motivation	227–230
Infer		• Make inferences from text clues	• Evaluate inferences	231–236
Visual Literacy	• Just the facts • Green questions	• Inferred facts • Red questions • Yellow questions	• Evaluative questions	211–214, 236–238
Poetry Analysis	• Visualize • Summarize • Identify literary elements	• Question the poet • Interpret literary elements	• Author's purpose	185, 238–242
Evaluate		• Fact/Opinion • Thesis-Proof	• Backtalks	242–244

Questions Teachers Ask About Fluent Guided Reading

Should the students write during the first reading or after they read?

Students should always write during the first reading because this will improve comprehension and provide you with a way to evaluate their understanding. It lets you know how you should scaffold. Having students write after they read an entire selection can also be beneficial as long as you have a purpose for the assignment. Guided writing is completed after the students read the text to provide writing support and to extend comprehension.

Can students write on a whiteboard instead of in their reading notebook?

I have students write in their notebooks because it is an artifact you can use for evaluating students. If they write on a whiteboard, you have no record of what they did.

What should I do while the students are reading silently?

You should have mini-conferences with each student. Look at their notes, ask them if there was something that confused them, ask them a question about what they read, ask them to tell you what they are going to write next, help them write bullets, help them use vocabulary strategies, etc. If there is nothing for you to do, then the text is too easy or you need to change your strategy focus so students are challenged.

Why should I teach children how to write in bullets?

Writing in bullets will help children identify the most important information. It also prevents them from copying word for word.

What do I do if my students cannot stay focused with independent reading while I am teaching my guided reading groups?

If children do not enjoy independent reading, they either have not found a book they like, or the book they have chosen is too difficult. Have a class meeting and explain why students need to read for 20–40 minutes each day. Ask the students to help you organize your classroom library so students can find books they like. Do book talks and book teasers. Ask the librarian to pick out some really good books and put them in a box so students can find them. Once books are available and students realize that is the only thing they will be able to do during the reading workshop, the vast majority will become eager readers. If this approach doesn't work, have students do three literacy activities during reading workshop, one of which is independent reading.

How do I assign a reading grade if I am using guided reading?

I recommend you use a combination of assessments from independent, instructional, and grade-level texts. It is best if you work with your students to develop the rubric you will use for grading, but I have included a sample rubric on page 266. If a student is reading below grade level, it should be indicated on the report card. However, I would not report the exact reading level. Here are some options you might consider as you construct your rubric.

* **Volume of Reading:** Determine the number of books students must read during each grading period in order to get an *A*, *B*, or *C*. You might require students to read from more than one genre in order to get an *A*. Since students are expected to read books at an independent level, every student, regardless of his or her reading ability, is capable of scoring an *A* in this area.

* **Response Journal**: Use a rubric to evaluate students' weekly (or biweekly) responses to their independent reading book. See Chapter 2 for response rubrics.

* **Good Faith Participation** (Rief, 1992): Students receive points if they have their independent reading book and read it silently during reading workshop. If students are off-task during independent reading, put a check by their name. At the end of the week, add the number of checks, multiply by 5, and subtract from 100. This would be the independent reading grade for that week. For example, if the student is off-task twice during the week, his or her independent-reading grade would be 90% for that week.

* **Guided Reading**: Each week students are given a grade for participation in guided reading lessons. Since students write short responses during each lesson, you have an artifact to evaluate.

* **New Word List**: Students keep a list of new vocabulary they have learned during their guided reading lessons. Test students every couple of weeks on ten of the words (new and old) to get a vocabulary grade.

* **Home Reading**: Students receive points for reading 25 minutes each night. Ask parents to sign a weekly time sheet.

✳ **Reading Strategies** (Robb, 2000): After you have taught a specific reading strategy to all of your guided reading groups, test the class on the reading strategy by using passages at each student's independent reading level.

✳ **Grade-Level Performance**: Evaluate the student's decoding, comprehension, fluency, and retell according to grade-level standards. You can use quarterly benchmark tests or a running record on any grade-level text.

✳ **Other Responses and Artifacts**: Assign a variety of literacy activities that provide evidence of reading proficiency. Possibilities include (but aren't limited to) these:

- ◆ Letters to characters or authors

- ◆ Book talks

- ◆ Performances—Readers Theater, speeches, dramatic presentations, debates

- ◆ Artistic responses—paintings, drawings, sculpture, poetry, media, etc.

- ◆ Self-Assessment—students reflect about their own growth, accomplishment, and performance

Sample Rubric for Reading Grade

Name:_____

Grading Period: _____ Score: _____ /100

	Exceeds 10	Meets 9–8	Nearly 7	Below 6–0
Volume of Reading: Reads at least 7 "just right books" from at least 2 genres				
Independent Reading: Maintains silent reading for at least 20 minutes during school				
Response Letters: Completes 7 quality response letters				
Home Reading: Reads at home for at least 80 min./week and maintains a home reading log				
Guided Reading: Participates and responds thoughtfully				
Use of Reading Strategies: Demonstrates skills and growth during guided reading lessons				
Decoding: Meets grade-level standards				
Comprehension: Meets grade-level standards				
Fluency Rate: Meets grade-level standards				
Vocabulary: Average grade from tests on the New Word List				
Total: Add the points in each column and total across for final reading grade.				

Comments:

chapter

chapter
7

Helping
STRUGGLING READERS

Because many issues affect learning, students will progress at different rates. Some factors, such as attendance, illness, family crises, and so forth are outside of your control. This chapter focuses on elements you can control: behaviors, strategies, and skills that can impede student progress.

Step 1: Analyze your teaching.
Have you provided consistent daily guided reading lessons? Have you been following the lesson framework? Have you emphasized one aspect of reading more than others? For example, you might have overstressed decoding skills and neglected to prompt for meaning. Or you might have targeted fluency, when the student is having decoding problems. You need to examine your prompts to make sure you are supporting a balanced processing system that includes meaning, decoding, fluency, and comprehension.

Step 2: Analyze student assessments.
Gather recent assessments such as running records, guided writing journals, dictated sentences, and high-frequency word charts. As you analyze the data, describe the student's reading process. Ask yourself, "What does the student do well? What cues, strategies, and skills does the student ignore?" If the student is an emergent or early

reader, check the high-frequency word chart to see if he or she knows enough sight words to process text quickly. Assessments, however, cannot reveal the entire story. There are behaviors (both teacher and student behaviors) that do not show up on a running record. The best way to gather other information is from an independent observer.

Step 3: Ask a colleague to observe the student.

Find an experienced colleague who can observe the student in the classroom. It might be another classroom teacher, a reading specialist, a coach, a Title I teacher, or a Reading Recovery® teacher. This extra set of eyes and ears might notice behaviors you have missed.

Observe the Student During Guided Reading

Ask your trusted colleague to observe the child while you teach his or her guided reading group. The observer should sit slightly behind the student but close enough to hear the student read. The colleague can record what the student does at difficulty, especially when you are not watching. Perhaps the child has developed coping behaviors such as skipping pages or copying the student sitting beside him. This observation can shed light on the child's problem. Perhaps you are too supportive and the student has become dependent upon your help. The observer should record the prompts you use and how the student reacts.

Observe the Student During Independent Reading

With transitional readers it is also helpful to observe the student during independent reading. First, you or your colleague watch the student from a distance. Does he or she seem interested in the book? Does the student stay focused? Do you notice avoidance behaviors such as flipping through the book, playing with items inside the desk, or walking around the room? After a few minutes of observation, sit next to the student and ask these questions:

1. Tell me about your book. What do you like about it?

2. Why did you choose it?.

3. How long have you been reading this book? When do you think you will finish it?

After you have asked the questions, invite the student to read a page so you can determine if the book is on an appropriate level. It is critically important that struggling readers select easy books for independent reading. Then check comprehension by asking the student to tell you what he or she just read.

Step 4: Develop an acceleration plan.

Now that you have analyzed assessments and observed the student reading, you and your colleague should establish a specific plan for acceleration. Keep the focus on the student's reading process and avoid issues such as classroom behavior, attention deficit, and failure to complete homework assignments. Above all, do not allow yourself to attribute the child's slow progress to a lack of parental support. Neither you nor the child can control that. Use the following guidelines to identify the needs of emergent, early, and transitional readers and to select one or two areas to work on next.

Analyzing Problem Areas for Emergent Readers

Use the following questions to identify areas that need to be targeted. Then refer to the problem-solving chart for activities that strengthen those behaviors, strategies, and skills. I have listed the problem areas in the order of importance. It makes no sense to prompt the student to check the picture if he or she does not have the vocabulary to identify the objects in the picture. Also, strategies will not be useful unless the student knows letters, sounds, and some sight words.

Oral Language

Does the student need to develop oral language? I can usually tell if oral language is a problem just by talking with a student. Does the student have the vocabulary to read the book? Some second language learners develop enough skills and strategies to read early text levels but struggle when they encounter words that are not in their listening vocabulary. Analyze the student's reading errors to determine if this is a problem. He or she may be lacking concepts such as colors, animal names, familiar objects, and so forth.

Risk and Independence

Does the student try unknown words or wait for help from the teacher (or other students)? Is the student working independently or trying to "hitchhike" off other students in the group?

Skills

Skills are items of information such as letters, sounds, patterns, and words. Assess the student's strengths and needs on the following skills:

* Does the student know the **letters and sounds**?

* Is the student learning **sight words**? Check the high-frequency word chart to see how many words the student can write. At Level A, the student should learn about ten words. At Level B, another ten. If the student is reading a Level C book and does not control about twenty sight words, the student is going to flounder during reading. There aren't enough known words to anchor his or her reading and the student will struggle with both decoding and fluency. Check the running record. Does the student miscue on a lot of sight words?

* Does the student **hear sounds** and record them in sequence in CVC words? The best way to analyze this skill is to dictate some simple unknown words. Does the student write the words phonetically? It is not unusual to find emergent readers who know letter sounds but do not apply the skill when writing.

Strategies

Use the following questions to determine which strategies the student uses and which ones he or she needs to learn.

* Does the student use the **picture** to figure out an unknown word?

* Does the student use **first letter cues** by getting his or her mouth ready for unknown words? Check the errors on a running record to see if they begin with the same letter as the correct word.

* Do you notice any **cross-checking**? Does the student use both the picture and first letters to predict unknown words or correct errors?

* Does the student **monitor** for meaning? The student should stop when the reading does not make sense. Of course, self-correction is the goal, but if the student is at least stopping, he or she is monitoring.

Problem-Solving Chart for Emergent Readers

The following chart lists problems that interfere with the progress of emergent readers. Once you identify the focus for the next two weeks, try the actions suggested to improve that skill or strategy. After two weeks, assess whether the student has made progress in that area. If there are no visible signs of progress, you might need to target a prerequisite skill. For example, if you don't see the student cross-checking, then perhaps you need to firm up the sounds. The student cannot cross-check if he or she doesn't know letter sounds.

Focus	Action
Oral Language	Many excellent books have been written about this topic. I, too, could go on endlessly about how important oral language is to reading development. However, let me offer just a few simple suggestions for children who are learning English as a second language and for others who have limited oral language. • Encourage conversations inside and outside the lesson. Ask the student to discuss the pictures in the book during the introduction. Avoid asking questions that require one-word answers. Instead say, "Tell me what's happening on this page." Make a special effort to have conversations with the student throughout the day. Use partners during read-alouds and shared reading so the student has the opportunity to speak to a peer. Students with limited oral language rarely raise their hand to answer your questions. • Send home a set of alphabet cards with pictures. Teach the parent how to use the pictures to encourage language. Allow the child to select a picture and make up a sentence about it. Once the child is able to create a sentence using one picture, ask her or him to select two pictures and create a sentence using both words. • Carefully construct the dictated sentence to match the student's language level. Students who are just learning English should write simple sentences without prepositional phrases. (e.g., *I like pizza. I can play games.*) As students gain proficiency with English, extend the length of the dictated sentence to include short prepositional phrases. (e.g., *I like to play with my cat. He can run to the park.*) Gradually increase the complexity of the sentence to include conjunctions and varied prepositional phrases. (e.g., *The dog went down the steps and ran after the car.*)
Risk and Independence	The student needs to experience success before taking risks. Use an easier book and praise the student for any problem-solving action, even if it results in an error. For a few days, do not attend to *any* errors the student makes. When the child begins to try unknown words, be gentle with correction. The student is still fragile.

Focus	Action
Letter Names	Follow the procedures for tracing the alphabet book on pages 57–59 of Chapter 3.
Sounds	Check the student's letter/sound checklist and systematically teach the sounds he or she doesn't know with picture sorts during word study. Teach the easy sounds first and use classmates' names or the alphabet chart to link the sound to a letter. Place an alphabet chart next to the student so he or she can refer to it for help while reading and writing.
Sight Words	Take stock of the words the student can write by dictating the words on the high-frequency chart. Put a plus (+) next to the words the student wrote quickly and accurately. Now teach one of the words the student doesn't know. Always teach the words at the lower levels first. Follow the four steps for teaching a sight word: What's Missing?, Mix & Fix, Table Writing, Whiteboards. Do not skip a step. Do not teach a new sight word until the student has firmly learned this one. Be sure to put the new word in the dictated sentence and have the student practice it during the sight-word review. One more suggestion: insist the student say the word as s/he writes it. Do not allow the student to spell the word. This can interfere with learning the word as a whole unit.
Phonemic Awareness/ Sound Boxes	If the student knows the sounds but is not using them in writing, use sound boxes during word study. Dictate a word with two phonemes such as *am, so, at, no.* Have students say each sound as they hold up a finger, /a/ - /m/. Then students segment the word again and write each letter as they say the sound. Do not let them spell the word. Be careful that you do not segment the word **for** the students. The children need to enunciate each word slowly as they write to help them hear sounds in sequence. During guided writing remind students to say the words slowly as they write.

Focus	Action
Use of Picture and Read for Meaning	Most children eagerly search the picture for help once it is modeled and prompted. Some students look at the picture but don't find the help they need. Perhaps the tricky word is a sight word or an unknown concept. Select books that have supportive pictures and known concepts. Do a richer book introduction that supports the meaning of the book. During individual prompting, ask the student to tell you about the picture before s/he reads the page. If the child forgets a concept that was discussed during the introduction, just tell him/her the word. It may take several experiences with the new concept before the student remembers it. When the student stops to problem-solve say, "What would make sense? Check the picture. Think about the story."
Initial Letters: Get your mouth ready.	If the student knows the letter sounds and does not sound the first letter when you say, "Get your mouth ready," it's possible the student is not looking at the beginning of the word. It's also possible that he or she doesn't know that particular sound. Sometimes it helps if the student puts his/her finger under the first letter of a tricky word. If this does not work, try sounding the first part for the child. The student should then be able to use the first letters and the picture to figure out the new word. Only sound the first part for a few days at most or the student will become dependent on you to do the work. Once you have modeled, release your support and prompt by saying, "Get your mouth ready." Ask the student to demonstrate getting his or her mouth ready on known words.
Cross-check	Make sure the student knows how to get his/her mouth ready and knows the picture concept. Then say, "Get your mouth ready and check the picture." Also, use the cross-checking teaching point described on page 78 of Chapter 3. Children will quickly apply this strategy as long as they know the letter sounds and the picture concepts.

Analyzing Problem Areas for Early Readers

It is common for early readers to have varying rates of progress. You might notice a surge in learning followed by a few weeks of staying at the same level. On average, early readers progress one alphabetic level per month. If you notice a student is staying at one level for longer than a month, you need to follow the intervention steps in this chapter. Most often the problem will be with decoding strategies, phonemic awareness, fluency, or comprehension. The following questions and charts will help you analyze the early reader and develop a plan for progress. Again, I have listed the problem areas in the order they should be addressed.

Risk and Independence

Does the student stop at difficulty and wait for assistance? Some students will immediately look at the teacher and not make any attempts to solve a problem. Check the text difficulty. The student should not make more than one error in every ten running words.

Decoding Strategies

Early readers will learn a variety of decoding strategies as you follow the teaching points described in the lesson plan. Some readers may abandon meaning while they are learning to use more of the print details. Others will coast along on their meaning and structure and avoid the print, hoping the word they say is the one in the book. Ask yourself the following questions and identify the strengths and needs of the student.

* *Does the student read for meaning?* By this level, most students check the picture without prompting, but they may still struggle with using meaning at difficulty. An efficient reader anticipates and predicts what might happen in the story and uses this information to process unknown words. Many challenging words will not be in the picture. The student must think about the events in the story to help him or her make meaningful predictions for unknown words. This is the feed-forward process (Clay, 1990). Check the running record to see if the student's errors make sense. If they don't, then this is a problem that needs to be addressed.

* *Does the student monitor for meaning?* The student should stop when a miscue does not make sense. Clay (1991) calls this process the "feedback mechanism." Check the running record to see if the student stops when meaning breaks down and attempts to fix the error by rereading, sounding the word in parts, or using other strategies. Monitoring for meaning is the most important decoding strategy because it is the basis for all comprehension. If the student is not aware of meaning-changing errors, he or she will probably not give an accurate retell.

✳ *Does the student monitor for visual information?* Although meaning is the most important aspect of reading, students should also develop visual scanning processes that help them notice when the error does not look like the word in the book. Early readers gradually attend to more of the details of print, generally focusing on the beginning letters, the ending letters, and finally the middle letters (Clay, 1991). When students ignore medial or final letters, they are not looking all the way through the word. Sometimes a student may have a serial order problem because he or she developed the habit of looking haphazardly at words rather than left to right. Check the errors on the running record. Does the first attempt make sense but not match the first letter of the word? Or perhaps the errors match first letters, but the student ignores the end of the word. If you see this behavior, then the student needs to use more visual information.

✳ *Does the student try to sound out every word letter by letter?* Sounding out short words at levels A–C will sometimes work. Students reading at early levels encounter longer words and words that are less phonetic. By the time the student finishes sounding out each letter of a long word, he or she has probably lost meaning, and the feed-forward process breaks down.

✳ *Does the student use known parts and endings?* Covering the ending and finding known parts is a more efficient decoding strategy than sounding out letter by letter. Watch the student problem-solve a word to see if he or she attends to a part of the word. Students who only sound the first letter and wait for the right word to magically pop out are not developing an efficient processing system.

Phonemic Awareness

✳ *Does the student hear short vowels and blends?* Look for evidence in word study and guided writing.

✳ *Does the student hear sounds in sequence?* Analyze the student during guided writing and word study to see if the student is segmenting sounds without your support and writing unknown words phonetically. You shouldn't expect perfect spelling, but you should be able to read the invented spelling.

Vocabulary

✳ *Does the student have enough oral language to understand the vocabulary in the early books?* Some second language learners develop enough skills and strategies to read early text, but struggle when they encounter words that are not in their listening vocabulary. Analyze the student's reading errors to determine if this is a problem.

＊ *Does the student have a large bank of function words that he or she can read and write?* Check the running record to see if the student miscues on sight words. Use the high-frequency word chart to find out how many words the student can write. If this is a problem, and it often is at the early levels, the student will struggle with fluency.

Fluency

＊ *Does the student read familiar texts with fluency, phrasing, and expression?*

＊ *Does the student read new material with some phrasing and expression?* You shouldn't expect the child to read the entire book quickly because the guided reading text should have words that need to be processed. However, there should be stretches of fluent, phrased reading when the student does not have to problem-solve.

Retell

＊ *Does the student recall what he or she read?*

＊ *Does the student participate in the discussion after reading?*

Problem-Solving Chart for Early Readers

Use the following chart to develop your intervention plan. Establish a specific focus for the next two weeks. After that time, determine if the plan is working. Revise if necessary.

Focus	Action
Risk and independence	Drop the text level for a few weeks so the student can experience success. If the student takes a risk but makes an error, ignore the error and praise the student for trying. Say, "That was a great try. Good for you. Keep going." This will be difficult for you because you want every word to be correct. But if you want to encourage risk-taking behavior, you must accept errors. Once the student is consistently taking risks, you will be able to target another decoding goal.
Read for meaning	When the student stops to problem-solve, prompt by saying, "What would make sense? Think about the story." If he or she still has trouble after you prompt for meaning, ask what is happening in the picture. Another suggestion is to do a richer book introduction and invite the student (not you) to talk about the pictures. If a student pauses at a new word and refuses to try, sound the first part of the word for him or her. This may help the student stay focused on the meaning of the story.

Focus	Action
Monitor for meaning	After the student makes a meaning-changing error, allow him/her to finish reading the sentence and then say, "Does that make sense? Reread that and think about what would make sense." Do not interrupt the student in the middle of the sentence. Give him/her the opportunity to self-monitor. If the student tells you that it does make sense say, "Listen to what you said." Repeat how the student read the sentence. Continue to make meaning your priority. This means you will ignore errors that make sense.
Monitor for visual information	Early readers should scan the word from left to right to make sure they are using the letters and sounds at the middle and end of the word. When a student makes an error that makes sense say, "That makes sense but does it look right? Check the middle (or end) of the word and try something that looks right *and* makes sense." Ask the student to check the word slowly by running his/her finger under the word as s/he says it. This helps the student check for an auditory and visual match. The sounds he says need to match the letters he sees.
Read in chunks or take words apart during reading	Discourage sounding out letter-by-letter, and show the student how to read in chunks. This would include covering the ending, finding a known part, sounding the first part (onset), and finding a chunk (rime) you know. Once you model these strategies, keep your fingers out of the book, and prompt the student to do the work. If the child chunks the word but ignores the meaning, prompt him or her to reread the sentence.
Hear short vowels and blends	Use picture sorts for words with short vowels in the middle of the word. Show the student how to say the word up to the vowel sound and "punch" the vowel (*fl-a-a-a-g*). This helps the student hear the vowel sound. If the student does not know the letter that makes the vowel sound, use a link with a short known word. I usually use *at* for short *a, egg* for short *e, it* for short *i, on* for short *o*, and *up* for short *u*. Say "That sound is the same sound you hear at the beginning of *up*."
Hear sounds in sequence	Use sound boxes and make sure the student says the word slowly as s/he writes. Students need to enunciate each word slowly as they write to help them hear sounds in sequence. Avoid saying the word slowly for the student.
Learn sight words	Take stock of the sight words the student can write using the high-frequency word chart for levels A–E. Most early readers know the words at Levels A and B because they are phonetically regular. You will notice problems occurring as you have them write words like *said, here, come,* and *what*. Students need to develop automatic recognition of these words so they can process text quickly. Follow the procedures in the lesson to teach unknown sight words. The goal is for the student to quickly write the word without prompting; however, you should prompt if the student starts to write the word incorrectly. You do not want the wrong spelling to become internalized.

Focus	Action
Vocabulary	Select books with mostly familiar concepts and discuss new concepts during the introduction. Encourage the students to turn and talk about the new word to the person sitting next to them.
Fluency	Check the text level. If fluency is your goal, there should be few unknown words in the book. Do not allow the student to point to the words. Prompt the student to read smoothly as you frame two to three words at a time. Use texts with interesting dialogue so the student can practice reading with expression. Read with the student if s/he needs support. Provide opportunities for the student to reread familiar books to a classmate, a parent, a reading buddy in another class, or even the principal.
Retell	Students who do not read for meaning cannot retell the story. Be sure you prompt these students to look at the picture before and while they read. Ask students to retell a page immediately after reading it. If they need more support, encourage them to look at the picture during the retell. Looking at the picture is a scaffold that should eventually be removed but not until they begin to visualize on their own.

Analyzing Problem Areas for Transitional Readers

Problem areas for transitional readers include motivation, self-monitoring, decoding, fluency, vocabulary, and retell. Before we tackle the processing challenges, let me offer a few suggestions for increasing the amount or volume of reading.

Increase Reading Volume

One reason struggling readers don't like to read is they can't find easy books that interest them. Use the information you collect from your observation during independent reading to help students find good, easy books. Make a big deal about selecting these books "just for them" because you think they will enjoy them. Tell them to let you know if they don't like the book you selected, so you can help them find others.

Another approach that may increase reading volume is to have students read with a buddy from the classroom. They sit beside each other and either read silently or take turns reading softly. As a last resort for motivating reluctant readers, I suggest taped stories. I am not sure how much a student actually reads with this approach since most struggling readers have a difficult time keeping up with the reading speed on the tape. Still, I would rather have a student listen to a story than do nothing, and it may eventually motivate the student to read the book on his or her own.

Readers Theater

Readers Theater motivates students to reread a text because they get to perform it in front of the class. Be sure the text is at an independent level. Students will not increase fluency by reading texts that are too difficult for them. Incorporate Readers Theater into your workstation rotations, especially if you have several students who need to improve fluency.

Neurological Impress (Adapted from Heckelman, 1969)

Neurological impress requires that a student read with an adult for 15 minutes every day for at least 21 days. Classroom teachers seldom have time to work individually for 15 minutes, so neurological impress is best performed by another adult. You may have a high school student, student teacher, instructional aid, parent volunteers, or even the building custodian who is willing to spend 15 minutes a day helping one student. I have trained parents how to use neurological impress, and if they are consistent, it works!

1. Use a text at the student's independent level. Begin with familiar texts and switch to new texts as the student gains confidence.
2. You and the student read the same material out loud together. Keep your voice a little softer than the student's.
3. Place your hand on top of the student's hand and run the student's finger under the words as they are being read. Make sure the finger and the voice are operating together.
4. Lower your voice on easy text and increase the volume when the student struggles. You might sound the first syllable of a challenging word to see if the student can figure it out. If the student doesn't respond immediately with the correct word, tell the word and continue to read with the student. At no time should you stop to correct or test the student. The objective is fluent reading, not accuracy or comprehension.
5. If the student falls behind or begins to mumble, stop the reading, tell the student to read with you, and reread that sentence.
6. Do neurological impress for 15 minutes a day for at least 21 days. You should notice a marked improvement in fluency although I have found that some students may require more than 21 days for the procedure to take effect.

Identify Processing Problems

Just increasing the amount of reading a student does will not solve processing problems. Use the following questions to uncover areas of strength and need. Then use the chart to find activities that address the problem.

Strategies

Analyze running records and observe the student during reading to determine the actions the student takes to solve problems. Transitional readers may not vocalize their processing, so you may need to ask some questions to help you identify reading strategies the student uses.

* Does the student **monitor for meaning** by stopping when the reading doesn't make sense? This is the most important reading strategy because it is the foundation for comprehension.

* Does the student **monitor with visual** information? Readers should notice when what they say does not look right. If students ignore medial or final letters, they are not scanning all the way through the word.

* Does the student **take apart big** words to find known chunks? This strategy is obvious if the student uses his/her finger to cover part of a word such as the ending. You may have to ask the student to show you the parts in a tricky word to see if the student knows how to break a word apart.

* What **skills** does the student know and apply during reading and writing? Use the Word Study Inventory on page 48 of Chapter 2 and writing samples to determine weaknesses. Assess students on short vowels, digraphs, blends, vowel patterns, and endings. Students who are weak in this area often have spelling problems. Either they write phonetically and ignore phonic patterns, or they try to remember the letters in a word but write them out of sequence.

* Does the student have a rich oral and listening **vocabulary**? You can discover a great deal about a child's vocabulary just by having a conversation. Does the student use simple vocabulary, or does he or she include interesting, rare words? Does the student use big words during independent writing, even when he or she doesn't know how to spell them? You can also analyze the student's reading errors. Does the student mispronounce unfamiliar words?

* Does the student read **fluently** with phrasing and expression?

* Does the student **recall** what he or she read and participate in the discussion after reading?

Problem-Solving Chart for Transitional Readers

Use the following chart to establish a goal and develop a plan for progress. In two weeks meet again with your colleague to share your observations and adjust your acceleration plan.

Focus	Action
Self-monitor	If students make errors that do not make sense, wait until they finish the sentence and say, "Does that make sense?" Usually they miscue on known words and can easily correct the error if they begin to listen to themselves. You must ignore errors that make sense until the student consistently monitors for meaning. Direct the student to look at the pictures before he or she reads. Prompt for meaning by saying, "Think about the story." Make a short comment just as the student is turning the page to direct the student's attention to the action on that page. For example, "Now you are going to learn how they solved the problem."
Decoding	Teach the decoding strategies from Appendix C (page 288). After you model each strategy, prompt the student to apply it when appropriate during guided reading. Teaching students to use analogies is an effective strategy for transitional readers, especially if they have trouble remembering phonics rules.
Skills (spelling & phonics)	Use sound boxes if the student does not write words phonetically. Use analogy charts if the student struggles with vowel patterns and endings. Always encourage the student to say each word slowly as he or she writes. Noisy writing helps students apply phonemic awareness skills.
Fluency	Use easy text for guided reading and support phrasing and expression. Follow the prompts for fluency on page 159–160 of Chapter 5. Add repeated readings and Readers Theater as a center activity. Find someone to do neurological impress with the student. Have the student practice a picture book to read to a student in a lower grade. If the student skips lines, let him/her use an index card to slide down the page.

Focus	Action
Vocabulary	Encourage conversations throughout the day. Use the "turn and talk" technique during read-alouds and content instruction and teach vocabulary in every subject area. During guided reading introduce unfamiliar vocabulary using the four steps on page 157. Use the New Word List to hold students accountable for learning useful and important words. After you teach the vocabulary strategies in Appendix C (page 288), prompt students to apply them during guided reading.
Retell	Some children with poor retell are rapid readers who read without thinking. Direct students to stop and look at the illustrations as they read a page. After reading, have them retell each page using the STP procedures on page 160. Use other activities listed in Chapter 3 to improve retelling.

Final Thoughts: Is Guided Reading Worth It?

The list of "add-ons" to your schedule is seemingly endless: extra physical activity, character development, assessment, collaboration, staff development, additional intervention, new initiatives, documentation, etc. Now I am asking you to add guided reading. It is true that whole-group reading instruction takes less time to prepare and deliver than guided reading instruction, but efficiency does not equate to effectiveness. Students differ in their reading development. Because students differ, teachers must use a variety of assessments to discover what their students need to learn. They must also provide differentiated small-group instruction that targets those specific needs. Whole-class instruction is part of a balanced literacy framework, but it is just not possible to meet every student's needs with a single lesson.

"A simple principle—children differ—explains why there can be no one best method, material, or program."

Dick Allington (2001), *What Really Matters for Struggling Readers*, p. 22

I have worked side-by-side in the classroom with hundreds, perhaps thousands, of teachers. I know that teachers want to provide the best possible instruction, and they are willing to go the extra mile if the effort will make a difference for their students. Does guided reading make a difference? Based upon data I have collected over the past ten years, the answer is a resounding "Yes!" To be powerful and effective, however, guided reading must be a year-long commitment that is part of the daily classroom routine. In addition to consistency, several other factors will maximize the effectiveness of guided reading instruction:

✴ **Understand the reading process**. "Learning to read depends on two critical factors: the teacher's thorough knowledge of the reading process itself, and his or her determination to understand and respond to each child's needs as a reader." (Keene, 1997, p. xiv.) Teachers need training in how to analyze assessments (especially running records) and how to use them to understand a student's processing system. Teachers should be able to describe a child's reading process and know what to do to help him or her become a better reader.

✴ **Use assessments to target needs and form flexible groups.** Not all assessments are useful for teaching reading. Some are a waste of time because they do not tell you anything you do not already know. An assessment that merely identifies whether a student needs intervention is not useful. You already know who needs help. Useful assessment tells you the strengths and needs of students so you can provide the kind of instruction that will accelerate them.

✴ **Choose appropriate texts.** It is important to select the right text for a guided reading lesson. You need to consider the reading levels in the group and the reading strategies students need to learn. Guided reading texts should be slightly challenging and provide opportunities for students to practice the target strategy.

✴ **Provide explicit, focused instruction.** Effective guided reading lessons are purposeful. You should know what you are teaching, and students should know what they are learning. You should explicitly state the purpose of the lesson by saying something like, "Today you are going to learn how to use picture clues to define new words." Keep in mind, the strategy should be one the students do not already know how to do. With the limited amount of instructional time available, we cannot waste time teaching something the students already know.

✴ **Teach appropriate skills during the guided reading lesson**. Many teachers opt to teach reading skills during whole-class components. Although it may be appropriate to teach the concept of contractions or a specific suffix to the entire class, the skill should be taught again during guided reading if students have not internalized it.

✴ **Include guided writing, especially with emergent, early, and transitional readers**. Although writing workshop is an essential instructional component, there is never enough time to meet with every individual. By spending a portion of the guided reading lesson supporting students' writing, you can help students internalize a skill or strategy that has already been taught during writing workshop.

✳ **Foster independence by providing a gradual release of support.** This is one of the most powerful elements of guided reading. During independent conferences, the teacher can provide just the right amount of support and gradually reduce that support until the student is independently applying the strategy.

✳ **Work within a balanced literacy framework.** Guided reading cannot be the entire reading program. It should be balanced with whole-group instruction and individual practice so teachers can make the best use of the instructional day.

The Next Step

Changing the way you teach reading is not easy. There will be days when you will think you will never get it right. The good news is you don't have to get it right in order for guided reading to work. You just have to do it—and then reflect on your teaching and on your students. Did they learn something new today? Did you help them become better readers? What should you teach tomorrow? Just by asking these questions, you have already taken the next step towards becoming a better reading teacher.

References

Allington, R. (2001). *What really matters for struggling readers: Designing research-based programs.* Boston: Pearson.

Allington, R. (2009). *What really matters in fluency: Research-based practices across the curriculum.* Boston: Pearson.

Beaver, J. (2006). *Developmental reading assessment.* Boston: Pearson.

Beck, I. L., McKeown, M. G., & Kucan, L. (2002). *Bringing words to life.* New York: Guilford.

Both-de Vries, A. C., & Bus, A. G. (2008). Name writing: A first step to phonetic writing? *Literacy Teaching and Learning, 12*(2), 37-55.

Boushey, G., & Moser, J. (2006). *The daily five: Fostering literacy independence in the elementary grades.* Portland, ME: Stenhouse.

Clay, M. (2006). *An observation survey of early literacy achievement.* Portsmouth, NH: Heinemann.

Clay, M. (2000). *Running records for classroom teachers,* Portsmouth, NH: Heinemann.

Clay, M. (1993). *Reading recovery: A guidebook for teachers in training.* Portsmouth, NH: Heinemann.

Clay, M. (1991). *Becoming literate: The construction of inner control.* Portsmouth, NH: Heinemann.

Cunningham, P. (2009). *What really matters in vocabulary: Research-based practices across the curriculum.* Boston: Pearson.

Diller, D. (2003). *Literacy workstations: Making centers work.* York, ME: Stenhouse.

Diller, D. (2005). *Practice with purpose: Literacy workstations for grades 3-5.* York, ME: Stenhouse.

Dorn, L. J., Soffos, C., & Lyons, C. A. (2005). *Teaching for deep comprehension: A reading workshop approach.* York, ME: Stenhouse.

Elley, W. B., (1989). Vocabulary acquisition from listening to stories, *Reading Research Quarterly, 24*(2), 174-187.

Fountas, I., & Pinnell, G. S. (1996). *Guiding reading: Good first teaching.* Portsmouth, NH: Heinemann.

Fountas, I., & Pinnell, G. S. (2001). *Guiding readers and writers: Grades 3-6.* Portsmouth, NH: Heinemann.

Fountas, I., & Pinnell, G. S. (2008). *The Fountas and Pinnell benchmark assessment system, K-8.* Portsmouth, NH: Heinemann

Hart, B., & Risley, T. (1995). *Meaningful differences in the everyday experiences of young American children.* Baltimore, MD: Paul H. Brookes.

Harvey, S., & Goudvis, A. (2000). *Strategies that work: Teaching comprehension for understanding and engagement.* York, ME: Stenhouse.

Harvey, S., & Goudvis, A. (2007). *Comprehension toolkit,* Portsmouth, NH: Heinemann.

Hasbrouck, J., & Tindal, G. A. (2006). ORF norms: A valuable assessment tool for reading teachers. *Reading Teacher, 59*(7), 636-644.

Heckelman, R. G. (1969), The neurological impress remedial reading technique, *Academic Therapy, 4,* 277-282. San Rafael, CA: DeWitt Reading Clinic.

Hoyt, L. (2007). *Interactive read-alouds.* Portsmouth, NH: Heinemann.

Ingraham, P. B. (1997). *Creating and managing learning centers: A thematic approach.* Peterborough, NH: Crystal Springs Books.

Keene, E., & Zimmermann, S. 1997. *Mosaic of thought: Teaching comprehension in a reader's workshop.* Portsmouth, NH: Heinemann.

Kucan, L. 2007. I Poems: Invitations for students to deepen literary understanding. *Reading Teacher, 60*(6), 518-525.

Leslie, L., & Caldwell, J. (2005). *Qualitative reading inventory IV.* New York: Longman.

Macon, J., Bewell, D. M., & Vogt, M. (1991). *Responses to literature.* Newark, DE: International Reading Association.

Manyak, P. (2007). Character trait vocabulary: A schoolwide approach. *Reading Teacher, 60*(6), 574-577.

Morrow, L. M. 1997. *The literacy center: Context for reading and writing.* York, ME: Stenhouse.

Nagy, W., Anderson, P., & Herman, R. (1987). Learning word meanings from context during normal reading, *American Educational Research Journal 24,* 237-70.

Nelley, E., & Smith, A. (2000). *Rigby PM benchmark kit.* Crystal Lake, IL: Rigby.

Palincsar, A. S., & Brown, A. (1984). Reciprocal teaching of comprehension-fostering and comprehension monitoring activities. *Cognition and Instruction, 1*(2), pp. 117-175.

Pearson, P. D., Roehler, L. R., Dole, J. A, & Duffy, G. G. (1992). Developing expertise in reading comprehension. In J. Samuels and A. Farstrup (eds.), *What research has to say about reading instruction,* (2nd ed.), 145-199. Newark, DE: International Reading Association.

Raphael, T. E. (1982). Question answering strategies for children. *Reading Teacher* (36)2, pp. 186-190.

Rief, L. (1992). *Seeking diversity: Language arts with adolescents.* Portsmouth, NH: Heinemann.

Appendix A
Behaviors, Strategies, and Skills by Level

Summary of Skill Focus and Word Study Activities

Level	Skill Focus	Sound Sorts	Magnetic Letters/ Whiteboards	Sound Boxes	Guided Writing
Pre-A	Letters, sounds, print concepts	Initial consonants	Sort letters by shape, color, size, etc. Make first/last name	none	Interactive writing
A **1**	Consonants Long vowels	Initial consonants Long vowels	Make sight words Exchange initial consonants with magnetic letters *cat, fat, mat, bat*	2 boxes (consonant and long vowel) *me, go, he, so*	Dictated sentence 3–5 words
B **2**	Consonants Short vowels *(a, o)*	Initial & final consonants short *a* & *o*	Make sight words Exchange initial & final consonants *pat, pan, pad, mad, man; hat, has, ham, jam,*	2 boxes (short vowel-consonant) *at, an, on, am, as*	Dictated or open-ended sentence 5–7 words
C **3/4**	Short vowels Hearing sounds in sequence (CVC)	Short vowels *(e, i, u)*	Make sight words Exchange initial, medial and final letters; include all short vowels *pot, hot, hop, mop, map; cap, map, lap, lad, mad*	3 boxes (CVC) *hop, mat, did*	Dictated or open-ended sentence 7–10 words
D **5/6**	Digraphs— *sh, ch, th* Endings: *–s, –ing, –ed* Contractions	Initial and final digraphs	Exchange first, medial, and final letters; include digraphs: *lot-hot-hop-chop-shop-ship* Add and delete endings: *–s, –ed ,–ing* Introduce simple contractions: *can't, I'm, didn't*	3 boxes (words with digraphs) *ship, chat, then*	Dictated or open-ended sentence Use two sentences Include endings: *–ing, –s, –ed*
E **7/8**	Initial blends Onset/rimes Contractions	Initial blends	Add and delete initial clusters. Break at onset and rime: *cap-clap-clip-grip-grin-spin* Make simple contractions.	4 boxes (initial blends, short vowels) *slip, clan, step*	Dictated sentence or beginning-middle-end

Appendix A (continued)

Level	Skill Focus	Sound Sorts	Magnetic Letters/ Whiteboards	Sound Boxes	Guided Writing
F 9/10	Final blends Onsets/rimes Contractions	Final blends	Add and delete final clusters. Break at onset and rime: *went-wept-west-lest-list-limp* Make more difficult contractions.	4 boxes (final blends, short vowels) *west, milk, sunk*	Beginning-Middle-End (B-M-E) (3 sentences)
G 11/12	Blends Silent *e* rule	None	Use magnetic letters and analogy charts to teach the silent *e* feature. *mat-mate-mane-man*	5 boxes (initial and final blends, short vowels) *stink, grunt, stomp*	B-M-E (4 sentences) Somebody-Wanted-But-So (S-W-B-S)
H-I 13-16	Vowel patterns *ee, ar, ay, oa, or, all, ow (cow)* Endings	None	Use magnetic letters, whiteboards and analogy charts to teach vowel patterns. *cow-clown-crown-crowd* Include blends and familiar endings such as *-er, -ed, -ing, -s* Break at onset and rime (cl-own)	5 boxes (initial and final blends, short vowels)	B-M-E (5 sentences) S-W-B-S
J+ 17+	Vowel patterns *ou, ew, ight, aw, ai, oi, ow* (low) Make a big word *e-nor-mous*	None	Use magnetic letters, whiteboards and analogy charts to teach vowel patterns. Include blends and more challenging endings: *-est, -ly, -y, -ful, -ness,* etc. Use magnetic letters to make a big word and then break it into syllables.	None	Retell Problem-solution Predict-support Character description Main idea and details Chapter summaries Microthemes

Strategies and Skills for Pre-A

Visual Memory	Phonological Awareness	Oral Language and Print Concepts	Interactive Writing
Work with letters and names to improve visual discrimination, visual memory, letter identification, and letter formation.	Students learn to hear syllables and identify rhyming words.	Students develop oral language skills and learn concepts of directionality, letter/ word, etc.	Students work with the teacher to write a short message. This activity improves oral language, concepts of print, letter formation, and sound-letter links.
Work With Letters	• Clap syllables – Use classmates' names and picture cards.	**Shared Reading**	
• Match letters to an alphabet chart.	• Rhymes – Orally identify words that rhyme.	• Use a simple guided reading book (Level A).	• Negotiate a simple sentence about the book that was read during shared reading.
• Sort letters by shape or color.	**Phonemic Awareness**	• Preview pictures and encourage discussion.	• The teacher and the students work together to write the message.
• Teach letter formation.	Students learn to hear initial consonants and link the sounds to letters.	• Chorally read the book with the students.	• Use a name chart and letter chart to help students make sound-letter links.
Work With Names	• Picture sorts with initial consonants	**Teaching Focus**	• Cut the sentence apart and support students as they remake it.
• Name puzzles	• Easiest letter sounds to hear: *b, d, j, k, p, t, v, z, f, l, m, n, r, s*	• Vocabulary development	
• Make names out of magnetic letters.		• Oral language (discussion)	
• Rainbow-writing — use colored markers to trace first names		• Left-to-right directionality	
		• 1:1 matching	
		• Concept of letter & word	
		• Concept of first & last	
		• Print contains the message	
		• Period at the end of a sentence	

Strategies and Skills for Level A

Use this chart to plan your lessons and guide acceleration decisions.

Students learn to . . .	Picture Sorts	Making Words	Sound Boxes	Guided Writing Dictated Sentence
• maintain 1:1 on one line of print. • use meaning (pictures) to predict, monitor, self-correct. • read and write about 10 words. • firm up letter knowledge. • hear and use initial consonant sounds in reading and writing. • hear and use long vowel sounds in writing. • orally generate rhyming strings (*fat, cat, mat,* etc.).	**Initial consonants** Students take turns sorting pictures by initial consonant sounds. Dd (desk) (duck) Hh (hangar) (hand) **Long vowels— medial** Ii (kite) (slide) Ee (leaf) (feet)	Students use magnetic letters to make rhyming words by changing initial consonants. Examples: *go, no, so* *cat, hat, mat, pat* *me, he, we, be* *hop, mop, top, cop* *pot, lot, hot, dot* *pan, man, ran, fan* *map, cap, tap, gap* *mad, had, sad, pad* *dog, fog, log, hog*	Dictate words with two phonemes, one being a long vowel. Students segment the sounds on their fingers and write one letter in each box. Encourage students to say the sound as they write the letter in the box. ┌─────┬─────┐ │ S │ O │ └─────┴─────┘ Examples: *me, we, he, go, no, so, lo*	Dictate a simple sentence (3–5 words) that contains the targeted sight words. It should contain at least one unknown word that students must stretch out. Encourage approximations on unknown words, but sight words that have been taught should be spelled correctly. Whenever possible, include other sight words that have been previously taught. Examples: *I like pizza.* *I see the turtle.* *I ran to my mom.* *I can go fast.* **Comprehension** <u>Before</u> reading, discuss the pictures and unfamiliar concepts. Support students to use a complete sentence to talk about the picture. <u>During</u> reading, prompt students to use meaning (pictures) at difficulty. <u>After</u> reading, discuss the story.

Strategies and Skills for Level B

Use this chart to plan your lessons and guide acceleration decisions.

Students Learn to . . .	Picture Sorts	Making Words	Sound Boxes	Guided Writing Dictated Sentence
• maintain 1:1 on two lines of print. • use meaning, structure, and known words to predict, monitor, and self-correct. • cross-check meaning and first letters with prompting. • read and write about 20 words. • hear and use initial and final consonant sounds in reading and writing. • hear and use short vowels (*a, o*) in writing.	**Short Vowels** (*a* and *o*) Students take turns sorting pictures with short, medial vowels. Encourage slow stretching of the word to emphasize the vowel sound in the middle. **a** (hat) (cat) **o** (mop) (box)	Using magnetic letters, students change final consonant or both initial and final consonants to make new words. To maximize power, avoid rhyming families. This forces students to attend to each letter in sequence. Change final consonant: *rat-rag-ram-ran-rap* *cat-cap-can-cab* *man-mat-map-mad* *hat-ham-had-has* *hot-hop-hog* Change initial and final consonant: *mat-map-man-pan-pat* *sat-sam-sad-mad-mat* *did-dig-pig-pit-sit* *cat-can-man-map-tap-tan*	Dictate words with two phonemes, one being a short *a* or short *o*. Students segment the sounds on their fingers and write one letter in each box. Encourage students to say the sound as they write the letter in the box. | u	p | Examples of words for Level B: *am, at, as, on, up, an*	Dictate a sentence (5-7 words) that relates to the story. It should contain the targeted sight words and other words that have been previously taught. Encourage invented spelling of unknown words. Examples: *The tiger is in the cage.* *Look at the pig in the road.* *The bear is at the* ____ *She is up on the* ____ *I like to go on the* ____ *Look at me. I am* ____ *Did you see the* ____? **Comprehension** <u>Before</u> reading, discuss the story using the pictures. <u>During</u> reading, prompt students to make sense. <u>After</u> reading, discuss the story and retell events.

Strategies and Skills for Level C

Use this chart to plan your lessons and guide acceleration decisions.

Students Learn to . . .	Picture Sorts	Making Words	Sound Boxes	Guided Writing Dictated Sentence
• use meaning, structure, known words, and initial consonants to predict, monitor, and self-correct. • cross-check meaning and first letters to problem-solve unknown words without teacher prompting. • read and write about 30 words. • hear and record short vowels during writing. • hear and record CVC sounds in sequence during writing with prompting. • maintain one-to-one matching, without pointing, in familiar books.	**Short Vowels** *(e, i, u)* Students take turns sorting pictures according to the medial vowel sound. **i** (pig) (stick) **u** (cup) (rug)	Students use magnetic letters to make new words by changing initial, medial, and final letters. Examples: *can-cap-map-mop-top-tip* *bag-beg-big-wig-win-bin* *sat-sad-mad-mud-bud-bug* *dog-dot-hot-hop-hip-dip* *jam-yam-yum-rum-rut-rat* *ran-run-gun-gut-get-net* *lap-lip-lid-lad-mad-map* *got-get-net-pet-peg-pig-* *his-hit-pit-pot-hot-hop-hip* *had-hid-rid-rig-wig-wag* *run-bun-bin-bit-bet* *sat-sit-bit-big-bug-beg* *fun-fan-fat-bat-bad-bed*	Dictate words with two phonemes, one being a short *a* or short *o*. Students segment the sounds on their fingers and write one letter in each box. Encourage students to say the sound as they write the letter in the box. | v	e	t | Examples of words for Level C: bag sit hop gum rap big job wet cab hop vet tag cap mob rid fog can jog get nod had rob mud wig map run log sad pet	Students write a dictated sentence with 7–10 words. Gradually extend the length of the sentence to increase auditory memory. Include known sight words and unknown words for students to stretch. Examples: *"Come and look at the red car," said Nick.* *We will catch the big fish in the water.* **Comprehension** <u>Before</u> reading, discuss the story line and encourage predictions. <u>During</u> reading, prompt for meaning and ask students to recall a page they read. <u>After</u> reading, support a retell and ask an inferential question.

Strategies and Skills for Level D

Use this chart to plan your lessons and guide acceleration decisions.

Students Learn to . . .	Picture Sorts	Making Words	Sound Boxes	Guided Writing Dictated Sentence
• maintain meaning while problem-solving new words. • cross-check without prompting. • use known parts with prompting. • attend to endings (–ed, –s, –ing) in reading and writing with prompting. • blend the sounds in small words. • reread to access meaning • read without pointing. • read in short phrases. • read and write about 40 words. • use digraphs and short vowels in reading and writing. • attend to bold words and read dialogue with expression. • hear and record sounds in sequence without support. • retell the story and respond to questions with support.	**Digraphs** Students take turns sorting pictures by the initial digraph. **sh** (ship) (sheep) **ch** (chicken) (cheese) **Whiteboards** Students use whiteboards or magnetic letters to add endings to words. Do not select words that end in silent *e* or require consonant doubling. *look-looked-looking* *go-going* *like-likes* *mash-mashing-mashed*	Students use magnetic letters to make new words by changing initial, medial, or final letters. Include initial and final digraphs. *hip-chip-chop-shop-shot* *bat-bath-math-mash-mush* *did-dish-dash-mash-math-math-mush-hush-hash-cash* *hat-chat-chap-chip-ship* *cat-chat-that-than-thin-this* *map-math-bath-bash-bush* *the-then-than-that-hat-chat*	Use three boxes and dictate words with a digraph. Both letters of the digraph go in the same box. **m a s h** Examples: *math shop* *chin this* *such dash* *chat dish* *then mash* *chop thud* *such shot* *path hush* *with chip*	Dictate two sentences related to the story. Include many sight words, digraphs, and endings. *Ben is looking for his bear. Mom said to check the chair.* **Comprehension** Before reading, invite students to talk about the storyline using the pictures. Encourage predictions and connections. Discuss unusual vocabulary and unfamiliar sight words. During reading, prompt students to reread to access structure and monitor for meaning. After reading, support an oral retell and ask a discussion question that requires inferential thinking.

Strategies and Skills for Level E

Use this chart to plan your lessons and guide acceleration decisions.

Students Learn to . . .	Picture Sorts	Making Words	Sound Boxes	Guided Writing Dictated Sentence
• maintain meaning and use known parts to problem-solve new words with little prompting. • cover the endings to problem-solve. • monitor with meaning, initial blends, and endings. • build automaticity in reading and writing a large bank of high-frequency words. • read familiar text with fluency and expression. • read new text with some phrasing. • attend to bold words and read with expression. • understand simple contractions made from known words. e.g., *can't, didn't, I'm, I'll, you're, we're, they're, he's, she's, it's, isn't* • orally segment one-syllable words at the onset and rime (st-ick). • hear and write a CCVC word in sequence.	**Focus: Initial Blends** Students sort pictures according to the initial blend. Select two or three blends that begin with the same letter to draw students' attention to the second letter in the blend (e.g., *pr-pl; gr-gl; sl-sw-st*) **fl** (flower) (flag) **fr** (fruit) (frog)	Students change letters to make new words that contain an initial blend. After students make each word, have them break the word at the onset and rime and say each part. Then students remake the word. *gr (onset)* *ab (rime)* . Examples of word sets: *bag-brag-brat-flat-flit* *lip-clip-slip-slit-spit-spot* *lap-clap-slap-slam-spam* *pet-pets-step-stop-spot* *rim-trim-trip-trap-strap* *tub-stub-stab-tab-gab-grab* *crab-slab-grab-grub-snub* *skin-skip-trip-trap-clap-clip* *plum-drum-drug-snug-snag* *step-stop-slop-slip-blip* *win-twin-twig-swig-swim*	Use four boxes and dictate words with an initial blend. Students say the word slowly as they write one letter in each box. | c	r	a	b | Students should check the word by saying the word slowly and pointing to the corresponding sound. To maximize power, use a series of words that contain different initial, medial, and final letters. This forces students to attend to each sound in the word. Examples: brag clip blob snug clam crib drop spun crop clap drip stub crab flip plop sled flop drag grin sped flag grip plot stem flap skid slot step flat skin spot swim glad skip stop twin grab slid trot snub plan slim club step slam slit spun sped slap drug snip plot	Dictate two sentences that relate to the story and contain many sight words. **B-M-E** After students orally retell the story as a group, have them write three sentences: One about the beginning, the middle, and the end. These sentences are not dictated by teacher. **Comprehension** Students learn to . . . - retell most of the events in sequence. - identify characters, problem, and solution. - respond to questions with interpretation and higher level thinking. - orally answer questions about the story.

Strategies and Skills for Level F

Use this chart to plan your lessons and guide acceleration decisions.

Students Learn to . . .	Whiteboards	Making Words	Sound Boxes	Guided Writing Dictated Sentence
• maintain meaning while using known parts and endings to problem-solve new words. • attend to the middle and the end of words with prompting. • use onsets and rimes to problem-solve with teacher prompting. • easily decode unfamiliar one-syllable words (*fast, chimp, splash*). • read new books with greater fluency and expression. • use punctuation to read with phrasing and expression. • understand more challenging contractions such as *couldn't, won't, we'll, we've, I've, who'll, they'll,* etc. • hear and record final blends in one-syllable words.	**Final Blends** Students identify the blend at the end of a one-syllable word. Select two final blends and dictate words for students to sort. Students write the two blends on their whiteboard and point to the blend they hear at the end of the word. Words to use for final blend sorts: **–mp** (*camp, lamp, lump, pump, jump, ramp*) **–nd** (*band, land, sand, pond*) **–ng** (*sing, bang, lung, hang*) **–st** (*nest, rest, west, rust, post*) **–sk** (*mask, tusk, desk*) **–nk** (*tank, bank, junk, pink, link*) **–ft** (*raft, gift, lift, sift*) **–nt** (*ant, mint, bent*) **–lt** (*felt, melt, belt, bolt*) **Contractions** Students write contractions by erasing letters and inserting an apostrophe. *could not = couldn't* *we have = we've* *who will = who'll*	Students work with words that have a final blend. After students make a word, have them break the word at the onset and rime and say each part. Then have students put the word together again. This activity draws students' attention to the middle of words and helps them develop efficient decoding strategies. melt = m (onset) - elt (rime) Examples: *ask-bask-bash-mash-mush* *bang-bank-band-land-lend* *camp-damp-dump-dust-dusk-gang-fang-pang-pant-past* *fast-last-lest-left-lent-went* *rang-sang-sank-tank-task* *raft-rant-pant-past-pest-rest* *belt-bend-bent-best-nest* *desk-dusk-tusk-must-mist* *went-west-test-tend-send* *lift-lint-list-last-cast-rant* *just-jest-rest-rust-runt-rent* *soft-sift-silt-hilt-hint-mint* *felt-belt-best-bent-bunt-bust* *milk-silk-silt-wilt-welt-pelt*	Use four boxes and dictate words with a final blend. Students say the word slowly as they write one letter in each box. For maximum effect, select words with different initial consonants, medial vowels, and final blends. | k | e | p | t | Students should check the word to make sure they have written a letter for each sound. Examples: *gust-pink-kept-fang* *band-desk-lift-hunk* *bang-film-lend-rung* *damp-lung-mend-mist* *belt-sang-risk-lump* *dusk-mend-sink-land* *task-lend-milk-just* *raft-self-lint-lamp-gift-next-hunk* *camp-rent-sift-tusk* *sunk-pond-tend-fang*	**Beginning-Middle-End** (3 sentences) After an oral retell, have students write three sentences about the story. Do not dictate the sentences, but support students who need help with orally rehearsing their ideas. **B** beginning (1 sentence) **M** middle (1 sentence) **E** end (1 sentence) **Comprehension** Students learn to… - retell events in sequence. - identify characters, setting, problem, and solution. - respond to the text with interpretation and higher-level thinking. - predict what might happen next in the story.

Strategies and Skills for Level G

Use this chart to plan your lessons and guide acceleration decisions.

Students Learn to...	Making Words	Sound Boxes	Analogy Charts	Guided Writing
• maintain meaning while problem-solving using known parts, endings, and familiar rimes. • read new books with greater fluency and expression, stopping only to problem-solve. • break words in parts to problem solve. (Discourage letter-by-letter sounding!) • monitor by attending to the middle and end of words. • use analogies to problem-solve during writing with teacher prompting: *If you know* like *you can write* hike. • hear and record initial and final blends in one-syllable words. • apply the silent e rule with prompting.	**Silent e rule** Students use magnetic letters to change vowel sounds in simple words by adding and deleting the silent e. *hat, hate, gal, gale, pal, pale,* *at, ate, mat, mate, rat, rate* *slid, slide, rid, ride, rip, ripe* *hop, hope, slop, slope* *dam, dame, dim, dime* **Initial and final blends** Students make new words by changing initial and final blends. *cash, clash, crash, crush, crunch* *band, brand, bland, blank, blink, bling* *gasp, grasp, clasp, clamp, camp* *lush, blush, brush, crush, crust, crest, chest* *pit, spit, split, splint, sprint* *think, chink, shrink, rink, risk* *ran, ranch, branch, brunch, crunch, scrunch* *went, west, wept, swept, crept*	Use five boxes and dictate words with an initial and final blend. You can also review digraphs. | s | p | e | n | t | | t | w | i | s | t | Examples: *brand, blank, clang, clank, cramp, crash, flash, grand, grasp, plank, plant, shaft, smash, spank, stamp, tramp, champ, clamp, clash, drank, stand, trash, thank, strap, scrap, branch, draft, crest, fresh, spent, swept, blend, spend, shelf, bench, blink, chimp, crisp, drift, drink, print, shift, stink, swift, swish, twist, think, pinch, shrink, split, chomp, stomp, cloth, plump, skunk, slump, slung, slush, stump, stung, thump, trunk, trust, crust, grump, grunt, stunt, blush, brush, crush, flush, punch, munch, lunch, bunch, crunch*	Students use analogy charts to sort words by their short and long vowel sounds. For maximum power use words with digraphs and blends. Gradually increase the challenge by dictating words with different rimes. Easy (rime is constant) hot · hope · pin · dime spot · rope · thin · slime trot · slope · grin · grime clot · grope · spin · crime Harder (rime changes, but vowel sound is constant) cat · same · hut · tune chat · brake · pump · flute champ · quake · rust · prune last · grave · shrub · brute Hardest (rime and vowel sounds change. Students sort words by their long or short vowel sound.) cat (short) · cake (long) slip · grape clot · slime shut · spoke See pages 166–168 for more examples.	**Beginning-Middle-End** (4 sentences) Students construct their own sentences about the story. Prompt students to orally rehearse each sentence before writing it. **B**eginning (1 sentence) **M**iddle (2 sentences) **E**nd (1 sentence) **Somebody-Wanted-But-So (S-W-B-S)** *The lion (somebody) wanted to eat the rabbit, but a deer came by, so the lion let the rabbit go.* **Comprehension** Students learn to . . . - respond to questions with interpretation and higher-level thinking. - orally do a B-M-E with little support. - orally do the five-finger retell with little support. - work towards a one-minute retell. - describe characters. - identify the problem and solution.

The Next Step in Guided Reading © 2009 by Jan Richardson, Scholastic Professional

Strategies and Skills for Level H & I

Use this chart to plan your lessons and guide acceleration decisions.

Students Learn to . . .	Making Words	Sound Boxes	Analogy Charts	Guided Writing
• maintain meaning while quickly problem-solving new words using a variety of strategies. • read new books with greater fluency. • use analogies to problem-solve during reading with the teacher's support. (For example, if the student is stuck on the word *fill*, the teacher shows the student how to use the known word *will* to read the new word *fill*.) • use known vowel patterns during reading and writing with support. • apply the silent *e* rule in writing with little prompting. • orally summarize the story with teacher prompting.	**Silent e rule** If necessary, continue working with the silent *e* feature. **Vowel patterns** Students use magnetic letters or whiteboards to write a sequence of words that differ by one or two letters. This activity sharpens phonemic awareness and visual scanning abilities. Include familiar vowel patterns and add simple endings (–s, –ed, –ing, –er) *day, say, stay, slay, play, pray, prayed* *car, card, cart, chart, charm, harm, hark, shark* *see, seed, weed, week, cheek, creek, creeps* *boat, boast, coast, coach, roach, roast, toast, toaster* *for, fork, pork, porch, scorch, scorching* *cow, clown, crown*	If necessary, use five boxes to work with initial and final blends. Also use words with three letter blends such as *scrub, strip, splash, shred, shrimp,* and *shrunk* | s	p	l	i	t | | s	c	r	u	b | See examples listed for Level G. When students can write a word phonetically, including blends, sound boxes are no longer necessary.	Use analogy charts to teach common vowel patterns such as *ay, ar, ee, ow, or,* and *oa*. Begin with two known words (key words) and dictate other unknown words for students to write using the pattern from the known words. As students write a word, they should underline the pattern that matches the key word. When appropriate, increase the challenge by including words with initial blends and endings. Examples: **day** / **and** *may* / *sand* *pray* / *stand* *stray* / *brand* **car** / **cow** *far* / *now* *card* / *plow* *started* / *crowd* **see** / **for** *tree* / *fort* *sweep* / *sport* *sleeping* / *stormy* **boat** / **all** *float* / *tall* *coach* / *stall* *toaster* / *smallest*	**Beginning-Middle-End** (5 sentences) Students write five sentences about the story. **B**eginning (1 sentence) **M**iddle (3 sentences) **E**nd (1 sentence) Students should not copy out of the book. **Somebody-Wanted-But-So** If there are several characters, the teacher can assign a different character to each student. *Victor wanted to fly his kite, but it was too small, so he made a better kite, and it carried him to the roof.* **Comprehension** Students learn to . . . • respond to questions with interpretation and deeper thinking. • orally retell the story, recalling events in sequence. • describe characters and how they change. • identify the problem and provide alternate solutions. • make several possible predictions. • make inferences.

Strategies and Skills for Level J+

Use this chart to plan your lessons and guide acceleration decisions.

Students Learn to . . .	Making Words	Analogy Charts	Comprehension	Guided Writing
• increase reading stamina. • flexibly use a variety of strategies to problem-solve new words and maintain meaning. • read new books with fluency and expression, stopping only to problem-solve. • use vowel patterns in reading and writing. • use the silent *e* feature in reading and writing. • chunk words with two and three syllables. • attend to prefixes and suffixes in reading and writing. • use vocabulary strategies to determine the meaning of unknown words. • respond to a story in writing with decreasing support. • use more complex comprehension strategies. • read and respond to nonfiction and poetry.	**Vowel Patterns** Students use magnetic letters and whiteboards to work with more vowel patterns. Increase the challenge by including words with endings and blends. Examples: *out, ouch, pouch, pound, round, around* *rain, train, strain, sprain, brain, brainy* *snow, show, shown, grown, growth* *night, right, fright, flight, slight, slightly* *oil, boil, coil, coin, join, joint, point, pointer* *new, few, flew, blew, brew, crew, chew, chewed* *saw, law, claw, crawl, drawl, draw, squaw, squawk, squawking* Explain the "e drop" when adding *–ing*. Ex. *come – coming* *have – having* *like - liking*	Students use charts to write words with vowel patterns such as *ew, ou, ight, aw, oi, ai, ow.* Gradually increase the difficulty of the task by using words with digraphs, blends, prefixes, and suffixes. Examples: **out** **snow** pout know sprout known about blowing found unknown **night** **oil** bright soil lightly moist mighty unspoiled **new** **saw** flew claw threw thaw chewed drawn unscrew crawling **rain** **eight** train weight paint freight painful neighbor unpaid eighty	Students learn to . . . • respond to questions with interpretation and reflection. • give alternative solutions to a problem. "How else could they have solved this problem?" • make predictions during and after reading. • orally retell using Five-Finger Retell. • orally summarize a story. • make personal connections while reading. • make inferences about characters. • determine cause of a character's feelings. • ask questions while reading. • determine main idea/details in nonfiction. • use visual information (graphs, charts, diagrams) to enhance comprehension. • make inferences about a character's action or dialogue. • understand figurative language in poetry. • evaluate texts using personal interpretations and opinions.	Students should be able to write a summary for fiction with little teacher support. As stories become more complex, students might connect two **S-W-B-S** statements with the word "then." Example: *Victor wanted to fly his kite, but it was too small so he built his own kite.* *THEN* *Victor wanted to fly his new kite, but it lifted him to the top of the roof so his dad had to get him down.* Students extend their understanding of the story through guided writing. Possible responses: • problem/solution • a character's actions (B-M-E) • a character's feelings (B-M-E) • chapter summaries • microthemes • new knowledge or understandings • reflections and wonderings

Appendix B

Word lists for each skill and level (to use with word study activities)

Level B & C CVC words					Level D Digraphs
A	**O**	**I**	**U**	**E**	**sh/ch/th**
cab	hog	bin	hum	fed	mash
dad	jog	fin	gum	beg	dash
cat	fog	pin	bum	yet	cash
sad	log	tin	mug	led	wish
cap	top	dip	tub	wed	dish
can	dot	win	cub	red	fish
had	got	did	fun	jet	ship
ham	cot	hid	sun	let	shop
hat	lot	bid	yum	pet	shot
mad	not	kid	gun	met	shed
man	hot	lid	mud	wet	rush
zap	pot	big	rug	set	mush
map	hop	dig	rut	net	hush
ram	mob	pig	gut	get	shut
rag	mop	rig	run	leg	
rap	pop	wig	nut	ten	chat
van	bob	dim	hut	hen	chin
rat	job	him	rub	peg	chop
had	rob	rid	sub	bet	such
ran	sob		bus	pen	much
wag	dog			den	
tab	cob			bed	that
mat				bet	this
jam				fed	then
pat					them
pan					thud
pad					path
yam					math
has					bath
					with

Appendix B *(continued)*

Word lists for each skill and level (to use with word study activities)

Level E Initial Blends		Level F Final Blends * endings may be added		
brag	skip	and	elf	limp*
clam	slid	ant	end*	link*
clap	slim	ask*	felt	list*
crab	slit	band	held	milk*
drag	spin	bang*	help*	mint
flag	spit	bank*	kept	mist*
flap	trim	camp*	left	pink
flat	trip	damp	lend*	risk*
flash	twig	fang	lent	sift*
crash	twin	fast*	melt*	pond
clash	swim	hand*	mend*	romp*
smash	blob	hang*	next	chomp*
trash	crop	lamp	nest*	dusk
glad	drop	land*	pest	dust*
grab	flop	last*	rent*	gust*
plan	plop	mask*	rest*	hump*
slam	plot	pant*	self	thump*
slap	slot	thank	send*	hunk
snap	spot	past	sent	jump*
stab	stop	rang	tend*	junk
swam	trot	raft	test*	just
trap	club	sand*	went	lump*
sled	drug	tank	west	lung
sped	drum	task	film	must
stem	plug	champ	fist	pump*
step	slush	shaft	gift	rung
clip	blush	belt	hint*	rust*
crib	crush	bend*	lift*	sung
drip	brush	bent	chest	sunk
flip	flush	best	shelf	tusk
grin	plum	desk	bench	
grip	plus		chimp	
skid	snug		shift	
skin	spun		think	
shrug	stud			

Appendix B *(continued)*

Word lists for each skill and level (to use with word study activities)

Levels G & H Silent *e* rule Initial and final blends		
at-ate	brand	shrimp
can-cane	blank	shrink
cap-cape	clang	split
hat-hate	clank	stomp
mad-made	cramp	strong
man-mane	grand	plump
mat-mate	grasp	skunk
plan-plane	plank	slump
rag-rage	plant	slung
rat-rate	spank	stump
tap-tape	stamp	stung
scrap-scrape	tramp	trunk
bit-bite	clamp	trust
dim-dime	drank	crust
fin-fine	stand	grump
hid-hide	strap	grunt
kit-kite	scrap	stunt
pin-pine	shrank	crunch
rid-ride	ranch	scrub
rip-ripe	draft	shrunk
slid-slide	splash	scrunch
spin-spine	spent	
strip-stripe	swept	
twin-twine	blend	
hop-hope	spend	
not-note	shred	
rob-robe	blink	
rod-rode	crisp	
slop-slope	drift	
cub-cube	drink	
cut- cute	print	
hug-huge	stink	
us-use	swift	
tub-tube	twist	
	strip	

Appendix B *(continued)*
Levels H and Higher:

Words to use for word study activities to teach vowel patterns.
May also be used for spelling activities.

–ay	–all	–ar	–or	–ee		–oo		–er, ir, ur	-ow
day	**ball**	**car**	**for**	**see**	**see**	**look**	**zoo**	**her**	**how**
bay	call	bar	born	bee	seem	book	boom	germ	now
hay	fall	far	cord	tree	seen	brook	bloom	fern	cow
jay	hall	jar	cork	beef	seep	cook	boost	stern	pow
lay	mall	tar	corn	beep	sheep	crook	boot	term	wow
may	tall	arm	fork	beet	sheet	foot	broom	clerk	town
pay	wall	arch	fort	deed	sleet	good	cool		plow
ray	small	art	forth	deep	speech	hood	food		gown
say	stall	bark	horn	feed	speed	hoof	loop	**girl**	down
way		card	north	feel	steep	hook	moo	sir	drown
gray		cart	pork	feet	sweep	shook	moon	bird	crowd
play		charm	porch	heel	sweet	stood	noon	chirp	crown
pray		chart	port	jeep	street	took	pool	dirt	clown
stay		dark	scorch	keep	teeth	wood	proof	firm	brown
tray		dart	scorn	meet	three	wool	roof	first	
spray		harm	short	need	knee		root	shirt	
		farm	sort	peel	kneel		school	skirt	**show**
		hard	sport	peep	queen		scoop	stir	blow
		march	stork	reed	screen		scoot	third	blown
		park	storm	reef	cheek		shoot	thirst	bowl
		part	sworn	seed	creek		smooth	whirl	crow
		scar	thorn	seek			snoop		flow
		scarf	torch	seem			soon		flown
		shark	torn				spoon	**fur**	glow
		smart	worn				stool	burn	grow
		spark					swoop	burp	grown
		star					too	curl	know
		start					tool	hurt	known
		yard					toot	nurse	low
		yarn						burp	own
								church	shown
								turn	slow
								spurt	snow
									stow
									throw
									thrown

Appendix B *(continued)*
Levels H and Higher:

Words to use for word study activities to teach vowel patterns.
May also be used for spelling activities.

-oa	-ai	-ea		-ou	-ew/ue	-oy/oi	-aw/-au	-igh/-eigh
boat	**rain**	**eat**	**eat**	**out**	**-ew**	**-oy**	**-aw**	**-igh**
coat	aid	bead	meal	loud	**new**	**boy**	**saw**	**night**
loaf	aim	beak	mean	ouch	blew	toy	claw	bright
loan	bait	beam	meat	pouch	chew	coy	crawl	fight
oak	fail	bean	neat	shout	crew	annoy	dawn	flight
oat	jail	beat	peach	south	dew	destroy	draw	high
road	faith	cheat	peak	spout	drew	enjoy	drawn	knight
boast	laid	clean	real	sound	few	joy	fawn	light
coach	maid	cream	reach	proud	flew	joyful	hawk	might
coast	nail	deal	teach	mouth	grew	loyal	jaw	right
croak	paid	dream	read	count	knew	oyster	law	sigh
float	pain	each	seal	cloud	screw	royal	lawn	sight
foam	paint	east	seam	round	stew	voyage	paw	slight
goal	rail	feast	seat	around	threw		raw	thigh
goat	sail	beast	sneak	ground		**-oi**	shawl	tight
groan	tail	heat	speak	pound		**oil**	slaw	
load	wait	lead	squeak	found	**-ue**	**oil**	sprawl	
moan	braid	leaf	steal	sprout	**blue**	boil	squawk	**-eigh**
oath	brain	leak	stream	grouch	glue	broil	straw	**eight**
roam	chain	lean	team	crouch	hue	coil	thaw	weight
roast	claim	leash	treat		clue	foil	yawn	freight
soak	drain	least			true	join	bawl	neigh
soap	faint				cue	joint		neighbor
toad	grain					moist	**-au**	eighty
toast	plain					point	**because**	weightless
throat	saint					soil	caught	
	snail					spoil	cause	
	sprain					poison	fault	
	stain					moisture	haul	
	strain					avoid	haunt	
	trail					toilet	launch	
	train						sauce	
	waist						taught	

Appendix C: Reading Strategies Cards

Decoding Strategies   ## Vocabulary Strategies

Reread & Think: What makes sense? Sound the 1st part of the word.

1. Reread (or read on) and look for clues in the text.

Check the Picture

2. Check the picture or visualize the sentence.

Cover the Ending and find a known part.

3. Use a **known part**. *courageous* *preventive*

Chunk the Word

pro/tec/tion

4. Make a connection to other words you know. *introductory* *introduce*

Connect: Does this word remind me of another word I know?

cloud   *proud*   *shroud*

5. Use the **glossary** (or other text features).

Appendix D: Alphabet Chart

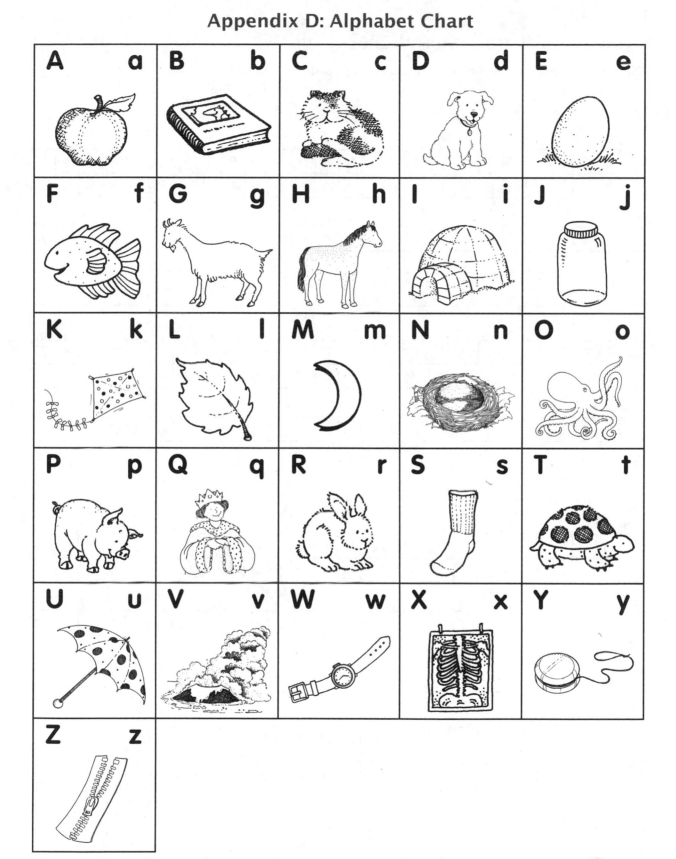

Appendix E: Letter/Sound Checklist

Directions: Highlight the letters and sounds each student knows.

Student: _____

Letters

A	B	C	D	E	F	G	H	I	J	K	L	M	N	O	P	Q	R	S	T	U	V	W	X	Y	Z
a	b	c	d	e	f	g	h	i	j	k	l	m	n	o	p	q	r	s	t	u	v	w	x	y	z

Sounds

a	b	c	d	e	f	g	h	i	j	k	l	m	n	o	p	q	r	s	t	u	v	w	x	y	z

Student: _____

Letters

A	B	C	D	E	F	G	H	I	J	K	L	M	N	O	P	Q	R	S	T	U	V	W	X	Y	Z
a	b	c	d	e	f	g	h	i	j	k	l	m	n	o	p	q	r	s	t	u	v	w	x	y	z

Sounds

a	b	c	d	e	f	g	h	i	j	k	l	m	n	o	p	q	r	s	t	u	v	w	x	y	z

Student: _____

Letters

A	B	C	D	E	F	G	H	I	J	K	L	M	N	O	P	Q	R	S	T	U	V	W	X	Y	Z
a	b	c	d	e	f	g	h	i	j	k	l	m	n	o	p	q	r	s	t	u	v	w	x	y	z

Sounds

a	b	c	d	e	f	g	h	i	j	k	l	m	n	o	p	q	r	s	t	u	v	w	x	y	z

Student: _____

Letters

A	B	C	D	E	F	G	H	I	J	K	L	M	N	O	P	Q	R	S	T	U	V	W	X	Y	Z
a	b	c	d	e	f	g	h	i	j	k	l	m	n	o	p	q	r	s	t	u	v	w	x	y	z

Sounds

a	b	c	d	e	f	g	h	i	j	k	l	m	n	o	p	q	r	s	t	u	v	w	x	y	z

The Next Step in Guided Reading © 2009 by Jan Richardson, Scholastic Professional

Appendix F: Pre-A Lesson Plan

Student: _____ Date: _____ Lesson# _____

Activity Options	Observations/Notes
Eight Ways of Working With Letters Letter Activity: #_____ Letter Formation: _____	
Working With Names (Choose 1) ☐ Use name puzzles ☐ Make names out of magnetic letters. ☐ Do rainbow writing with names.	
Working With Sounds (Choose 1) Clapping syllables 1 2 3 Rhyming words _____ Picture sorts _____	
Working With Books Do shared reading with a level A book. Encourage oral language and teach print concepts (choose one or two): ☐ Concept of a word (students frame each word in a sentence) ☐ First/last word (students locate in text) ☐ Concept of a letter (students frame a letter or count the letters in a word) ☐ First/last letter (students locate in text) ☐ Period (students locate in text) ☐ Capital/lower case letters (students locate in text)	Title: _____ Observations: _____ _____ _____ _____ _____
Interactive Writing & Cut-Up Sentence Sentence:	

Appendix G: Emergent Guided Reading Lesson Plan

Title: _____ Level: _____ Lesson #_____

Day 1 Date: _____	**Day 2** Date: _____
Sight Word Review–Writing _____ _____ _____	**Sight Word Review–Writing** _____ _____ _____
Introduce New Book: This book is called _____ and it's about _____ _____ **New vocabulary:**	**Rereading of Yesterday's Book (and other familiar books)** Observations:
Text Reading With Prompting: ❏ Check the picture. What would make sense? ❏ Get your mouth ready for the first sound. ❏ Get your mouth ready and check the picture. ❏ Could it be _____ or _____? ❏ Show me the word _____. ❏ Check the word with your finger. Are you right? ❏ Try reading without pointing. ❏ How would the character say that? (show expression)	

Teaching Points After Reading (choose one or two each day):
- ❏ One-to-one matching (at level C, discourage pointing)
- ❏ Use picture clues (meaning)
- ❏ Monitor with known words
- ❏ Get mouth ready for initial sound
- ❏ Cross-check picture and first letter
- ❏ Visual scanning (check the word left to right)
- ❏ Fluency and expression

Discussion Prompt (if appropriate):	**Discussion Prompt (if appropriate):**
Teach One Sight Word: _____ • What's missing? • Table Writing • Mix & Fix • Writing on a whiteboard	**Teach Same Sight Word:** _____ • What's missing? • Table Writing • Mix & Fix • Writing on a whiteboard
Word Study (Choose just one): ❏ Picture sorts: _____ ❏ Making words: _____ ❏ Sound boxes: _____	**Guided Writing:** Dictated or open-ended sentence

Appendix H: Early Guided Reading Lesson Plan

Title: _____ Level: _____ Strategy Focus: _____ Lesson #_____

Day 1 Date: _____	**Day 2** Date: _____
Sight Word Review–Writing (optional) _____ _____ _____	**Sight Word Review–Writing** (optional) _____ _____ _____
Introduce New Book: This book is called _____ and it's about _____ _____ **New vocabulary:**	**Continue Reading Yesterday's Book (and other familiar books)** Observations:

Text Reading With Prompting:
- ❑ Check the picture. Does it look right and make sense? Reread the sentence.
- ❑ Check the end (or middle) of the word. What would look right and make sense?
- ❑ Cover the ending. Is there a part you know?
- ❑ Break the word into parts.
- ❑ Do you know another word that looks like this one?
- ❑ What can you try? What can you do to help yourself?
- ❑ Put some words together so it sounds smooth. (fluency)
- ❑ Read it like the character. (expression)
- ❑ What did you read? What's the problem? How might the characters solve it? (comprehension)

Select one or two teaching points each day after reading.

Word-Solving Strategies:	**Fluency & Expression:**
❑ Monitor	❑ Attend to **bold** words
❑ Reread at difficulty	❑ Reread page _____ for expression
❑ Attend to endings	**Comprehension**
❑ Use known parts	❑ Recall information
❑ Contractions	❑ Retell events in sequence
❑ Use analogies	❑ Five-finger retell
❑ Chunk big words	❑ Discuss characters' feelings

Discussion Prompt:	**Discussion Prompt:**

Teach One Sight Word: (optional after level E)
- What's missing?   • Table Writing
- Mix & Fix   • Writing on a whiteboard

Word Study (Choose just one):	**Guided Writing:**
❑ Picture sorts: _____ ❑ Making words: _____ ❑ Sound boxes: _____ ❑ Analogy chart: _____	

Appendix I: Transitional Guided Reading Lesson Plan

Title: _____ Level: _____ Strategy Focus: _____ Lesson #_____

Day 1 Date_____ Pages_____ **Introduce New Book:** This book is about _____ _____ **New vocabulary:**	**Day 2** Date_____ Pages_____ **Continue reading the book.** You will read about _____ _____ **New vocabulary:**

Text Reading With Prompting (use prompts that target each student's needs).

Teaching Points: Choose one or two each day (decoding, vocabulary, fluency, and/or comprehension).

Decoding Strategies: ❑ Reread & think what would make sense ❑ Cover (or attend to) the ending ❑ Use analogies ❑ Chunk big words	**Fluency & Phrasing:** ❑ Phrasing ❑ Attend to **bold** words ❑ Attend to punctuation ❑ Dialogue, intonation & expression
Vocabulary Strategies: ❑ Reread the sentence and look for clues ❑ Check the picture ❑ Use a known part ❑ Make a connection ❑ Use the glossary	**Comprehension** (oral): ❑ B-M-E　　　❑ Five-Finger Retell ❑ S-W-B-S　　❑ Describe a character's feelings ❑ Who & What　❑ STP (Stop Think Paraphrase) ❑ Problem &　　❑ VIP (very important part) 　 Solution Other:
Discussion Prompt:	**Discussion Prompt:**
Word Study (if appropriate): Sound boxes–Analogy chart–Make a big word	**Word Study (if appropriate):** Sound boxes–Analogy chart–Make a big word

Day 3 Date_____ **Reread the book for fluency (5 min.) and/or engage in Guided Writing**

Options for Guided Writing

Beginning-Middle-End　　Five-Finger Retell　　　Somebody-Wanted-But-So (SWBS)　　Character Analysis

Problem/Solution　　　　Compare or Contrast　　Other: _____

　　　The Next Step in Guided Reading © 2009 by Jan Richardson, Scholastic Professional

Appendix J: Prompts for Guided Reading

Use the following prompts when working with individual students. Attend to monitoring, decoding, and fluency before you prompt for vocabulary and comprehension.

Helping students <u>self-monitor</u>

❑   *Are you right?* (Ask this question even when the student is correct.)

❑   *Does that make sense?* (If the student says, "Yes," reread the sentence the way the student read it and ask, "Does that make sense? Try that again and see if you can fix it to make sense.")

❑   *Does it look right? Check it with your finger.*

Helping students <u>decode</u> unknown words

❑   *Sound the first part and check the picture. What would look right and make sense?*

❑   *Cover the ending. Is there a part you know that can help?*

❑   *Can you break it into parts?* (Chunk it.)

❑   *Reread the sentence and think what would make sense.*

❑   *Do you know another word that looks like this one?*

Helping students read with <u>fluency</u> and phrasing

❑   *Try reading it without pointing.*

❑   *How would the character say that? Can you read it like you're talking?*

❑   *Put some words together so it sounds smooth.*

❑   The teacher uses his or her fingers to frame 2–3 words at a time, helping the student read in phrases.

❑   The teacher slides his or her finger over the words to push the student's eye forward.

❑   The teacher reads with the student to model expression and intonation.

Helping students understand the meaning of words (<u>vocabulary</u>)

❑   *Is there a word you don't understand?*

❑   *Have you heard that word before?*

❑   *Are there clues in the sentence or illustration to help you?*

❑   *Is there a part in that word that can help?* (for example, *"landslide" has "land" and "slide" in it.*)

❑   *Do you know a word that is similar?* (for example, *"mysterious" is similar to "mystery".*)

Helping students <u>comprehend</u> the text

❑   *What is happening on this page? What happened at the beginning of the story?* (retell)

❑   *Is there a confusing part? What don't you understand?* (clarify)

❑   *What is the most important idea or event?* (determine what is important)

❑   *Can you summarize what you read in one sentence?* (summarize)

❑   *Can you ask a question about what you read?* (question, clarify)

❑   *What do you think might happen next? Why do you think that?* (predict)

❑   *What are <u>you</u> thinking now?* (think aloud)

❑   *What are you thinking about the character? What might the character be thinking or feeling right now?* (inference, character analysis)

❑   *Why do you think the character did (or said) that?* (inference, cause-effect)

❑   *How do you think the character feels now?* (inference)

❑   *What was the effect of . . .? What do you think caused that to happen?* (cause-effect)

Appendix K: Reading Workshop Contract

Name: _____ Date: _____

	Literacy Activity #1	**Literacy Activity #2**
Monday Independent Reading Title: _____ Pg. _____ to _____	❑ guided reading ❑ writing ❑ word study ❑ other: _____	❑ guided reading ❑ writing ❑ word study ❑ other: _____
Tuesday Independent Reading Title: _____ Pg. _____ to _____	❑ guided reading ❑ writing ❑ word study ❑ other: _____	❑ guided reading ❑ writing ❑ word study ❑ other: _____
Wednesday Independent Reading Title: _____ Pg. _____ to _____	❑ guided reading ❑ writing ❑ word study ❑ other: _____	❑ guided reading ❑ writing ❑ word study ❑ other: _____
Thursday Independent Reading Title: _____ Pg. _____ to _____	❑ guided reading ❑ writing ❑ word study ❑ other: _____	❑ guided reading ❑ writing ❑ word study ❑ other: _____
Friday Independent Reading Title: _____ Pg. _____ to _____	❑ guided reading ❑ writing ❑ word study ❑ other: _____	❑ guided reading ❑ writing ❑ word study ❑ other: _____

Appendix L: Class Progress Chart

Name	Pre-A	A	B	C	D	E	F	G	H	I	J	K	L	M	N	O	P	Q	R	S	T	U	V	W	X	Y	Z
1																											
2																											
3																											
4																											
5																											
6																											
7																											
8																											
9																											
10																											
11																											
12																											
13																											
14																											
15																											
16																											
17																											
18																											
19																											
20																											
21																											
22																											
23																											
24																											
End of Year Benchmark			K							1st			2rd				3rd			4th			5th				6th

Appendix M: Reading Buddy Strategies

PAUSE

Wait five seconds.

1 . . . . 2 . . . . 3 . . . . 4 5

Let your buddy finish the sentence.

PROMPT

"Try it. What would make sense?"

"Reread the sentence."

"Look at the picture."

"Is there a part in the word that you know?"

"Can you break the word into parts?"

PRAISE

"That was a good try!"

"I like the way you tried something!"

"You are close!"

The Next Step in Guided Reading